DATE DUE

7-22-11			

Demco

Returning to Religion

Jonathan Benthall is an Honorary Research Fellow in the Department of Anthropology, University College London. He has served as Director of the Royal Anthropological Institute, Founding Editor of *Anthropology Today*, and Chair of the International NGO Training and Research Centre, Oxford (INTRAC). His previous books include *Disasters, Relief and the Media* (1993) and *The Charitable Crescent: Politics of Aid in the Muslim World* (co-authored with Jérôme Bellion-Jourdan, 2003), both published by I.B.Tauris, and the edited *The Best of 'Anthropology Today'* (Routledge, 2002).

Returning to Religion

Why a Secular Age is Haunted by Faith

Jonathan Benthall

LONDON · NEW YORK

Published in 2008 by I.B.Tauris & Co Ltd
6 Salem Road, London W2 4BU
175 Fifth Avenue, New York NY 10010
www.ibtauris.com

In the United States of America and Canada distributed by Palgrave Macmillan,
a division of St. Martin's Press, 175 Fifth Avenue, New York NY 10010

Library of Modern Religion: 1
ISBN: 978 1 84511 718 4

A full CIP record for this book is available from the British Library
A full CIP record is available from the Library of Congress

Library of Congress Catalog Card Number available

Printed and bound in Great Britain by TJ International Ltd, Padstow, Cornwall
from camera-ready copy edited and supplied by the author

To
Julian Pitt-Rivers
(1919–2001)

CONTENTS

INTRODUCTION

This book is based on the presumption that the religious inclination, the need for a framework of orientation or object of devotion, is a human universal. In industrial societies whose survival needs are, at least for the time being, generally satisfied, traditional religious authorities are increasingly weakened or adopt defensive positions, while new transnational spiritual movements abound, from neo-oriental cults to Scientology – often aspiring to global relevance. Hybrid movements have emerged that set out to achieve combined religious and secular aims, or to make the distinction between the two open to question. We see many of the features associated with religion coming to animate what are normally seen as secular movements.

I have set out to review the growth of 'religioid' movements from the point of view of social science, drawing on the work of anthropologists such as Mary Douglas and Alfred Gell and on current American and French scholarship that rejects attempts to define religion precisely. I propose detailed criteria by which a family resemblance between all kinds of religious movements can be identified, and suggest how a variety of movements may each be assigned to a strong or a weak religious field. It is already commonplace to argue that political doctrines such as communism and nazism, some movements in the arts, and intellectual schools such as psychoanalysis, all have religioid aspects. I extend the argument to include some other social movements. It is encouraging to note that others agree with this approach: for instance, the distinguished American physicist, Freeman Dyson, who has written that 'environmentalism has replaced socialism as the leading secular religion'.[*]

As an exercise in social research, this book sidesteps the issue of truth-values. It asks practical questions. How is 'civil society' based on shared

---

[*] *New York Review of Books*, 12 June 2008, p.45.

moral values developing across national borders? What are the outlooks for conservative theologies in both Christianity and Islam? Can the Chinese regime retain its political stability without establishing an ideological successor to Maoism? How would spiritual movements in the West adapt in the event of serious threats to its sense of material security?

Chapter 1 sets out the general argument on 'religion and parareligion'. Chapter 2 explores the 'family resemblance' between religious movements, outlining 19 criteria for identifying a movement as religious or religioid – though not all the criteria have to be satisfied for the identification to hold. Chapter 3 introduces the concept of the 'religious field', in which a particular movement's position may be strong, medium or weak; and then explores the shifting boundaries between the religious field and other fields of human activity. The same chapter goes on to consider briefly how first, political ideologies and second, artistic movements fit into this model.

The three following chapters describe particular social movements and their religioid features. Chapter 4 covers the humanitarian movement, with Médecins Sans Frontières (MSF) as a detailed case study. Chapter 5 discusses the animal liberation and rights movement and environmentalism, including the latter's relationship to religious movements. Chapter 6 covers three humane disciplines at both the scholarly and the popular levels: psychotherapy, archaeology and anthropology.

The concluding Chapter 7, 'Throw Religion Out of the Door: It Flies Back by the Window', deals with three issues that emerge from the study: the contradiction of militant atheism in relying on science but not being scientific enough in studying the religious field; orthodoxy and conservatism as movements reacting against what Raphaël Liogier has identified as 'individuo-globalism'; and the present Chinese regime's search for legitimacy. The chapter closes with a postscript suggesting how an apparent exceptional case, the former East Germany, may nonetheless be accommodated within the model proposed.

The book ends with a brief Envoi addressed to readers of whatever beliefs and backgrounds.

Acknowledgments

This book owes much to Raphaël Liogier's publications and discussions with him, and to his invitation to give some lectures at the Observatoire du Religieux, University of Aix–Marseille, France. I am also specially grateful to Daniel Stoekl ben Ezra for reading some of the chapters in draft; to Bron Taylor for exchanges on environmentalism and for reading drafts; and to I.B. Tauris's commissioning editor, Alex Wright, and their editorial co-ordinator, Jayne Hill.

Thanks are due for personal exchanges with Jean-Yves Tadié (on Proust), Rabbi David Goldberg (on Judaism), Joseph Rykwert (on twentieth century architecture), James Beckford and Jean-François Mayer (on new religious movements), Ulrike von Pilar, Rony Brauman and Hugo Slim (on MSF), Erica Bronstein and Peter Redfield (on humanitarianism), John Knight (on animals), Krov Menuhin (on cetaceans), Richard Fardon (on Mary Douglas), Benson Saler (on Loren Eiseley), George Appell, Chris Knight, Roslyn Poignant and Gustaaf Houtman (on various aspects of anthropology), Bishop Hilarion Alfeyev (on the Orthodox Church), Stephan Feuchtwang and Jon Halliday (on China), and Paul Froese (on the former East Germany).

None of the above bears any responsibility for the content.

Many other debts are acknowledged in the text and the Notes and References.

Parts of the arguments set out in Chapters 5 and 6 were published in summary form as guest editorials in *Anthropology Today*. The material on MSF in Chapter 4 was presented in a seminar in the anthropology department, University College London, in November 2005. Some of the more general argument in that chapter was worked through in an article on 'relief' in the Palgrave *Dictionary of Transnational History*.

I am grateful above all to Zamira for her support and patience.

1

RELIGION AND PARARELIGION

The Religious and the Secular

'Cometh the man, cometh the hour' reads an old portrait postcard of David Beckham. Alcoholics Anonymous, widely regarded as offering one of the best programmes for mastering addiction, claims to serve 'the ultimate authority – a living God as He may express himself in our group conscience'. A management consultant in personal growth advertises himself as 'one of life's runaway experiments who goes around scaring people until they either ascend to a higher level of consciousness or flee naked into the desert screaming, "The horror, the horror" '. The Princess of Wales's death in a banal street accident takes on a sacrificial meaning, causing parts of London to be carpeted with flowers and Cellophane. A blockbusting novel and film are concocted from a clever counterfactual to the standard history of Christianity. 'Saint' Bob Geldof, as he is called in the press, stirs his fellow-musicians to try to give a new impetus to Third World aid. A more highbrow musician, the revered concert pianist Gregory Sokolov, waits till the audience has settled down and stopped coughing and snapping their handbags, before the lights dim and he prowls onto the stage, then seems to lift the whole of the Barbican concert hall out of earthly time with a Beethoven sonata. Yes – and politicians accuse their opponents of reciting 'mantras' or being 'true believers' or 'not singing from the same hymn sheet'. The vocabulary of religion and its imagery and overtones have spread across our society's secular institutions. Is this just a matter of surface vocabulary, or a sign of deeper infiltration? Has religion become a metaphor for everything but itself? And what do we mean by the 'religious' and the 'secular' anyway?

Thirty years ago, the 'secularization thesis' dominated sociology. It was a catch-all thesis with a number of variants. It could mean that secular spheres differentiate from religious norms and institutions, and gain ascendancy over them. It could mean that religion is marginalized or becomes a purely private choice. It could mean that religious beliefs and practices decline: this is sometimes called 'disenchantment' or 'desacralization'. It could mean that religions come to be seen as human creations. It could mean that religious movements adapt to the here-and-now world rather than otherworldly aspiration. It could mean that religions have to compete in a market of consumable ideologies. It could mean that correct practice rather than belief is emphasized – sometimes called orthopraxy as opposed to orthodoxy, or pejoratively (disregarding the view that good behaviour has moral value in itself) as 'formalism', that is to say adherence to outward observances at the expense of what are claimed to be their inward spirit and meaning.

I use the past tense because 'secularization' is no longer a buzzword: we might indeed call it a plonk-word. Social scientists taught, thirty years ago, that the main markers that divided people were class, ethnicity, gender, age, language and political ideology. Few of them predicted such events as the Islamist revolution in Iran, the *Satanic Verses* controversy in 1988, the important contribution of the Roman Catholic Church to defeating Soviet communism, the revival of the Orthodox Church in Russia, the continuing power of the religious Right in the USA. It is now commonplace to warn that – along with the risks of global warming, the precariousness of the financial system, and pandemic diseases – the risk of a clash of religious civilizations is one of the greatest facing the world, much to the disgust of most academic analysts, who despise the theory either as simply misguided or as possibly becoming a self-fulfilling prophecy.

There is some degree of truth in many plonk-words. All the aspects of secularization mentioned above are observable realities in various contexts; but this is tricky territory to argue on. Formal, regular religious observance is far more widespread in the world's leading industrial nation, the USA, than in Europe. It has been argued that Britain and western Europe, not the USA, are the world exception with their pronounced secularizing trend, especially among the young. But even in England – where only some 10 to 15 per cent of the population regularly attend Christian churches, and the 'established' State church faces financial pressures with dwindling congregations and a top-heavy hierarchy – it has been estimated that at least 80 per cent of funerals still include some kind of religious service. This book does not aspire to compete with many distinguished texts in the sociology of religion that have argued against simple versions of the secularization thesis. Any study of American religion has to take account, in particular, of the synthesizing force of Robert Wuthnow's publications, especially his analysis of the transformations of religion in the United States since the Second World War. He emphasizes the accelerated social experimentation of the 1960s and 1970s that resulted from the State's expansion of higher education and threatened the authority of traditional denominations; the political polarization (between conservative and liberal) of the traditional Christian churches; and the continued role of religion in fostering community spirit and compassion. The social experimentation which Wuthnow describes included a new spirit of tolerance and egalitarianism, freer life-styles and an awareness of civil rights – and a spate of new religious movements. Whereas religious conservatives reacted, sometimes fiercely, against these trends, 'liberal churches and liberal religious periodicals, in contrast', Wuthnow writes, 'have been much more likely to ask what can be learnt from the new religions'. If California was the capital of social experimentation in the 1960s and 1970s, a comparable restructuring of religion may be observed in most industrial countries. Whereas it is common to write of religious affiliations as obeying market forces, we must also note an element of convergence as different suppliers compete to offer rather similar products.

We have adopted here a well-tried manoeuvre of cultural anthropology – following a number of writers on religion rather outside the sociological mainstream – which is to set out to unsettle prior assumptions; in particular, about the definition of religion. It is, I suggest, only through recognizing that it cannot be precisely defined that we can begin to understand it.

Secularization is sustained by many intellectual trends. Darwinism in particular is perhaps the only 'big idea' of the nineteenth century to have survived relatively intact, confirmed and refined by the advance of genetics, and it is a guiding force behind modern biology. The Roman Catholic Church made a fuzzy peace with Darwinism many years ago, but Pope Benedict XVI has been too intelligent not to put out signals that he recognizes serious problems of compatibility between Catholic doctrine and natural selection as applied to human beings. (One problem is that, according to Catholicism, no animal has a soul, but if I am descended from hominid and primate ancestors, at some generational point in time God must have intervened to grant them one.) Many American Protestant churches, supported by some other Christian affiliations, promote creationism or the more euphemistic 'intelligent design' as an alternative to the disruptive threat of Darwinism. Some Muslim intellectuals have made their point more rawly and view Darwinism as the main obstacle to faith and spirituality, on the grounds that it elevated a 'bestial postulate' to the status of dogmatic truth. I have seen an Islamist shop window in Istanbul wholly devoted to posters in various languages denouncing Darwinism as responsible for all the ills of the twentieth century including Stalinism and nazism.

The word 'secular' (in French, laïque) stands for everything that is not religious, and all of us know what religion is. But do we? Originally, the distinction between 'religious' and 'secular' was a distinction within Christendom between the monastic orders and extra-monastic churches and priests. A growing body of research suggests that whereas everyone knows what he or she means by religion, it is more of a 'folk category' than an objective term. (Much would-be-subtle discussion of the relationship between the secular and the religious could have been avoided if it had been grasped that, just as the word 'religion' has changed its precise meaning in different times and places, so the word 'secular', basically its antonym or opposite, has mirrored the changes.) A number of linked arguments have been put forward that should make one feel nervous when using the term.

First, precise definitions of religion are leaky. It is often claimed that religion necessarily entails belief in a divine being or beings. But Buddhism does not entail such a belief. Ritual is probably an essential component of religion – albeit pared down and mistrusted by some groups such as the Quakers – but it is also essential to many other spheres of life such as warfare, law and the arts, all of which have historical links with the sphere of religion but are now, in industrial societies, largely autonomous.

Second, the definition of religion is political. It is a legitimating claim, a discursive strategy. For instance, is Scientology a religion? No according to the Charity Commissioners in Britain, as we will see in Chapter 2, but yes according to the tax authorities in the USA, while the authorities in France and Germany are actively hostile to it. The same ambiguity applies to the Brazilian fusion of popular Catholic and west belief systems, Candomblé, to the syncretic Vietnamese movement, Cao Dai, to the Falun Gong in east Asia and to many others. Defining the limits of religion – as against 'cults' and 'sects' and 'superstitions', with their pejorative overtones – is to exercise a form of power. Religion used to be an intrinsically coercive activity, as its Latin etymology, 'binding', suggests, and the emphasis on subjective spirituality as the presumed essence of religion is relatively recent in history.

Third, it is owing to the specialization of roles and discourses in the West that 'religion' has come to occupy a defined sphere. In medieval Indian temple sculpture, for instance, religion and aesthetics and eroticism seem to have been inseparable from one another. The thirteenth century Surya Temple at Konarak on the east coast, probably the centre of a Tantric cult, is embellished by a multitude of filigree sculptures of men and women in couples, whose erotic physicality cannot be separated analytically from their spiritual significance as symbolizing ecstatic reunion with the divine. The concept of Hinduism as a singular religion is only a few centuries old, borrowed from the Arabic name for India (al-hind). The concept of religion is indeed peculiar to language families influenced by Latin, and has no exact equivalent elsewhere. The European concept of privileged institutional religion, after being imposed as a consequence of European hegemony on countries such as India, China and which it did not fit exactly, has now come to be accepted as operative on a global scale. Yet many Muslims contend that Islam is not 'merely' a religion but also a seamless whole encompassing politics, economics and morality. Judaism, too, is often seen as culture rather than religion.

Fourth, Christianity, especially in its Protestant forms, and much of mainstream Islam, attach more importance to belief, as an essential of religion, than, say, Judaism (which emphasizes particularly the moral law) and Confucianism (which emphasizes the proper exercising of social roles). The Catholic Church enjoins assent – to its own institutional tradition, the 'magisterium'. This is close to one of the dominant connotations of the Arabic noun *islām*, i.e. submission to the will of God – and does not necessarily imply that believers have explored for themselves every item of their creed.

It has even been argued that religion has no valid existence as a concept outside the academic discipline of Religious Studies, and that the term should be avoided completely. The ingenious argument may be put that there is no such thing anyway as strictly analytical categories: according to this view, analytical categories are merely the 'folk' categories of a particular group, i.e. in this case academic students of religion. This however is a counsel of despair. It is an illusion to think that extreme precision is indispensable or even possible when one is discussing the subtler aspects of human experience. Nor can one escape the problem of definition by substituting for 'religion' other words such as 'faith' or 'spirituality'. These terms import their own problems: to start with, both exclude the institutional aspects of religion. Indeed, when citizens of advanced industrial societies say, as many of them do, that they are by inclination spiritual, but not religious, I argue that those who feel affinity with the former as opposed to the latter are merely saying that they would like to decant the pure essence of religion from its institutional sediment. (In fact, new institutions emerge to compete with the more established ones.) It is a fallacy to think that by defining words precisely one can guarantee lucidity of thought, for thoughts are expressed in sentences rather than words. Most non-European languages had no word exactly corresponding to our 'religion' until the nineteenth century.

Moreover, contrary to the view of some religious apologists that questioning of religious dogma began only with the eighteenth century Enlightenment, the anthropologist Jack Goody has shown that a 'kernel of doubt' can be detected in diverse historical traditions. These include not only some of the Sophists and Sceptics of the ancient classical world, but also the Sanskrit *Rigveda* of the second millennium BCE:

Non-being then existed not nor being:
There was no air, nor sky that is beyond it,
What was concealed? Wherein? In whose protection?
And was there deep unfathomable water?

According to Goody, gods can only be described in language, and doubt about their existence is built into the language used to describe them. The historian Georges Minois has even argued – though his selection of data is limitingly Christocentric – that atheism, since the origins of humanity, was 'one of the two big ways of seeing the world: a world without the supernatural, a world where man stands alone to confront himself and a nature ruled by immutable laws. The atheist detects the subterfuge behind the concept of God, and denounces it'.

The problem here is to convert the 'folk category' of religion – which always means different things to different people – into an analytical category; in other words, to borrow the jargon of anthropology, to turn an 'emic' (insider) category into an 'etic' (outsider) category. I think this can be done, and attempt to do so in Chapter 2.

The Religious Inclination

The starting-point of this book is that a 'religious inclination' is essential for the functioning of any society. Many writers from different viewpoints have argued this. (It may be that this inclination is biologically determined, but such a view is speculative and my argument does not depend on it.)

Erich Fromm (1900–80) was both a psychoanalyst and a member of the Frankfurt School of critical social theorists. However, unlike nearly all his distinguished colleagues, he was sympathetic to religion. If every society, he thought, needs what he called a 'framework of orientation' or 'object of devotion', the consequences, when traditional objects of devotion are withdrawn or disappear, can be disastrous – leading to such aberrations in the twentieth century as nazism and Stalinism. He described this condition in a figurative way as a form of 'necrophilia'. Other examples of this, for Fromm, were worship of false gods such as megamachines, or treating people as things, or reckless consumerism.

For Clifford Geertz the anthropologist, it is an intrinsically human trait to try to make sense of our lives and to ward off the threatening experience of meaninglessness:

> Bafflement, suffering, and a sense of intractable ethical paradox are all, if they become intense enough or are sustained long enough, radical challenges to the proposition that life is comprehensible and that we can, by taking thought, orient ourselves effectively within it.

All schools of Marxism have adopted a reductive approach to religion, which is held ultimately to reflect economic relations of domination, though on occasion to provide opportunities for challenging domination – as in the historical cases of the English nonconformist churches or Latin American guerrilla priests. Neo-Marxism uses a powerful intellectual tool when it claims that the ruling class represses – in the psychoanalytic sense – what determines it, that is to say economic relations of domination. This applies not only to religion as such but to all 'ideology', in the pejorative Marxian sense, that is to say systems of ideas that make the interests of the ruling class appear to be in the interests of all. It is possible to apply this insight not merely to traditional capitalist societies but to communist and post-communist societies, which in practice are equally stratified. But according to neo-Marxism, all analysis eventually comes back to the primacy of political economy over ideas. Neo-Marxism considers 'idealism' – in the technical philosophical sense of non-acceptance of materialism, not the other, popular sense of a quest for perfection – to be an intellectual fallacy.

However, I would like to turn this argument on its head and suggest that the 'religious inclination' is repressed in a secularizing society. Freud used the metaphor of energy displacement to account for the flow of individual emotions. We may feel a surge of unexpected anger, directed against another person, when – as Freud has made it easier for us to see – the real cause for it may well be found in some emotional frustration of ours that has nothing to do with that individual. Freud conceives the psyche as a system of underground water pipes under pressure. Borrowing the structure of the Freudian metaphor but not the content, I suggest that the religious inclination is like a hydraulic system. If the taps are turned off at one outlet, and if the water finds a weak point in the pipes, it is likely to well up unexpectedly somewhere else. Or as Wuthnow puts it, 'Religious sentiment does not simply wax and wane; it changes clothes and appears in garb to which we are sometimes unaccustomed. It may well be all around us, and yet we have not trained ourselves to recognize it'.

We may call these outlets or overflows parareligions. Other names that have been suggested are 'quasi-religions' or 'religioid forms', or 'analogical' or 'implicit' religion. The word parareligion has sometimes been used with pejorative intent to characterize 'cults' or 'sects' of which the writer disapproves, but I try to use it with strict neutrality, to mean movements or institutions that have some but not all the characteristics of religions in a stricter sense.

For the sake of this analysis, consideration of the truth-values of religions (or parareligions) will be sidestepped. This is the only tenable starting point for social scientists, because the aim of social science must be to find common ground for discussion. As a leading sociologist of religion, David Martin (though himself an ordained Christian), has observed, it is not feasible to 'give a systematic account of the divine activity in our world'; so a kind of methodological agnosticism is necessary for social research. Clearly, the various religious doctrines disseminated in the world cannot all be true, but we can put in brackets for the time being the question of whether any particular one is true. On the other hand, we do not need to assert that any particular religious doctrine is false. Even a doctrine that may appear far-fetched or implausible may be defended as an expression of a metaphorical or oblique truth. Nor, taking an agnostic position, do we need to argue, as some philosophers do, that the burden of proof ought to lie with religious believers rather than with atheists, atheism being according to this argument considered as a default position. Methodological agnosticism is, admittedly, a difficult position to maintain consistently – as will become clear later in this book when we come to consider parareligious phenomena that are widely considered to be contemptible or even evil.

Choice of any religious commitment is strongly influenced by social determinants as well as individual preference. A religious choice has two aspects. First, a choice of narrative, which may variously be characterized as a divine revelation, a prophecy, a historical record, or a myth (again, not in any pejorative sense). Second, an aesthetic choice. By aesthetics we mean in part the arts and ceremonies that have always fortified religion, and have often succeeded in stretching official doctrine into new and original shapes. But at a deeper level we equally mean all the acquired, embodied dispositions included in the sociological term 'habitus'. Habitus has been well defined by an anthropologist as:

> the self-developable means by which the subject achieves a range of human objects – from styles of physical movement (for example, walking), through modes of emotional being (for example, composure), to kinds of spiritual experience (for example, mystical states).

The concept of habitus therefore has both objective or observable, and subjective or phenomenological, aspects. One might suggest commonalities between the physical deportment of religious dignitaries across a range of cultures. Typically, they walk at a deliberate and slow pace, and allow themselves to smile or frown only in a restrained way, never to break into laughter or anger in public. Unless acknowledging or bestowing a greeting, they look straight ahead of them, as if lacking peripheral vision; and they wear special clothes indicating their status. By contrast, mystics and visionaries are expected to display signs of social marginality such as unkempt hair, a more rolling gait, a roving gaze, and contempt for finicky detail. (Jesus was evidently humorous by nature, especially when dealing with hecklers.) These may however all be 'fronts', in the nature of assumed theatrical roles, and deceptive as to the person's state of mind. Subjective states of mind are continuously and no doubt necessarily brought into being by representations of other persons and their respective habitus: parents and siblings, friends and lovers, teachers and pupils, exemplary figures, such as the Buddha or Jesus or Muhammad, whose behaviour in life the faithful seek to emulate.

Detours of the Religious Inclination: the Communist Period

Let us take a simple example of how the religious inclination finds new outlets when under compression: the life-cycle rituals and similar ceremonies developed in Russia and Bulgaria during the atheistic communist period. These hark back to the short-lived calendrical experiments of the French Revolution, with a series of annual holidays, the *sans-culottides*, dedicated to Genius, Labour, Noble Actions, Awards and Opinion – this last an intellectual saturnalia permitting unrestricted criticism of public figures.

In the 1970s Bulgaria was among the other socialist countries that copied the Soviet Russian system of 'socialist holidays and rituals'. Ethnographers and folklorists helped a National Commission for Socialist Holidays and Rituals to introduce guidelines and a calendar based on Marxist theory, intended to cover all aspects of Bulgarian social life. Rituals associated with the 'sphere of material production' included, for instance, special days for the shepherd or the construction worker. The 'sphere of familial consumption' included a name-giving ritual instead of baptism. Emphasis was placed, according to a German scholar who analysed the system just before the restoration of multi-party democracy in 1990, 'on the mother, on the local community and on the "Bulgarian fatherland". The room was decorated with flowers and the national colours, and the female officials might wear "elements of stylized national costume" '.

The narrative promoted by the Bulgarian State was the creation of a new humanity superseding Christianity, coupled with patriotism. Used to the elaborate sensorial appeal of the ceremonies of the Bulgarian Orthodox Church, with its exaltation of the person of the priest as God's representative, the population failed to respond whole-heartedly to these civic rituals, and their efflorescence was short. After 1990 the church soon regained its supremacy – albeit weakened by schism on account of the Patriarch's record of alleged compliance with the communist authorities.

The Bulgarian communist example is one of attempted top-down imposition of parareligion on the people in the aid of a political ideology, with the help of pliable scholars. The nazis had attempted something similar, for instance trying to replace Christmas by a 'winter festival'. But it would be a mistake to think that all such detours of the religious inclination are entirely top-down.

During the earliest phase of the Soviet regime, 1917–23, the Bolshevik leaders introduced new names for towns and streets, new forms of address ('Comrade'), new flags and badges, and also new calendrical and life cycle ceremonies, often borrowing some of the 'folk' features of the past. A sensitive chronicler of the ceremonies of these years, Christopher Binns, comments that they had 'a fresh, spontaneous, improvised quality and an atmosphere of chaotic enthusiasm and communal feeling…'.

For instance, the May Day demonstrations of this period evoked not only the French Revolution with red banners, scarves and armbands, but also the Orthodox 'Way of the Cross'. 'In the early years country people often mistook Bolshevik processions for religious ones; the untutored peasants of one remote village, according to a contemporary report, "took off their hats and devoutly crossed themselves" on seeing the approach of people carrying colourful banners and portraits of august bearded figures', in fact of Lenin and other Bolshevik leaders. The Komsomol (Union of Soviet Youth) activists organized ceremonies such as 'renaming the factories'. After speeches and singing indoors, and the presentation of a banner,

> … the crowd of people filed out of the shed, preceded by the banner, into the dark, autumn night and carrying firebrands, walked round the whole huge area of the Putilov works, stopping at the gates. To the accompaniment of singing and blows on an anvil the old sign was taken down and the new one put up. The procession moved on, stopping at the various workshops and sections. At other factories they carried a portrait of the new factory manager instead of a banner.

Trotsky argued that anti-religious propaganda alone could not satisfy 'man's desire for the theatrical' and 'his strong and legitimate need for an outer manifestation of emotion', and predicted that over the decades new customs would develop through a process of natural selection, 'without bureaucratization, i.e. compulsion from above'.

It was not to be. During a second Soviet phase, after the death of Lenin in 1924 till 1928, Trotsky began to be discredited and the carnival aspects of ceremonies were replaced by strict discipline. Meanwhile Lenin came to be deified. During a third phase, 1928–53, that of terror and punishment, numerous festivals were introduced but the cult of the leader, Stalin, came to be the principal embodiment of the hopes of the nation. Anti-religious propaganda was muted between 1941 and 1954, when Khrushchev resumed it and a new panoply of life-cycle rituals was introduced, but without the communal enthusiasm of the early Bolshevik period. Binns, writing at the end of the 1970s, showed how, though the framework of the ceremonies was imposed from above, the introduction of such institutions as 'wedding palaces' was highly popular and allowed for considerable regional and personal variation, sometimes incurring complaints from the Soviet press about extravagance: 'It is sweet indeed for once to be treated with warmth and politeness by Soviet officials and to savour briefly the regal splendour of these Palaces ..., where the carpeted staircase and elegant halls make the cramped fifth-floor flat seem far away'. In the post-Stalin period the effort to instil the glum doctrine of Marxism-Leninism among the people – whatever its appeal to intellectuals – proved a failure, and in Binns' words '…whatever the regime's intentions of extending its ideological control into family life and leisure, the actual conduct of these ceremonies has given expression to, and thereby encouraged, pluralism, individualism and consumerism, which undermine a centralist ideology'.

Detours of the Religious Inclination: Limiting Cases

A clear example of religioid activity avidly supported by the people is football, by which is here meant soccer – the dominant version of the game except in the USA, which is resistant to colonization by non-American sports. Huge financial interests dominate the game and the head of the much-criticized controlling institution, FIFA, has the influence of a head of State. Popular susceptibilities are undoubtedly manipulated by FIFA as much as by successful political movements. However, the extraordinary success of football as a transnational, transcultural movement evidently has the deepest roots. It is now a commonplace that football has some of the characteristics of a religion: demigods, hymns, ritual vestments, ecstatic experience, tribalism, visible praying by the players (with the palms joined for Christians, raised in the air for Muslims). In Glasgow, football still overlaps with Scottish Christian sectarianism in that one of the two leading clubs, Celtic, is still associated with Catholics and the other, Rangers, with Protestants. Like religion, football both unites and divides. At the time of the World Cup, a visiting Martian might be forgiven for inferring that Goal had replaced God. In Britain, football results are announced at the end of virtually every television news bulletin.

But if football has some clear religioid characteristics, and many of its supporters would claim that it does offer a kind of spiritual uplift (indeed it is known as 'the beautiful game'), it is clearly lacking in others. It cannot be said to offer a moral code or to enjoin altruism, for instance, though its bosses take some hesitant steps in this direction. Nor does it try to explain human beings' place in nature or help us come to terms with death. Its rules and folklore do not amount to a doctrine. It also belongs to the wider category of 'sport', which is both a major sector in the economy and part of the sphere of 'leisure', the antonym of 'work'. Another example would be the Olympic Games, with their opening fire ceremony and their historical roots in Ancient Greece, and the efforts by the movement to introduce a politically progressive and human rights dimension. So football and the Olympics are limiting cases. Is there any way that we can discuss parareligions more carefully?

Commerce and industry offer many examples of the religioid. Take the chorus of the IBM Rally Song of the 1930s:

> EVER ONWARD – EVER ONWARD
> That's the spirit that has brought us fame!
> We're big, but bigger we will be,
> We can't fail, for all can see
> That to serve humanity has been our aim!
> Our products now are known in every zone,
> Our reputation sparkles like a gem!
> We've fought our way through – and new
> Fields we're sure to conquer too
> For the EVER ONWARD I.B.M.

Company songs are now out of fashion. However, today's extremely successful multi-level marketing (MLM) companies, which while being perfectly legal have a similar hierarchic structure to pyramid schemes, display religioid characteristics. Here is some of the wisdom of Mary Kay Ash (1918–2001), revered founder of the Mary Kay cosmetics company, which now has a global sales force of 1.6 million Independent Beauty Consultants, and an associated charitable foundation devoted to fighting cancers and ending domestic violence:

> Do you know that within your power lies every step you ever dreamed of stepping, and within your power lies every joy you ever dreamed of seeing? Within yourself lies everything you ever dreamed of being. Become everything that God wants you to be. It is within your reach. Dare to grow into your dreams and claim this as your motto: Let it be me.

Another large MLM corporation, Nikken, specializing in magnetic therapy and other 'wellness' products, announces the Five Pillars of Health: a healthy body, a healthy mind, a healthy family, a healthy society and healthy finances. Amway (short for American Way), with more than 3 million distributors worldwide selling a range of products from dietary supplements to scouring sponges, has had to fend off charges of milieu control, pseudo-science, suppression of critical thinking, 'love-bombing' new recruits (with displays of group affection), and mafioso methods of dispute resolution and control.

These are also limiting cases of the religioid, and we lack useful tools for discussing them. But why should this matter?

Making Sense of Parareligion

Some movements, such as Scientology, lay claim to a religious status that is widely denied it by outsiders. Others, such as football, lay no claim to such status but they may appear to outside analysts to have several of the characteristics of religion. Again, other organizations, such as Mary Kay or Amway, appear to be deliberate attempts to mimic the more hierarchic forms of religion for purposes that are mainly commercial, though sometimes tinged with philanthropy.

Of special interest are those movements and organizations that may believe themselves to be motivated by purely rational considerations, whereas the truth is that their would-be rationality is haunted by the shadow of the irrational. The question also arises as to whether religion is fundamentally rational, as Pope Benedict XVI contends on behalf of Catholicism, and hence presumably wholly compatible with science, or fundamentally irrational, as Kierkegaard contended, or somewhere between the two. It seems unarguable, however, that even if Pope Benedict's controversial position is accepted, the rational is constantly apt to be undermined by the irrational.

To establish this point we can go back a hundred years to a lecture that Sir James Frazer gave to mark his appointment to the first chair in social anthropology in Britain, in which he wrote:

> The smooth surface of cultured society is sapped and mined by superstition. Only those whose studies have led them to investigate the subject are aware of the depth to which the ground beneath our feet is thus, as it were, honeycombed by unseen forces. ... The surface of society, like that of the sea, is in perpetual motion; its depths, like those of the ocean, remain almost unmoved.

Frazer was thinking however of the 'grosser beliefs' of 'the vulgar' and assumed that scientific progress would eventually displace superstition and magic. For instance, he discussed in his great work *The Golden Bough* the supposed curative properties of mistletoe:

> Whereas the Druids thought that mistletoe cured everything, modern doctors appear to think that it cures nothing. If they are right, we must conclude that the ancient and widespread faith in the medicinal virtue of mistletoe is a pure superstition based on nothing better than the fanciful inferences which ignorance has drawn from the parasitic nature of the plant, its position high up on the branch of a tree seeming to protect it from the dangers to which plants and animals are subject on the surface of the ground. ... As mistletoe cannot fall to the ground because it is rooted on the branch of a tree

high above the earth, it seems to follow as a necessary consequence that an epileptic patient cannot possibly fall down in a fit so long as he carries a piece of mistletoe in his pocket or a decoction of mistletoe in his stomach. Such a train of reasoning would probably be regarded even now as cogent by a large portion of the human species.

Indeed mistletoe traditions survive in the broad European folk memory, as well as being a focus of modern druidism. Mistletoe extracts are a widely used form of complementary medicine today, believed to have a value in strengthening the immune system against cancer and other diseases, though clinical tests so far have been inconclusive.

For a modern anthropologist, Alfred Gell (1945–97), the truth is more vertiginous than for Frazer. Gell argues that irrationality or magic haunts our most seemingly rational activities like a shadow. For Gell, magic is a way of getting something for nothing. He wrote of the 'technology of enchantment', which pervades our modern technology so that the two can be hard to distinguish. It includes mind-control, all the arts and creeds, advertising, public relations, 'spin'. This is an extremely broad category, then, which includes not only most of the things that make life worth living, but also all the mechanisms – short of brute coercion – whereby people can be enslaved. Gell's personal philosophy is that we can protect ourselves from this enslavement by means of play, willing submission to enchantment, and humour.

The proper disposal of human remains – almost a cultural universal – is a clear example of 'magical' defiance of brutish mortality, as if this could be defeated by the murmuring of sacred texts or the donation of wreaths. Reason tells us that what separates human beings from animals is precisely – short of some future extraordinary discoveries by neurobiologists – the elusive stuff, whether it is poetry or electronic bank transfers. So our cherishing of our loved ones' perishable remains becomes one of humanity's weakest points for ideological manipulation. All the major recognized religions prescribe funerary ceremonies. Insofar as these depend logically on explicit doctrinal premises, they cannot fairly be called 'irrational': for instance, the Eastern Orthodox Church and Orthodox Judaism require burial and forbid cremation as it defies the doctrine of the general resurrection of the body (the Catholic Church having somewhat relaxed its position on the matter). However, it is also clear that much contemporary concern with burials and bones is closely related to nationalism, for instance with the televising of military funerals, or the demands for repatriation of the bones of indigenous people such as the Maori from Western museums where they had been preserved as scientific specimens. The case of Israel, strongly committed towards repatriation of Jews for burial in the Jewish homeland, is merely an extreme example because of the Zionist movement's need to vindicate what has been called the 'will to rebirth of this old–new people in its old–new land'. Even in the secularizing West, indifference to the proper treatment of dead bodies or body parts is generally condemned as an outrage, regardless of any specific religious beliefs.

Death is widely 'brushed under the carpet' in Western consumer societies, where the prolongation of youth is a major industry that includes cosmetics and perfume, plastic surgery, dieting and exercising. Arguably, keeping old age, decay and death at bay with the aid of this huge industry is a means of confronting death through its negation, and therefore has a parareligious aspect, with Elizabeth Arden the beautician and Pierre-François Guerlain the perfumer exemplifying a line of prophets.

Public concern for the proper treatment of a dead body, even among those who practise no formal religion and count themselves unsuperstitious, is one example of magical thinking in Gell's sense. We may also argue that when groups of mourners gather at a funeral to pay respects to the memory of someone we respect and love, we are capable of rising to a height of moral awareness that few other occasions inspire. We willingly submit to a ceremony that acknowledges the irrational in all of us in its concentration on mortal remains, according to the aesthetic preferences with which we feel socially comfortable, while the mourning ritual does its work not for the dead but for the living in stimulating cohesion and empathy.

The same is true of an institution that is deeply vulnerable to criticism on purely rational grounds, and incorporates a marked element of magical thinking: monarchy. Rationalist arguments against it include the following. Monarchies emerged in hierarchic societies based on the hereditary principle, and are anachronistic in our contemporary meritocracies. In traditional monarchies, the throne was closely associated with the State religion – as it still is in Buddhist Thailand or Muslim Morocco, and still was in Britain when Queen Elizabeth II was anointed as the sovereign in 1953 – and it begins to be less sustainable in secularizing, multicultural societies. It is hard for a child crown prince to be brought up in the media spotlight of celebrity worship without psychological risk. The bounty of monarchs is a confidence trick, as their money is not actually earned in the normal way. And so on. However, a monarch who well understands his or her role, as do Queen Elizabeth or even the Emperor of Japan (though his powers are sharply circumscribed as a result of the Second World War), is sometimes able to underwrite political stability, and many believe that the value of this makes all the disadvantages of monarchy tolerable. A major part of that role is one of responding to magical thinking and maintaining the aura of majesty while also embodying a commitment to cohesive moral values. A similar role is fulfilled in republics: in the United States or France by the rhetoric of freedom, human rights and democracy; in Indonesia, by that of *pancasila* or religious tolerance. These are on the face of it more rational political values than those of monarchy, but are no less liable to be used to obfuscate political and economic relationships of domination.

Europe's surviving monarchies do not seem to be under threat. In the Ancient Near East, gods had the characteristics of kings, but they did not only inspire fear and reverence: they were also seen as defenders of the disinherited and downtrodden. It would be a mistake to sentimentalize this role, for one of the penalties of occupying a throne is the risk of becoming a scapegoat when things go wrong, or even of being sacrificed – as Frazer famously described in *The Golden Bough*, and as the beheadings of Charles I of England and Louis XVI of France exemplify. In a limited monarchy such as the British, the incumbent is wise to allow ambitious politicians to aspire to the sacred status of sovereignty, rather than seeking to monopolize it for the throne itself, because eventually the politicians are likely to overreach and be deposed. Political power is always closely allied to the numinous.

It is no part of my argument to belittle the importance of science and scientific method. Science is the application of reason, but reason must include the rational study of the irrational. This is not to glorify the irrational – which leads to aberrations such as fascism that wilfully exploit violent human emotions – but to seek to understand it rationally. Moreover, claims to rationality are frequently used as bludgeons in an argument – just as much as invocations of God, Nature or human rights. Some anthropologists, such as Paul Rabinow, have devoted much of their careers to studying expressions of modernizing rationality – whether urban planning or laboratory science – with a similar method to that which more traditional anthropologists have applied to exotic societies. Yet the aim of anthropologists such as Rabinow, on the whole, is not to undermine science but to enrich it by exposing how its practice is influenced by power relations and metaphysical complacency.

The next chapter will propose a more precise way of discussing religion and parareligion, accepting that total precision is impossible.

2

THE FAMILY RESEMBLANCE OF
RELIGIONS

A Polythetic or Fuzzy Category

We shall follow here the classic sociologists of religion in arguing that no rigorous definition of religion is valid cross-culturally. Instead, we will adopt a 'fuzzy' definition according to a score or so of criteria, and refer to a religious 'field' on a spectrum between strong and weak.

As an alternative to fuzziness, we may sometimes refer to 'polythetic' or 'family resemblance' classification. To advocate fuzzy classification is not necessarily to be guilty of sloppy thinking. Linguists have developed the idea of 'prototype semantics', whereby the applicability of a word to a thing is not a matter of 'yes or no', but rather of 'more or less'. In labelling something, we implicitly compile a checklist of criterial properties, a list of features that it is supposed to satisfy if it is to be deemed properly labelled by some word. These criteria may be graded. For instance, a chair or a bed may be deemed more 'prototypical', i.e. representative, of the category 'furniture' than a lamp or a telephone. This can be established by questionnaires and similar techniques. It might be argued that one or two criteria, such as a belief in supernatural entities, should be treated as 'prototypical' for religion. However, as made clear in Chapter 1, we are exploring in this book the possibilities of the term religion as an analytical ('etic') category rather than a folk ('emic') category. It is possible that a conclusion might be reached that certain criteria are more central to the category of religion than others. I did try at first to devise an ordering of the criteria that might prioritize some of them as more prototypical than others, but have abandoned the attempt, as it seemed to be begging the question. Thus a very important criterion – what I have called 'patina', the hallowing of a religion over centuries – I have placed last. In any case – as we are setting out to clarify an 'etic' concept – the question is to be resolved through analysis and interpretation of comparative data, not by polling language-users as to how they understand the term 'religion' when applied or not to different social movements (which would give folk or 'emic' results).

Here is a list of 19 criteria for the polythetic category 'religion', together with some comments intended to illustrate sketchily both the elusiveness of some of them, and also the wide variety of phenomena that must be considered if we are to grasp the issue comparatively. There are overlaps between some of the criteria. In considering them, we must remember not only the variety of beliefs and practices to be found within each major religious tradition – particularly, the contrast between elite and popular forms – but also that arguably every doctrine contains within itself the seeds of its own negation. (For instance, declaring that there is only one God admits linguistically of the contrary proposition that there are more than one. To publish militant atheist tracts is to stage a rebellion against patriarchal doctrines that would not occur to those educated in traditions such as Buddhism which are more equivocal as to the objective reality of divine forces.)

1. Appeal to Supernatural Entities

A wide variety of supernatural entities appears in the world's belief systems. For the Aymara of the Bolivian Andes, Mount Kaata is a human body consisting of three parts, each a separate community: the mountain breathes and must be fed with animal blood and fat. For the Uduk of Sudan, ebony trees are able to overhear and record conversations. Animals are frequently anthropomorphized. A provocative theory has been put forward by one anthropologist, Pascal Boyer, that religious representations of supernatural entities typically include a salient counter-intuitive part, but the remainder works by default. Thus a spirit may have non-standard physical properties – for instance, invisibility and ability to be in various places at once – but standard psychological properties enabling us to guess the motives for its behaviour. A zombie, by contrast, has special psychological properties – it is remote-controlled by a spirit, witch or god – but standard physical properties. One may hold to the idea of a God that listens everywhere, but if one wants to pray to a statue one must be within hearing distance. According to Boyer, supernatural entities are selected from a 'catalogue of the supernatural'.

Divinization of individuals during their lifetimes is possible, and the anthropologist Roland Littlewood has adduced the cases of Jean-Jacques Dessalines (c.1758–1806), the first Emperor of independent Haiti, and François 'Papa Doc' Duvalier (1907–71), who ruled the same country for fourteen years. According to the doctrine of Incarnation set out by St John and St Paul, Jesus was already God in human form at the time of his birth, which is the reverse of apotheosis or 'upwards divinization'. Islam resisted divinization of the Prophet Muhammad, as the deism of the French Enlightenment and, later, Unitarianism were to reverse the divinization of Jesus.

The Buddha taught that belief in gods was unnecessary for salvation, but in the popular Buddhism of a country such as Thailand his images are treated with veneration and are the site of prayers and supplications; so it would be hair-splitting to deny that he has at least semi-divine status in that society. In Sri Lanka, according to the anthropologist Edmund Leach,

> the orthodox theological view that the Buddha is an example of enlightenment and not a god is far too difficult for the ordinary imagination of the ordinary Sinhalese villager. In village practice, as distinct from orthodox theory, the Buddha is unquestionably the supreme God.

But another ethnographer of village Buddhism in Sri Lanka, Martin Southwold, with maybe a higher opinion of the intellectual capabilities of his informants, reports that they are perfectly able to combine their belief in the Buddha as an exceptional human being – not a god – with a belief in various gods who have the power to bestow worldly benefits but have little to do with Buddhism as such.

Divinity has often been ascribed to monarchs. Until the eighteenth century, English and French kings and queens were thought to inherit the power to cure by touch those suffering from the 'king's evil' (scrofula or tuberculosis of the neck).

In the twentieth century, the Cult of Personality emerged in communist and fascist States. Unusually, the popular cult of Mao Zedong has survived both his death and the virtual abandonment of the political principles for which he stood. His birthplace, Shaoshan, has become a pilgrimage site, selling amulets engraved with his portrait rather than the traditional images of Buddhist or Taoist holy men. He is revered above all for his projection of personal power and for his messianic egalitarianism. The more some Chinese intellectuals, committed to economic reform, hate Mao, the more many of the poor people like him. Pope John Paul II, having done so much to defeat communism, proceeded to permit a cult of his own personality almost unprecedented in the history of the Papacy.

In capitalist societies, divinity has been replaced by the superbranding of footballers and entertainers. By buying toiletries or watches endorsed by David Beckham or Brad Pitt, we identify ourselves with these demigods' magical aura; or, to borrow Alfred Gell's terms, money spent on the most functional and material things such as a razor blade is magically transmuted into spiritual value, without the necessity to earn it by effort. Personal items that Beckham or Pitt has used will eventually command a high price as relics. Monotheists should be reassured by the thought that this is what is warned against in the Hebrew Bible when it inveighs against idolatry.

Much Western history is dominated by an explicit or implicit assumption that monotheism – as developed by the Ancient Hebrews, or perhaps a little earlier by the Egyptian king Akhenaten in the fourteenth century BCE – was a step forward in human progress, facilitating the rise of science and liberal humanism. This is by no means self-evident to non-monotheistic Asians, and a glance at the Ancient Near East may be instructive. Our view of the religions of the Ancient Near East is heavily coloured by the negative view that the Hebrews took of polytheism and idolatry. It has not been widely appreciated that the gods of the Mesopotamians, Phoenicians and Egyptians were seen as keepers of the 'inner, rational harmony of the universal order' (in Giorgio Buccellati's words), and fate was seen as an inert principle of that order 'communicating through its very predictability'. By contrast, the God of the Israelites made unpredictable demands – suddenly prohibiting the fruit of the tree of knowledge of good and evil, for instance, or calling on Abraham to break away from polytheism or to sacrifice his son. This God was also accustomed to communicating his will at a given time and expecting obedience, placing all revealed religions in opposition to others. Thus, according to Buccellati, the Israelite conception of the divine is arguably the less rational of the two traditions. In the Egyptian cosmology, the gods had to be continuously propitiated to prevent them from leaving Egypt and allowing the State to fall apart.

2. Appeal to an Ideal World

For the Greeks and Romans the world had deteriorated since the Golden Age that had immediately followed its creation. During the Golden Age, there was no conflict, no technology, no meat eating. Many religions look back to an age of primal innocence, or forward to a future spiritual fulfilment (such as the return of the Hidden Imam in Iranian Shiism), or to a holy land which may be either metaphorical (Arcadia or Eden) or located in actual present-day geography: Jerusalem (for Jews), Mecca and Medina (for Muslims), and in India Varanasi (or Benares, for Hindus) or Bodhgaya in southern Bihar (for Buddhists). In Buddhism, Nirvana is an ideal state of peace where earthly passions and illusions have been shed. Some religions such as Islam give a richly detailed account of the paradise that will greet the blessed, but its confessional cousin, Judaism, though generally accepting the idea of bodily resurrection after death, is reticent as to the details.

Dreamtime, a fundamental concept of Australian Aboriginal religion, is a condition beyond time and space that gives expression to the spiritual experience of groups and individuals. Arguably the glimpse of an ideal world must be a universal experience that may or may not be codified into a religious system – as these lines by the atheist Thomas Hardy suggest:

> Whence comes Solace? – not from seeing
> What is doing, suffering, being,
> Not from noting Life's conditions,
> Nor from heeding Time's monitions;
> But in cleaving to the Dream,
> And in gazing at the gleam
> Whereby gray things golden seem.

If the most powerful and basic feeling of attachment, across all cultures, is the child's attachment to the mother, then the loss of the original sense of unity with the mother as an irrecoverable reality is a universal experience, which religion and the arts try to recover throughout our lives. The charms, amulets and (in industrial cultures) key-rings or fridge magnets that are so widespread all over the world may be thought of as mentally retaining what psychoanalysts call the 'transitional object' – the blanket or stuffed animal to which young children after weaning become emotionally attached. In a higher register, the philosopher Charles Taylor writes of the sense of 'fullness' or 'richness', the sense that life is 'more than what it should be' – 'something we just catch glimpses of from afar off'.

The 'New Age' movement takes its name from the astrological Age of Aquarius, which has either arrived or is about to arrive – heralding a new stage in human evolution. At a more everyday level, consumer advertising and branding offer a ticket to an ideal world symbolized by the Rolex watch, the Chanel perfume, the Nike shoes.

As has often been pointed out, this appeal to an ideal world has morphed into many political utopias. John Gray has founded his deeply pessimistic philosophy on the proposition that not only the obviously religioid political ideologies such as communism and nazism (which will be discussed in Chapter 3) but also free market economics, for instance, or the Bush–Blair mission to spread democracy and good conduct through the 'war on terror', are kinds of religion – in that they depend on utopian thinking rather than realism. He has a fair enough case, but I suggest that to isolate only one of the criteria for a religion is to underestimate the complexity of the phenomenon.

3. Totalizing Discourse, Creeds, Master Dogmas and Scriptures

This is a difficult topic, because of the wide gap that can separate learned doctrines – often articulated in languages accessible only to the educated – from everyday religious practice. A large proportion of people brought up in a particular religion assent to its tenets as part of a diffuse cultural heritage in which formal doctrines and popular traditions are merged. For instance, Christmas trees are now popularly regarded as an integral part of Christmas celebrations – even to the extent of being officially banned in some multi-cultural contexts in Britain so as not to offend non-Christians – whereas they clearly derive from 'pagan' festivals of seasonal renewal.

The old historical religions have devoted much intellectual effort to trying to resolve doctrinal difficulties, such as the relationship of body and soul. St Thomas Aquinas was concerned by the puzzle of what happens in the resurrection of cannibals and those whom they have eaten. He taught that in the case of a cannibal who ate only human flesh, what would resurrect in him would be 'that which he drew from those who generated him [his parents], and what is wanting will be supplied by the creator's omnipotence'. St Augustine considered that aborted foetuses would be resurrected in the after-life as beautifully formed and mature. Until recently, the Roman Catholic Church held that those who died before the Coming of Jesus, as well as children who die before baptism, went to Limbo, which was neither Heaven nor Hell. Divinity students were instructed that if an unborn child was not expected to survive, intra-uterine baptism should be performed through a tube on the part of the child's body that was most accessible. Only at the end of 2005 did the Vatican announce that Limbo, now regarded by Pope Benedict XVI as merely a 'theological hypothesis', would be officially dropped as having no place in modern Catholic doctrine.

Elaborate rules in Islamic law define what animals are legitimate to eat and whether or not they must be killed in a ritual sacrifice. A strict Muslim may properly eat no land animals killed by 'polytheists'. Fish, being wild rather than domestic and caught with nets or hooks rather than killed outright, may be eaten whoever catches them. However, some schools of Islamic law decree that game animals which live on the land may not be eaten if they have been killed by a Christian or a Jew, whereas domestic animals killed by a Christian or a Jew may be eaten.

These are instances of the intellectual effort put into theological debates that are of acute concern for members of a particular faith, but of no interest to those who do not share its premises. Some religious people, on the other hand, argue that the essentials of their faith are very simple. In the case of Islam, the five 'pillars' or duties of religion are often held to sum it up: *shahada* (the profession of faith), regular prayers, *zakat* or alms, fasting and (once, if possible, in one's lifetime) the pilgrimage to Mecca. For nearly all Christian churches, the Incarnation is essential, while most of them insist on further dogmas such as the Virgin Birth and the Resurrection of Jesus. Many contemporary Christians – led by the Anglican Church with its genius for soft adaptation – have gratefully grasped the New Testament text 'God is love. Whoever lives in love lives in God, and God in him' (*1 John* 4:16), so as to reverse the equation and assert that if God is love, love is God. In this view, there is not much to separate a Christian commitment from the 'almost-instinct' described in the atheist Philip Larkin's well-known poem 'An Arundel Tomb': that 'what will survive of us is love'. A corollary in liberal Jewish religious observance today is the idea of God as the ultimate 'power for good'.

As for Buddhism, it has voluminous doctrinal texts, particularly concerned with monastic rules, though they were memorized orally and not committed to writing till the last century BCE, some four centuries after the Buddha's death. By contrast, some practitioners of western Buddhism argue that the essential doctrine of Buddhism is absence of doctrine.

If we turn to indigenous or 'tribal' belief-systems, many of these have been hailed by anthropologists as embodying sophisticated interpretations of human relationships with land and the cosmos. Some earlier anthropologists tried to compile systematic accounts of these belief-systems, with the laudable aim of demonstrating the philosophical acumen of peoples regarded at the time as 'primitive'. One famous such anthropologist of the 1930s and 40s was Marcel Griaule, who during his fieldwork among the Dogon of Mali in west Africa documented an all-encompassing creation myth with the help of a Dogon informant, Ogotemmeli. Subsequent research has shown that other Dogon people do not recognize many elements in this myth, and that it was to a great extent fabricated imaginatively by Griaule's Dogon teachers in order to satisfy his investigative desires – their own beliefs being transmitted orally rather than in writing, and much more flexible than systems committed to writing. It is due to the work of anthropologists such as Claude Lévi-Strauss, for the Amerindians, and W.E.H. Stanner, for the Australian Aboriginals, that we have come to appreciate the subtlety of many indigenous belief-systems, so that whether or not they are granted the label of 'religion' is a matter of cultural politics rather than anthropology.

Islamic law grants special concessions to 'People of the Book', mainly Christians and Jews, which are denied to polytheists and atheists. A poignant instance of the prestige attributed to written texts comes from the Kalasha of the Islamic State of Pakistan, or as they are pejoratively named the Kalash Kaffirs, thought to be the only group in the Himalayas who have resisted conversion to Islam, Hinduism or Buddhism. About 4,000 of them live in three valleys of the Hindu Kush mountains, with a subsistence economy based on grains, fruit and walnut trees, and goat-herding. Their culture resisted the conquest of the Kalasha kingdoms in about the sixteenth century. Non-Muslim Kalasha were enslaved. Their religion is a form of polytheistic shamanism, characteristic of the central Asian region, with influences from Muslim and Indo-Aryan sources. Conversion to Islam by an individual is considered a source of contagion to the household.

A hint of how the non-literate Kalasha have succeeded in surviving as a 'pagan' enclave may be found in an attempt by one of their shamans at the beginning of the twentieth century to resist the power of the written word wielded by Muslims. A man called Tanuk declared himself a shaman and produced a book written on birch bark and apparently dropped from the sky. He used to consult it while sitting alone on a stool on the roof of a stable. This prestigious book was reputed to fly like a crow, circle three times in the air above the place where an omen was buried, and return to Tanuk, who would then summon people to dig for an omen in the place indicated. When Tanuk died in the 1950s, the power of his book died with him. It was seen and photographed by a European ethnographer in 1956, stored carefully in a granary and treated with veneration. Its twelve pages of wooden strips were covered with systematic designs similar to those seen on the columns of Kalasha sanctuaries. Tanuk's revelatory book was evidently designed to enhance the self-confidence of the Kalasha vis-à-vis their proselytizing neighbours, and to put them on the same footing as Muslims.

Illustrating the same principle of the prestige of books, the anthropologist Raymond Firth tells how he was asked in 1952 by one of the 'pagan' chiefs of the remote Tikopia island in the Western Pacific, where Christianity had been making inroads for some decades, about the view that after death the souls of pagans were lowered into fire. The chief was pleased to hear from Firth that according to many modern Christians, this was only a traditional story of a figurative kind. 'Ah', said the chief, 'so it is just a lie. I thought it must be true as it was written in a book'.

In a number of traditions, such as Taoism, specially important texts have been handed down in obscure languages or coded form, so as to be inaccessible to the profane.

4. Ontology, or an Explanation of Human Beings' Place in Nature

Speculation on the two big ontological questions is inevitable: first, why is there anything at all rather than nothing? and second, how do human beings fit into the wider nature of which we are part? Comparative study of religions suggests that tensions between official doctrinal affirmation and free-floating reflection are virtually universal. Within the history of Islam, for instance, we find at one extreme the rigorist Wahhabi school that still dominates Saudi-Arabia – with its utter faith in the Prophet Muhammad, insistence on rules of visible behaviour, and opposition to popular forms of effervescent piety – and at the other extreme a far more adaptative version of Islam that grew up in, say, Indonesia. Here for instance is a prominent eighteenth century Javanese teacher, Seh Bari, setting out to present orthodox Islamic doctrine:

> The Primordial Void is the … Essence of the Adored Lord, but this Divine Nothingness, this Divine Void is not empty. … but before the creation of Muhammad the Apostle, the only one in existence was the Lord and he alone without any servant. … He had created the Apostle of Allah, there was no one beside him, and He was comparable to Nothing, The Essence of Allah as the Void was like that.

How different from the mainstream Sunni view that Muhammad was the last of a line of true prophets, beginning with Abraham! For Seh Bari, the Muslim's spiritual goal should be not only to participate in Allah's attributes of love but also to be lost in the sea of one's own non-being – to be distinguished from a third non-being, that of things before they came into existence. The soul in ecstasy is overwhelmed and replaced by God. The anthropologist Stephen Headley has argued that such a Javanese theology managed to integrate three strands: an indigenous cosmic pantheism, Indian-influenced 'radical Monism' according to which all creation is an illusion, and Islamic orthodoxy.

Claims are made on behalf of some religious traditions that their teachings resonate impressively with the findings of modern physics with regard to the origins and functioning of the universe. David Bohm the quantum physicist (1917–92) found that he had much in common with the theosophical philosophy of J. Krishnamurti, and he reached conclusions about the interpenetration of everything in the universe and in the mind which are close to the views of the Dalai Lama, with whom Bohm had meetings.

Whereas the biblical and Islamic traditions appear to place humanity well and truly above nature – but more on this later when we come to consider the environmental and animal liberation movements – the Asian religions are much more ambiguous and on the whole the line between human beings and the other animals seems to be less rigidly drawn. This is at least in part a result of the doctrine of transmigration (rebirth or reincarnation or metempsychosis) – *samsāra* in the Indian tradition, though it can be traced back also to the Greek philosopher Pythagoras (fl. 530 BCE) and has had sympathizers among Christians and in the esoteric Jewish Qabbala. In the Indian traditions, *samsāra* and *karma* (which means, among other things, the ethical concept of transcendental retribution) constitute a rigid system of reward and punishment. It has attracted many people as apparently compensating for the world's manifest injustices, while avoiding the permanence of judgment as taught by the Abrahamic monotheisms. It may also be argued that the doctrine of transmigration was a kind of intuitive foreshadowing of the scientific theory of evolution. Indeed the nineteenth century American essayist Ralph Waldo Emerson consciously attempted to fuse a belief in transmigration with pre-Darwinian evolutionary theory, though he never came to terms with Darwinism itself.

In a remarkable passage, the narrator of Marcel Proust's *À la Recherche du Temps Perdu* transmutes the routine experience of deep sleep and reawakening into an evocation of esoteric mysticism:

> Suddenly I was asleep, I had fallen into that deep slumber in which are opened to us a return to childhood, the recapture of past years, of lost feelings, the disincarnation, the transmigration of the soul, the evoking of the dead, the illusions of madness, retrogression towards the most elementary of the natural kingdoms (for we say that we often see animals in our dreams, but we forget almost always that we are ourself then an animal deprived of that reasoning power which projects upon things the light of certainty; we present on the contrary to the spectacle of life only a dubious vision, destroyed afresh every moment by oblivion, the former reality fading before that which follows it as one projection of a magic lantern fades before the next as we change the slide), all those mysteries which we imagine ourselves not to know and into which we are in reality initiated almost every night, as we are into the other great mystery of annihilation and resurrection.

Here, then, in the offering of an explanation of our very being, is one of the strongest criteria for religion. The Victorian poet Browning evokes how determined unbelief can be thrown off balance by a sudden intuitive flash:

> Just when we are safest, there's a sunset-touch,
> A fancy from a flower-bell, some one's death,
> A chorus-ending from Euripides…

Philosophies can become religions when they are socially organized, but a philosophy of agnosticism or one of nihilism is unlikely to underwrite a religion. The most we can say is that some extremely articulate exponents of an ultra-sceptical negation, such as the dramatist Samuel Beckett or the painter Francis Bacon, can become cult figures – in the religioid fields of literature and visual art respectively. The work of both is steeped in religious themes, and energized by a creative power that seems to undermine the act of negation. This power erupts with even more florid Christian allusiveness in the films of Buñuel.

Atheism, the active rejection of all gods, can exhibit some of the characteristics of a religion if it becomes a collective enterprise – as in the heyday of the Soviet revolution, when it was allied to the destruction of old social hierarchies, and churches and mosques were converted into 'museums of atheism'.

It is an intriguing feature of Judaism, and perhaps of some other religions, that an intense apprehension of human beings' need for religion may sometimes seem to qualify as a religious sensibility. One scholar of rabbinic thinking, Aharon Agus, has written:

> Religious man, perhaps, can convince himself that his own suffering is bearable, but he is infinitely perturbed by that of others. ... Religious man is forever restless with fear of a threatening chaos, unlike his secular brother who faces life with the serenity of utter insensitivity, or so it seems to his religious peer. ... Religious man withstands encroaching absurdity and nothingness with a sense of the overwhelming necessity of his being. ... Though religious man's beliefs continually lose their clarity, though they gray and shrivel up in the winter of today, religious man today is called upon to gather up what is left of his faith and plunge into the now of action.

Something of the same sense of struggle, but in a humanist or existentialist idiom, is expressed in Saul Bellow's novel *Herzog*:

> [This] is the unwritten history of man, his unseen, negative accomplishment, his power to do without gratification for himself provided there is something great, something into which his being, and all beings, can go. He does not need meaning as long as such intensity has scope. Because then it is self-evident; it *is* meaning.

An element of this mode of thought informs the tortured musings on religion written by Tolstoy after 1880. A similar sensibility may be detected in the literary and cultural criticism of George Steiner, who has argued that '[p]olitically, morally perhaps, little, very little in this twentieth century, one of the cruellest, most wasteful of hope in human record, gives motive for anything but a lucid "forgetting about" God'. In recent art and thought, however, 'it is not a forgetting which is instrumental, but a negative theism, a peculiarly vivid sense of God's absence or, to be precise, of His recession'.

Many religious traditions develop elaborate parallels between the human body and the natural world. In Taoism, for example, the body has the same structure as the cosmos, and is governed by administrative cadres in the same way as the imperial Chinese State. In the Qur'an, some beautiful passages ask how people can have doubts about the resurrection of the body after death, when we have all seen an apparently parched earth revived by rainfall. The Catholic sacrament of the Eucharist is based on produce from wheat-fields and vineyards being changed into the sacrificial body and blood of Jesus and ingested into the worshipper's own body.

Given that the human body is the meeting-point of the mental and the physical, religions frequently take a stand on the inescapable issues of reproductive and sexual morality. These issues, far from being merely mundane occasions for individual choice, surely have the widest ontological pertinence. If the Christian churches are sharply divided on questions such as contraception, *in vitro* research and homosexuality, it is because these questions throw a harsh light on the fundamental ambiguity of human existence in the natural world. The philosopher Merleau-Ponty has well summarized this ambiguity:

> It is impossible with human beings to superimpose a first layer of behaviour patterns that one could call 'natural' and a fabricated cultural or spiritual world. With human beings, everything is fabricated and everything is natural, so to speak, in that there is no word, no act which does not owe something to the simply biological state of being, and which does not at the same time slip away from the simplicity of animal life, and turn its behaviour patterns from their paths, by a sort of escape and a genius for the equivocal that perhaps might serve to define the human being.

5. Foundation Narratives

We must distinguish narratives about the creation of the world and the origin of gods on the one hand, from narratives on the other hand about the foundation of a religion. Ancient Near Eastern theogonies referred to the origin of the various gods themselves, together with the origin of the cosmos, not to the human recognition of their divine world. In the Syrian–Palestinian region, each political community singled out one or two gods on which it focused its worship. 'The religious pluralism that is implied in a polytheistic society', writes Karel van der Toorn, 'was counterbalanced, to some degree, by a particularism in the devotion'. Israelite monotheism was a unique development in its time, but has to be understood against the background of the contemporary exaltation theologies. Each community strove to promote its own god to the highest rank of the pantheon. The Israelite God, Jahweh, began as a national deity, then proved himself more powerful at war than other gods, then claimed absolute obedience against other gods, finally came to be regarded as the one and only God. David Pocock the anthropologist points out that in what came to be known as the Ten Commandments (*Exodus* 20 and *Deuteronomy* 5), we still find the demand for loyalty ('Thou shalt have none other gods before me') rather than the affirmation 'I am the God'; and he reminds us that monotheistic culture is 'a sport on the tree of human experience ... a unique departure in human thought'.

A similar form of monotheism to that of the Israelites emerged in Babylonian religious thought, with the suggestion that all male deities are simply manifestations of Marduk. Monotheism during this early period, according to van der Toorn, was 'at the heart of a polemic; not so much against the theological problem of polytheism, but against the pretenses of political rivals'.

Most formal religions had a historical founder, but there are exceptions – such as the cults and practices that grew to be known as Hinduism. Shintoism began in Japan as the set of indigenous religious practices honouring an innumerable range of *kami* or spirits that inhere in all kinds of natural phenomena. It was given a name around the sixth century CE in order to distinguish it from the foreign influences of Buddhism and Confucianism, and has always coexisted in Japan with Buddhism while also asserting its Japanese identity – and becoming so integrated with the State after the nineteenth century as to underwrite the cult of the emperor and militarism.

The more recently founded religious or parareligious movements vary in their approach to the past. Scientology claims to build on the religious experiences of the past, but it has a revered founder, L. Ron Hubbard, and its language is determinedly high-tech. The novice Scientologist's goal is to become an Operating Thetan, that is, to achieve a high state of spiritual awareness after achieving the intermediate state of Clear through a process of 'auditing' (consultation with an expert) which includes use of an electropsychometer to measure spiritual distress or travail. By contrast, the Rosicrucians, known in America as the Ancient Mystical Order Rosae Crucis – who unlike the Scientologists claim not to be a religion – are a partly secret association steeped in Ancient Egyptian myth, pre-Socratic philosophy, alchemy and similar intellectual ingredients. Freemasonry also claims not be a religion but has many characteristics in common with religions.

6. Conversion Experiences

Conversion is an integral aspect of all religious movements that seek to be more than local and 'particularist'. The best-known story of individual conversion is that of St Paul, who as Saul of Tarsus in Asia Minor was a fierce persecutor of the first Christians until his volte-face which resulted in his becoming the most influential early expositor and interpreter of the Christian message. According to the *Acts of the Apostles*, Chapter 9, he was blinded by a bright light on the road to Damascus, and lost his sight for three days until the blessing of a Christian disciple restored it, whereupon he was baptized. The 'road to Damascus' became a catchphrase denoting any dramatic change of heart.

We must distinguish between conversion as a reported individual experience and conversion as a collective phenomenon. The history of religion would have been very different if Judaism, which has tended to become an 'ethnoreligion' based on descent, had decided to abandon its ethnic grounding and aspire to become a universal religion in the sense of seeking to transcend ethnic boundaries. That it did not do so must be largely due to its having been persecuted as an ethno-religious minority. Yet even Judaism leaves open the possibility for non-Jews to convert; and at times Jews have embarked on missionary programmes – for instance, after the Second World War, when an admittedly marginal World Union for the Propagation of Judaism was founded by an Israeli professor (and it has recently been revived).

Christianity and Islam are the proselytizing, expansionist religions par excellence. It is clear that economic, political and military pressures have had much to do with religious conversions in history at a collective level. But it would be a mistake to exclude the individual's experience of change of belief, transposition of values, or discovery of a new self. St Paul's psychosomatic crisis, the experience of being reborn, has been amply recapitulated in Christian history. Calvin the Protestant reformer wrote as follows of his own conversion from Catholicism: 'I at length perceived, as if a light has broken in upon me, in what a sty of error I had wallowed, and how much pollution and impurity I had thereby contracted'. Over half the Moonie (Unification Church) converts studied by Eileen Barker in the 1980s claimed that they had had a deeply spiritual experience lasting typically between five minutes and half an hour. However, a substantial minority reported no conversion experience at all.

Raymond Firth has distinguished three major aspects of conversion:

1. a change in the system of general cosmological beliefs, and/or a change in the system of symbols in which those beliefs are expressed;

2. a change in the system of social actions related to such beliefs and symbols;

3. a change in the system of persons operating and controlling the symbols and benefiting from the actions.

He stresses that people converting from a 'pagan', ancestor-oriented religion may cease to worship their traditional gods, without ceasing to believe that those gods are still in existence, because the new God may seem more powerful. In the island of Tikopia which Firth studied, the first substantial conversions to Christianity were effected on the orders of a chiefly family in the 1920s. But gradually the traditional gods came to be thought of as being in limbo, having proved to be relatively inefficient in confrontation with the modern external world; and after an influenza epidemic in 1955 which carried off some pagan chiefs, a 'minimum cultic body', as Firth puts it, was no longer available. To those who deserted the old gods it felt more like a kind of betrayal than the awakening of a new 'me'.

The spread of Islam in Africa and India has resulted in complex mosaics of devotional practice. Michael Lambek, ethnographer of the French island dependency of Mayotte in the western Indian Ocean, prefers to write of 'acceptance' of Islam rather than conversion, and suggests that maybe the indigenous belief system has incorporated or converted Islam, rather than the other way round. The two traditions are discordant but manage to co-exist without an obvious sense of contradiction, owing to the islanders' 'cumulative embracing of opportunities'.

If conversion experience of the all-or-nothing Damascene type is far from being a universal constituent of religion in the strict sense, there are parallels in the sphere of parareligion that we shall examine later. One reason why conversion experience cannot be said to be an essential part of religion is that most religious affiliation is inherited from the cradle or at least from early upbringing. However, it is a widespread phenomenon, and needs to be analysed and interpreted both at the social level and in terms of individual psychology.

The corollary of the conversion experience is deconversion, whereby a taken-for-granted belief system comes to seem untenable. This is a common experience and can be just as disorienting. A.N. Wilson in *God's Funeral* writes of the profound agony experienced by Victorian intellectuals who lost their faith. Much of the enthusiasm for Marxism and similar dogmatic political ideologies among European intellectuals in the 1960s and 1970s may be put down to lapsed Christianity or Judaism.

7. Acceptance of Doctrinal Paradox

If we persist in our analysis of religious systems as, at least, human art-forms (leaving open the question of their truth-value) there is a striking contrast between what we might call their philosophical–aesthetic content and what seems to the outsider to be their counter-intuitive content. (Firth refers to their 'exalted' as opposed to their 'bizarre' aspects.) The philosophical–aesthetic content deals with the crises of individual lives, with relations between human beings, and with relations between human beings and the cosmos – calling on the rich resources of language and the arts. Deep commonalities between apparently very different religious traditions may emerge – for instance, in the architecture of temples, or in the organization of pilgrimages – enabling their philosophical–aesthetic content to be appreciated, to a large extent, across cultures. Religious ceremonies such as naming of babies, weddings and funerals, and pleas for intercession on behalf of the sick and suffering, enact a universal affective message. In multi-confessional societies in the Middle East such as Lebanon, Christians and Muslims and others traditionally invite one another to share their calendrical festivals (though sensitivity of this kind has been placed under great pressure by political turbulence over the last decades). And yet religious systems also disconcert those who do not share in their specific traditions, when they insist on dogmatic propositions at odds with everyday experience.

The monotheistic traditions generally rely on the concept of a God who is at once unknowable (especially in Islam and in the Eastern Orthodox Churches), all knowing, wholly good, and able to intervene at will in human affairs. This is an immense paradox in itself. Mediation between this God and Man has been effected by great prophets, and in the case of Christianity by the Incarnation and God's sacrifice of his son to redeem sinful humanity – which many Jewish and Islamic theologians find a repugnant idea, as contradicting the love of one's children that ought to be a paradigm of morality, but which Christian apologists generally regard as the cornerstone of their belief. Fourth century church councils entrenched the doctrine of the Trinity in which God the Father, God the Son and God the Holy Spirit have equal status, branding as heresies those (the Arians) who considered Jesus to be merely a human messenger of God – as well as many other ingenious solutions to a problem that had not been explicitly addressed in the New Testament. It was settled that the three Persons of the Trinity are consubstantial and co-eternal, 'Three in One and One in Three'. A schism between the creeds of the Roman Catholic and the Eastern Orthodox Churches survives to this day on the *Filioque* question: whether divine Grace proceeds from the Father and the Son, or (as the Orthodox Church maintains) only through the Son.

In Buddhism, the concept of Nirvana is equally mysterious. In Liogier's words, it has

> an immanent nature, to the extent that it cannot be preached about as an external, distant place to be reached by submission to a transcendent order. However, Nirvana does have a transcendent nature to the extent that it is external to space–time – not in terms of place or situation, but in terms of essence. One may have some kind of presentiment of Nirvana, but one may not experience it completely because it is not a phenomenon …

Many believers, when challenged on such matters, fall back on the argument that ultimately these are mysteries to which human beings have only limited access. It would be presumptuous however to call these doctrines irrational, for two reasons.

One is that in their own terms immense intellectual work has gone into building them up and debating them. The controversy within Islam as to whether the Qur'an was 'uncreated' or 'created' was a subject of major schism. The majority view among scholars has been that the Qur'an is 'uncreated', that is to say co-eternal with God. The Mutazilites, however, denounced the cult of the eternal Qur'an as endangering the thesis of the unity of God: the Qur'an was not the word of God, but created by Him. Equally divisive was the controversy within Christianity on whether the bread and wine in the Mass or Eucharist are actually transformed into the 'real presence' of the body and blood of Jesus (transubstantiation, according to the Catholics), or co-exist with them (consubstantiation, according to the Lutherans) or merely serve as a symbolic memorial (according to many other Protestants).

The second reason is that however scientific we may aspire to be, we cannot avoid paradox on a cosmic scale. Popular astronomy convinces us that the billion-fold galaxies extend as far as one could imagine, but we also learn that the universe is probably finite. The universe, or time itself, is said to have come into being at some point, but what happened beyond time remains mind-stretching. The physical constants that once permitted the development of life on earth appear to be so fine-tuned that the traditional view that an Unmoved Mover must have originally designed them has come to be philosophically respectable again. The concept of the infinite is riddled with philosophical holes (as exposed in Cantor's transfinite mathematics), as is that of pure logic (subverted by Gödel's theorems). No theory about the ultimate nature of Creation can be ruled out until science comes up with convincing answers. It has even been hypothesized that we are all living in a computer simulation.

It remains a puzzle – though of a lesser order of difficulty, one on which anthropologists may eventually come to agree – how counter-intuitive ideas have come to be transmitted from one generation to another. Steven Mithen, an influential archaeologist, contends that religious ideas – originally, in his view, 'anthropomorphism' or reading human motivation into non-human entities such as animals or mountains – are the evolutionary result of 'cognitive fluidity', whereby our specialized neural circuitry for understanding the natural world draws spontaneously on the 'social intelligence' module, and vice versa. For him, religious institutions have little or any 'adaptative' value – that is, survival benefits to balance their high cost in energy and resource use – and, in order to be transmitted in time, have to be dinned into each generation by means of elaborate rituals, often of a painful kind, and symbolism expressed in clothing, buildings and the like. Some who pursue this line of analysis argue that the very implausibility of religious doctrines has been used coercively to bond groups into fighting forces. In other words – on this dark interpretation of what may motivate soldierly morale – loyalty to the in-group, marked by totemic symbols, is the primary value in itself. The more of a puzzle the underpinning belief-system is, the better, since a belief-system that may be tested against reality stimulates rational thought and hence the possibility of disloyalty. The induction of recruits into military life, and also to some extent into semi-coercive institutions such as monasteries or teaching hospitals or boarding schools, includes a strong element of dissuading the novice from independent thought. The more old-fashioned theological seminaries in Russia that survive even today have been criticized – by a reforming Orthodox bishop strongly opposed to coercive education – as a mixture of a monastery and an army barracks, where discipline was maintained by the students themselves and informers were given power over their fellows.

Tolerance of paradox, or celebration of mystery? It depends on one's point of view. In any case, acceptance of paradox is widespread in all religious systems. Mark Lilla contends that Christianity, because of the doctrines of the Incarnation and the Trinity, is exceptionally subject to plural interpretations; but Islam is surely no less so, for instance in teaching that Allah has foreknowledge of all but can yet respond to prayer. However, we cannot say that paradox is an essential defining criterion of religion. That would leave out such movements as Unitarianism and Quakerism, or some forms of western Buddhism, which set out to reduce what they see as the 'superstitious', that is to say illogical, elements in religion, yet hardly deserve to have the label of religion withdrawn.

8. Ceremonies, Rituals and Spiritual Disciplines

A huge amount has been written on ritual, whose study is indeed one of the specialties of social–cultural anthropology. Certain key modes of analysis established early in the twentieth century have survived, with modifications, all the recent innovations in theory. These include Durkheim's powerful idea that in ceremonies ostensibly addressed to God, society is in fact celebrating itself, in a sublimation of concrete individual limits by means of the abstract permanence of the collectivity. This is clearly a valuable way of looking at a wide range of ceremonies – from State occasions such as coronations, jubilees and calendrical holidays to private occasions such as weddings and funerals. Another powerful contribution was the threefold analysis of rites of passages proposed by Arnold van Gennep: separation, transition and reintegration. Ritual can actually change the status of an individual, turning a maiden into a wife, a student into a graduate, an apprentice into a craftsman, a powerful office-holder into a pensioner, a free citizen into a convict, a stage actor into a tragic hero.

An influential trend in anthropology, influenced by Marxism, has presented ritual as an essentially conservative mode of social action, using repetition and sensory aids such as music and dance to instil obedience and assent to the powers-that-be – essentially, to obfuscate power relations. This is surely an over-generalized view, for political ritual can equally be used by revolutionary movements, for instance in recent years the Irish Republican Army or the Middle East opposition groups. Gell's broader concept of the 'technology of enchantment' does more justice to the facts.

Ceremony and ritual form a vital part of most religious traditions, but also in contexts that seem far removed from religion. Religion may however loom rather closer than appears at first sight. Opposing armies still invoke the blessing and protection of their respective gods. The elaborate procedures of the auction-room may be seen as a sequel to mortuary ritual, when the deceased's possessions are divided by the heirs – as brilliantly dramatized in the Auden–Stravinsky opera *The Rake's Progress*. The investiture of knights at Buckingham Palace by the British sovereign harks back, according to Sir Edmund Leach (who wrote a paper about his own experience of it) to the ordination of priests and the enthronement of bishops. So does also the inauguration of professorial chairs in European universities, which until the first half of the nineteenth century were all closely tied to the Christian religion. To take but one further example: modern tourism has much in common with religious traditions of pilgrimage, especially the cultural tourism that singles out sites such as Luxor, the Alhambra, Borobodur, Angkor and the Mont Saint-Michel, or – for the musical cults of Mozart, Wagner and Britten – Salzburg, Bayreuth and Aldeburgh.

Most major religions instituted procedures for meditation in which discipline of the bodily senses is enjoined in order to effect a liberation of the soul. St Ignatius, founder of the Jesuit Order in the sixteenth century, recommended as part of his elaborate system of Spiritual Exercises a kind of rhythmical prayer in which a word of the 'Our Father' was linked to each breath. This has parallels with Buddhist meditation techniques (and may even have been indirectly borrowed from them as well as from earlier Christian sources), though with a difference cleverly pointed out by Roland Barthes. Whereas one of the main aims of Zen Buddhist meditation – in common with those of Christian mystics such as St John of the Cross – is to dissolve the categories imposed by language so as to apprehend directly the mystery of being, St Ignatius has more in common with modern psychotherapists who set out to stimulate their subject's linguistic imagination. The emotional relationship between the patient under psychoanalysis and his or her analyst, technically known as 'transference', is analogous to the Jesuit retreatant's relationship with God – except that under St Ignatius's system (according to

Barthes) the 'patient' is inducted into a quasi-obsessive state of blaming himself for failure to obtain a reciprocal sign from God.

One of the most physically dynamic spiritual disciplines on record is the dance of the Sufi 'whirling dervishes' of the Mawlawi brotherhood, founded in the thirteenth century in Turkey: it was suppressed in Turkey in 1925, but still survives in a few other Muslim countries such as Egypt. The dervishes hold their arms extended like wings, the right hand extended towards the sky to collect grace or energy from above, the left hand towards the earth to spread it there. Their turning movements have many levels of representation: union in plurality; the descent of souls into matter and their rising again towards God in the whirlwind of mortality; the orbital paths of souls revolving around the Supreme Reality without being able to reach it. In Islam as in other major religions, mystical traditions of this kind have often been seen as a threat to established religious authority.

The Quakers (Society of Friends), once a persecuted sect, have no ritual at their meetings except that a Bible is placed on a table, with chairs set out round it. The meeting is deemed to begin as soon as one person enters the room. Much of the meeting takes place in a meditative silence. However, the silence itself is a form of ritual (just as all musicians know that silences or 'rests' are invaluable parts of a musical repertoire, and the musical authority of conductors may be measured by how long their raised baton is able to maintain the audience's silence, after a performance's final chord.) Every individual is held by Quakers to be able to find in the silence a 'divine light' within himself or herself, directly inspired by God. Of Buddhist rituals, Liogier writes that they are not important in themselves:

> ...they are relative to the results that people can get from them. They are in a way therapeutic and thus not at all indispensable to practice: someone who no longer suffers from a migraine can stop taking aspirin, and likewise you can be a Buddhist without any ritual practice.

Spiritual disciplines for the laity, such as long, arduous church services on Good Friday, have lost ground in the major Christian churches, but have found a new lease of life in the 'New Age' adoption of practices such as yoga and the Taoist *tai chi*. Scientology offers 'the Bridge', to enable novices to pass from a lower to a higher stage of existence.

9. Solace in the Face of Death and Suffering, and Eschatology

It may be argued, as Epicurus did, that the fear of death is irrational (since death is something that 'I' cannot experience), but such a fear seems to be hard-wired into our species. One of the roles of all religions is to compensate for and explain the terrible certainty that we are mortal, which children acquire not long after learning to speak. In ancient China, a classic text written in 320 CE by the Taoist master Ge Hong included receipts for immortality pills – favoured ingredients being gold, arsenic, lead and mercury. It is thought that some emperors poisoned themselves accidentally.

Hinduism and Buddhism teach that the soul is reincarnated in subjection to the law of *karma*. Judaism teaches that individuals will be judged after death, and enjoins careful rituals for the remembering of the dead as a religious duty. Some Jews, in particular the Chabad–Lubavitch movement, look forward to the coming, after a period of catastrophes, of a Messiah who will set up a kingdom that will end on the Day of Judgment. Traditional Christianity and Islam both proclaim the resurrection of the body, and both have developed elaborate eschatologies, that is to say the 'four last things': death, judgment, heaven and hell – a set of finalities that the doctrine of reincarnation rejects. Early Christianity seems to have been preoccupied by the belief that the world would end soon with the second coming of Christ – but later this belief was generally surrendered to fringy millennial groups by the mainstream churches, which came to reinterpret the advent of the kingdom of Christ on earth as a metaphor for spiritual redemption. For Christians, Jesus's humiliation, his torture and his execution represent both the reality of suffering and its potential transformation into joy for those who follow him.

However, elements in the religious Right in the United States have felt no need to worry about environmental matters, because the Apocalypse and Armageddon will intervene well before the exhaustion of natural resources; and as recently as 1990 Cardinal Lustiger, Archbishop of Paris, wrote:

> Today, the West – and no doubt the whole world – has become such a puzzle to itself, finds itself confronted with such formidably new problems, is exposed to the judgment of such an ordeal, that one must consider the hypothesis that only the coming of Christ will offer it the concepts and strengths to assume its destiny.

Excrement, universally associated with decay and death, is close in the mammalian body both to the main sites of the erotic – as Yeats wrote, 'Love has pitched his palace in / The place of excrement' – and also, in the female, to the source of new birth. This contiguity has provoked rich associations of values and symbolism in all cultures, as well as imaginative efforts at explanation by psychologists and anthropologists. The polluting values of excrement are often transferred, in religious thought-structures, to the adjacent sites that produce semen and menstrual blood. Disgust with menstrual blood is thought by many anthropologists to be at the heart of the traditional downgrading of women, and hence of their restriction to virginal or maternal roles, which has been characteristic of the traditional Roman Catholic Church and many other conservative religious systems. The monk – by sublimating his erotic desires in the service of God, rigorously avoiding contact with women, and devoting himself to an institution that will long outlast him – becomes a living embodiment of the divine.

Music and the other arts originated for the most part in religious ritual, but have succeeded in breaking free from their moorings so as to compete with religion – as a resource, particularly, for defying death. Many cultures represent spiritual life as being transmitted in a way analogous to physical procreation, but without the taint of carnality. Till recently, the institutions of this spiritual procreation were largely controlled by men, and it has been estimated that some 90 per cent of the world's religious officials are still men. The association of women with spiritual defilement, though not universal, is very common.

Religion and spiritual procreation are not the only solaces against the fact of death. Capital accumulation is another, and so is the cult of youth. We cannot ignore this aspect when we think of religion.

10. Martyrdom

Martyrdom is a frequent theme in the history of religions. It was a central concern of early Christian communities, praised as the emulation of Christ's victory over sin and the ideal form of baptism into the coming kingdom of God. Tertullian (c.150–22) said that Christians should go so far as to invite martyrdom, and Origen (c.185–254), the first biblical scholar, who was eventually condemned on the charge of heresy in 553, wrote an Exhortation to Martyrdom portraying the martyr as the 'athlete of piety'. St Clement of Alexandria, however, Origen's teacher, took a more reserved view, arguing that deliberately offering oneself for martyrdom was cooperating with the persecutor's evil deed. He legitimized the watered-down, now prevailing view that true martyrdom is a life lived according to the Christian ethic of spiritual love. Martyrs were a favourite theme of Europe's mediaeval and Renaissance art, and of European folk history to this day.

The most prominent martyr in Muslim history was Husayn, the second son of the Prophet Muhammad's son-in-law Ali, who became the third imam of the Shiites and was killed with other members of his family at Karbala, near Baghdad, in 680. The anniversary of his death is a period of mourning for Shiites comparable to the Christian Holy Week. Another analogy with Christianity was the imprisonment, torture and death of the Persian Sufi mystic Al-Hallaj (Abu Abdallah al-Husayn ibn Mansur) in Baghdad in 922. His sobriquet means 'comber of consciences'. Al-Hallaj's preaching of union between the soul and God, and his claim 'I am the Truth', were condemned as heretical. The Arabic word for martyr, *shahid*, has the same etymology as the English word derived from the Greek, i.e. 'witness', and has acquired considerable political and military importance because of its association with suicide bombing. Islam teaches that the *shahid*, who goes straight to heaven, is whoever is killed in *jihad* – usually taken as a synonym of another Qur'anic expression, the 'way of God', but the term *jihad* has a much broader range of meanings than physical fighting and must always be interpreted according to its context. It can be said however that martyrdom in Islam has generally been embraced in aid of achieving some practical goal, rather than as a spiritual end in itself.

Whole nations have embraced the ethos of martyrdom, one of the prime examples being Catholic Poland, whose sufferings under both nazism and Soviet communism justified its self-image as the 'Christ among the nations' or indeed 'Christ crucified between the two robbers'. Contemporary religions have their martyr-nations too: Israel for Jews; Palestine, Bosnia, Kashmir and Chechnya for Muslims; Tibet for Lamaist Buddhists and their sympathizers worldwide, citizens of a 'virtual' Buddhist State presided over by the Dalai Lama and spiritually encircling China.

Martyrdom is by definition ascribed by survivors, and may be so ascribed for political causes. Remembered today in the resistance to communism are Jan Palach, the student aged 21 who doused himself with petrol and set fire to it in Prague in 1969, as his protest against the Soviet occupation of Czechoslovakia; and Father Jerzy Popiełuszko, the charismatic young Catholic priest who was tortured and killed by the Polish security services in 1984 because of his stirring up of political opposition. Relegated to a footnote in history, however, is Horst Wessel, the young brown-shirt street fighter who was killed by a communist in Berlin in 1930 and promoted as a legend by Goebbels, with a song commemorating him that became the nazi anthem.

11. Demonology

The prevalence of suffering is perhaps the hardest stumbling block for all theologies. A belief in evil spirits is extremely widespread, and in traditional 'pagan' religions usually operates at a local and practical level. In a polytheistic system such as that of the Ancient Greeks or Egyptians, good and evil are scattered among different gods that may be capable of both. The Hebrew Bible by and large relieves God of the responsibility for evil by positing the existence of bad angels. God does not distribute good and evil directly but allows the chief of the bad angels, Satan, to do evil as a test, and He also allows Satan to tempt human beings. In the Jewish conception, which has been called 'qualified semi-dualism', the bad angels are creatures of God, whereas in fully dualistic systems such as Manichaeism and Zoroastrianism the universe is governed by conflict between good and an autonomously evil force. The accent in the New Testament changes to emphasize Jesus Christ's power of liberation from Satan's empire over 'this world' that resulted in the Original Sin of Adam. Islam took over the idea of Satan (*al-Shaytan*) except that there are many of them: their leader, Iblis (a contraction of the Greek *diabolos*) was the only one of the angels who refused to prostrate himself before God. But Islam rejects the Christian doctrine of Original Sin, claiming that individuals are responsible for their own actions and do not bear the guilt of others: justice ultimately prevails.

Sin has not disappeared from the lexicon of contemporary Christianity. In the early summer of 2007, the Anglican Bishop of Carlisle, the Right Rev. Graham Dow, speculated that floods in the north of England could be God's punishment for the government's passing of the Civil Partnerships Act that gave rights to homosexual couples. But the mainstream Christian churches today speak much less than before of sin and its traditional consequence, hell. One theologian, Henri Rousseau, has asked 'Can one think about evil without personalizing it? Does Satan's "incognito" indicate his ultimate stratagem or his inexistence?'

The evil qualities ascribed to supernatural entities may also be transferred to stigmatized groups, in extreme forms of racial, religious or political stereotyping. Much of this is to be found in the Old Testament, the writings of early Christian Fathers such as Chrystostom, and the Qur'an, and it has sometimes been argued that the Abrahamic faiths are specially prone to demonize others. This is doubtful: Hindu nationalists can be equally hostile to Muslims, and the historical Buddhism of Cambodia, Sri Lanka and Burma has not provided any vaccination against engaging in political violence.

12. Moral Imperatives Based on Altruism

All, or nearly all, religious systems embody an element of altruism – that is to say, a recognition of other persons as more than instruments to one's own interests – on which are built a moral code and philanthropic institutions. The relative weight to be given to matters of belief as opposed to practical action is a theme for comparative analysis. For instance, one of the divisions between Protestants and Roman Catholics during the Reformation hinged on convoluted arguments as to whether human beings may be justified by faith alone (as Luther maintained) or good works before justification have some merit (the traditional view, more or less). This broadly parallels an earlier sectarian dispute within Islam. The Murjiites held that serious sins are offset by faith, while good works are secondary. The Kharijites downgraded faith and held that major sins forfeited salvation. Both the Christian and the Islamic religious systems eventually settled down to teach that faith and works are mutually embedded. Raymond Firth has suggested an analogy with the split between the older Theravada ('doctrine of the ancients') or

Hinayana (pejoratively, 'small vehicle') Buddhism, still dominant in south-east Asia, which linked salvation with the acquisition of merit by self-effort, and the later Mahayana ('large vehicle') school, which held that vicarious salvation is possible through faith in the Buddha alone.

A particularly salient feature of mainstream Sunni Islam is its contention that all aspects of life – religion, law, morality, economics, politics, art and so forth – form a seamless whole. This is perhaps not so very different from the ambition of Roman Catholicism in its heyday when it claimed hegemony over all aspects of practical and intellectual life. The famous Christian maxim 'Render unto Caesar the things that are Caesar's; and unto God the things that are God's' (*Matthew* 22:21) is often taken to indicate a radical difference between Christianity and Islam, but this has probably been exaggerated. Both religious systems have achieved periods of ideological hegemony, but both have had to, and are having to, give ground and accept a division between spiritual and temporal spheres of life.

Confucianism cannot be reduced (as some have suggested) to a merely social philosophy, for it embraces the cosmic theory that everything in existence – heaven, earth, human and divine beings – is made from the same vital substance, *qi*. However, one of its chief traits that distinguish it from the Judaeo-Christian tradition is the contention that individuals have no existence apart from their social relationships. As James Spickard writes:

> One's web of relationships creates a self, which changes as one's relationships grow and fade. As my father's son, I have different responsibilities in old age than I had previously; this changes me, as does my changing relationship with my own son as he approaches adulthood. Western social thought recognizes this, but does not make it primary; Confucianism does.

This principle leads to a quest for harmony through ritualized relationships and a virtuous civil administration.

As Spickard notes, it is often argued that classical Confucianism is not a religion, but he suggests that this is a political issue, and that we should ask what the social study of religion would look like if it started from the standpoint of Confucian rather than Western patterns. This debate is paralleled by an intellectual movement in cultural anthropology led by Marilyn Strathern, inspired by Melanesian ethnography, which emphasizes relationality as opposed to the individual self. It also chimes with strong arguments, arising from the intellectual history of biology and psychology, that the concept of a unified self persisting through time, like the concept of the 'soul', has little if any backing in natural science, and is in a sense a fictional though maybe indispensable entity. This has profound implications for the future, since (as Martin and Barresi write):

... there are a great many very fundamental practices, of great importance to society, that depend on the integrity of the notion of a unified self. Among these practices are self-reference, ownership, responsibility, personal persistence, and belief in the rationality of prudence.

It is likely that Asian philosophies, and other systems of thought less dependent than Judaeo-Christianity on a rigid distinction between body and soul, will have increased relevance in helping us come to terms with the facts of modern biology and neuropsychology. However, the principle of relationality also has an important place in the Christian ethic of spiritual love (*agapê*) and in particular the injunction to love one's neighbour as one loves oneself (originally Hebraic, as in *Leviticus* 19:18), as well as in the Islamic concept of the *umma* or nation of Muslim brothers and sisters.

The Judaeo-Christian world has sometimes tended to assume that it has a virtual monopoly on philanthropy; yet traditions of almsgiving and charitable institutions are common to all the world religions – as will be further explored in Chapter 4. We will examine in particular the double-edged nature of religious philanthropic morality – its potential for conservatism as well as for political innovation – which is probably a sociological constant.

13. Internalization of a Moral Code

By 'conscience' is meant an internalized sense of right and wrong, presumably universal in all cultures. Though it is not a concept that appears as such in the Old Testament or the Christian Gospels, it has been given a very high place in traditional Christian theology as the ultimate court of appeal. According to the influential eleventh century Islamic theologian Al-Ghazali, the word in the Qur'an usually translated as 'heart', *qalb*, means not a physical organ but the moral conscience.

Freud's concept of the 'superego' – whereby the ego seems to be able to monitor and judge itself, starting in early childhood – overlaps with the Christian idea of the conscience, but it also offers a negative critique of religion. Freud drew general conclusions as to the structure of the ego from the 'delusions of being observed' experienced by paranoiacs, to argue that all children internalize the judgments and criticisms of parents and others as a part of normal upbringing. But for Freud, the superego goes further in harshness and aggressiveness than is necessary for human beings to get some control over their destructive instincts, and can lead to psychological distress. It is also intimately concerned with control over sexuality.

One of the complaints often levelled, under the influence of Freud, against established religion is that it unduly fosters the sense of guilt (and in order to argue that his experience of the religious sensibility was limited it is often adduced that his therapeutic practice was among the Viennese bourgeoisie). Wherever conscience enjoins obviously good actions such as charity and kindness, it is unproblematic. However, when moral codes are controversial, an appeal to conscience can intensify dilemmas: as when a political leader says he is guided by his conscience to lead his country into an unpopular war, or when masturbation is still harshly condemned by strict traditional moralists whereas some medical opinion holds that it may be a positively healthy habit.

Most Christian theologians regard Freud's concept of the superego as too restrictive. Emphasis by the churches on the supremacy of the individual conscience has opened the door for New Religious Movements that deny the need for institutions and hierarchies. In the teaching of one of these, for example, the Monde du Graal – founded in 1932 to propagate the work of a German writer, Oskar Ernst Bernhardt or Abd-Ru-Shin, and now claimed to have a membership of some 11,000 in twenty countries – we find the idea of reincarnation presented as a universal truth which was not abandoned in Christianity till the Nicaean Council in 325, when any notion of the pre-existence of souls became taboo. The Monde du Graal denies the possibility of reincarnation by humans in animal form, and its doctrine is close to the theory of Origen, who held that originally all souls were equal in the contemplation of God, but some of them declined into a state of brute matter. God however created a second universe, the material world, which allows these embodied beings to earn promotion to their original purity – but also to risk further abasement in materiality. Salvation is earned only through the individual's efforts to reach a series of progressively purer worlds after each death, culminating in the restoration of the luminous garden of our origin – through avoiding impure thoughts and actions, looking to the future rather than the past, and obeying the universal teaching of religions, which is love and forgiveness.

A characteristic Buddhist view of the external voice of conscience speaking to the Ego is to regard it as an illusion, but one that can be made use of to do good. If one feels the emotion of hatred, one should not fight against it but examine it and look for the source.

14. Sectarianism

The history of religion is to a great extent a history of sectarianism. Both Christianity and Islam may profitably be seen as offshoots of Judaism. Factions have proliferated within Christianity, Islam and Buddhism – also within Hinduism, though scholars are divided as to whether it should be seen as unitary tradition at all.

A caveat is in order here with regard to the tendentious word 'sect'. The older sense of the term referred to a body of believers distinct from the orthodox or majority norm, but within the same religion. Such a usage clearly reflects a standpoint of power and is far from objective. Jesus's followers would certainly have fallen into the category of a sect, in this sense, during and shortly after his lifetime. A more scientific usage was proposed by the Protestant church historian Ernst Troeltsch, who differentiated between sects and churches as 'ideal types'. On this definition, a 'sect' is

> a particular type of religious organization which, by combining and applying in a distinctive way theological doctrines that in themselves may be quite orthodox, forms small, intimate, exclusive, voluntary societies based on explicit faith; resistance to compromise with 'this world'; participatory, protodemocratic, or populist leadership; and a normative metaphysical–moral vision, demanding rigorous ethical standards. ... Sects can ... be centers of prophetic change or reactionary resistance to change.

By contrast, a 'church'

> ... takes on a normative social form that is a compound of religious convictions, apologetic, pastoral, and cultic needs, functional organizational requirements in coordinating right teaching and practice, and compromise with secular institutional realities of the context in which it finds itself.

This distinction, highly Christocentric as it stands, has been adapted and transformed by the social anthropologist Mary Douglas (1921–2007) into a model – grid–group analysis – designed to help understand all kinds of social institutions. I shall touch in this book on how secular institutions can display some of the characteristics of Troeltschian sects and churches. But no 'church' starts its life as a well-formed adult. Sects have been constantly emerging since the dawn of history: most of them die away, some have a prolonged life as sects – witness the Plymouth Brethren, founded in 1827 and still surviving – while a tiny proportion become hierarchic organizations or 'churches'. Max Weber's luscious phrase 'the routinization of charisma' aptly summarizes this historical process.

Though the word *culte* in French is semantically neutral (meaning simply a form of religious practice, whereas the French word *secte* is generally pejorative), the English word 'cult' has acquired pejorative overtones, associated with allegations of 'brainwashing' and exploitation of the gullible. In a number of countries, anti-sect or anti-cult associations have been set up to protect the public from exploitation. Attempts have been made by sociologists of Western religion to distinguish between 'cults' and 'sects'. However, a serious sociological – as opposed to faith-based – approach must surely strive to put on one side these prejudiced assumptions and to make allowance for any personal bias which the researcher may bring to bear on the topic. Sociologists of religion have recognized this in substituting the admittedly catch-all and imprecise term 'New Religious Movements', or sometimes 'emerging religions', for 'sects' or 'cults'. One of the difficulties with this term is that it would seem to exclude sects in the older sense of schismatic groups within major religions. An example of this is the Society of Saint Pius X, founded by Archbishop Marcel Lefebvre in 1970 in protest against liberalism in the Catholic Church. It has been in effect welcomed back to the fold by Pope Benedict XVI. To the Right of the Lefebvrists, who still recognized the Pope, are the 'sedevacantist' groups who hold that the Papal seat has been vacant since the election of Paul VI, and that he founded a new church.

Tragic incidents, such as the collective deaths in Guyana in 1978 of the adherents of Jim Jones's People's Temple, or in the 1990s of members of the Ordre du Temple Solaire in Switzerland, France and Quebec, attract great notoriety but are not common. The unregulated exercise of charismatic spiritual power over naïve subjects can be extremely dangerous. This is a strong argument in favour of supporting established religious hierarchies with multiple sources of authority and built-in checks and balances. However, the paedophile scandals in the Catholic Church – a kind of abuse of which 'sects' and 'cults' have only rarely been accused of – show that abuses can also take place even in highly regulated religious systems, when the short-term interests of the institution are given priority and when it is accustomed to a high degree of deference and trust. Whereas some of the New Religious Movements are sharply criticized for their authoritarianism and intolerance of dissent, it is only since Vatican Council II (1962–65) that the Roman Catholic Church officially accepted the human right of freedom of religion, and some Islamic States such as Saudi-Arabia are only now groping towards acceptance of the principle.

Western States vary considerably in their policies towards New Religious Movements. In Germany, Scientology is monitored by the State intelligence agencies. The Charity Commissioners of England and Wales refused in 1999 to grant Scientology the status of a religion for purposes of charity law, in a complex legal document relying principally on the following arguments: that it does not engage in organized worship of a Supreme Being; that its training and counselling are oriented more towards the private benefit of individuals than towards public benefit; that is it is new; and that it has a number of critics in the public sphere. The Commissioners reached this decision despite the submission by the late Bryan Wilson, one of the best-known sociologists of religion of his time and a strong proponent of religious freedom, that Scientology was indeed a religion. Scientology itself has is schismatics, known as 'freezoners' or colloquially 'squirrels', who separated from the church in the 1980s but still practice Scientology and are themselves divided among various groups, one of which is 'Ronsorg'.

15. Identity Politics

Religion goes with ethnicity, class, gender (formerly known as 'sex'), age, language and political ideology – as the main identity markers recognized by sociologists. They disagree on how it fits with the others. Some would deny religion the status of an independent determinant, claiming that confessional adherence is always determined by economic and political factors. All are agreed that religion is never the only determinant, which is especially clear in the case of conflicts such as those in Northern Ireland and the Middle East.

Most nation-states are dominated by one ethno-religious group that has come to power, showing more or less respect for the rights of its minorities. In some, such as Lebanon, two or more coexist together in a permanently fragile coalition. A less fragile exception is the Swiss Confederation, and it is likely that one of the reasons for the relative political harmony which has prevailed there for one and a half centuries is that the two dominant identity markers in that country were cross-cutting rather than coinciding: religion (Catholicism and Protestantism) and language (mainly German and French).

In England, the national Established Church, inaugurated in order to solve Henry VIII's divorce problems vis-à-vis the Church of Rome, still has the monarch as its titular head. In France, the official State policy of *laïcité* or secularism was introduced by the Republic as a counterbalance to the dominant weight of French Catholic culture. The phrase 'civil religion' is sometimes used to characterize the presence of religious vocabulary and symbolism in national cultures: as in oaths of allegiance, national flags, war memorials, State ceremonies and the like. Conversely, minority religion is often correlated with subordinate class status, which can feed into political opposition. However, ethno-religious minorities have also been able on occasion to achieve a lead in specific sectors of the economy: European Jews and French Protestants in financial services, Parsees in Indian industry, British Quakers in confectionery. Syria is unusual in being dominated by a minority sect within Islam, the Alawites, who are thought to comprise as little as 11 per cent of the population.

Politicians frequently mobilize religious identity, but they are frequently hoist on their own petard. The United States' experience with their co-optation of the Afghan Muslim *mujahidin* against the failing Soviet Union, which led to the rise of bin Laden, is a clear example. So is the Saudi government's political commitment to financing radical Islamic movements in other States, which have returned to challenge the Saudi monarchy. The British authorities in Egypt encouraged the radical Muslim Brotherhood in the 1920s, and it has since been one of the principal influences on today's political Islam.

Britain created the province of Northern Ireland in 1921 with a built-in Protestant majority as a way of partitioning the island between Catholic and Protestant hegemonies, but sectarian conflict lasted for eighty years and has only recently seemed to come to a halt. Israel's commitment to accepting Jews from all over the world as immigrants has resulted in the creation of a substantial minority of religious parties, including the ultra-orthodox, which has forced the mainstream secular parties on many occasions to negotiate their way into unstable coalition administrations. As Liogier comments on religion as a weapon:

> The handle of the knife adapts to just about every hand, but never completely: the weapon is slippery, not to be seized like a cold and passive thing, for it is founded on active and burning subjectivity, endlessly recast in the heat of fluctuating affective relationships.

Hence the politics of religious identity can override the laws of the market and confound predictions.

16. The Sacred–Profane Distinction

Much has been written about the sacred–profane distinction, but the concept of the 'sacred' is ambiguous. For Durkheim, who saw the distinction as fundamental to religious thought, it meant a special kind of beliefs and ritual activity that promotes social cohesion, as opposed to the 'profane', by which he meant the mundane or everyday. We might be led to the belief that the most sacred things are always the most pure and unpolluted – like the image of the nun as the 'bride of Christ', or the Buddhist monk who avoids all physical contact with other human beings, or copies of the Qur'an which are treated with reverence in devout Muslim households. Yet the anthropologist Edmund Leach pointed out that the result of cleansing is sterility, and it is in the 'dirt' which is removed that resides the indispensable stuff of life. Hence sacredness may paradoxically be ascribed to extrusions of the human body, such as fingernails or hair clippings, or the detached human phallus and its evocations in sculpture and architecture.

The Latin word *sacer*, from which 'sacred' derives, was double-edged since it could also mean 'accursed', dedicated to one of the infernal deities. In Ancient Rome, *homo sacer* was the phrase used to denote a malefactor whose blood could be shed with impunity. Though one should not fall into the trap of arguing by etymology, it would seem that the 'set-apartness' of the sacred makes it inevitably a double-edged concept, and one which can nourish inter-religious conflict.

Liogier argues that

> if the fundamental criterion for religion is the sacred – sacred space, rituals, prayers and dogmas – then Buddhism is not a religion … Salvation is everyday. If the sacred is whatever in religion symbolizes the possibility of salvation, then the everyday in Buddhism is the sacred par excellence.

Whereas admittedly the concept of the sacred has inspired much outstanding creativity in the arts, it has also lent authority to the sanctimonious. Many writers and artists would agree on the importance of the everyday. Nabokov, for instance, writes of the 'sensual sparks' of everyday existence and of the writer's need to 'caress the details, the divine details'. This is the sensibility that, in terms of visual art, gives a special appreciation to Vermeer's domestic interiors, Hals's portraits and Chardin's still lifes.

Proust writes that 'The poet's way of life should be so simple that the most ordinary influences gladden him, his gaiety might be the effect of a ray of sunlight, the air should be enough to elate him'. Though he was not a believer in the conventional sense, and religious office-holders are virtually unrepresented as characters in *À la Recherche du Temps Perdu*, Proust's novel is shot through with a kind of personal theology, a recognition of the possibility that everyday life can be spiritualized. He achieves this in part through using religious, mainly Catholic, doctrine as a recurring metaphor. The goodnight kiss given to the narrator as a child by his mother becomes the sacramental host 'for a communion of peace whereby my lips might draw her real presence and my ability to go to sleep'. Cider and cherries in the countryside, brought from a farm, can be transmuted into the divine wine and bread; as can, in the city, the morning coffee and a copy of the daily *Figaro*. The display of a famous writer's books in a bookshop window just after his death, illuminated in groups of three, becomes a group of angels with their wings unfurled, 'the symbol of his resurrection'. Proust systematically dismantles the opposition between sacred and profane.

Stephen Dedalus in Joyce's novel *A Portrait of the Artist as a Young Man* does something similar, angry with a girl for flirting with a young priest:

> To him she would unveil her soul's shy nakedness, to one who was but schooled in the discharging of a formal rite rather than to him, a priest of the eternal imagination, transmuting the daily bread of experience into the radiant body of everliving life.

17. Trance States

Trance states – 'altered states of consciousness' – are a feature of religions all over the world. In trance, ordinary consciousness is blurred and the individual no longer has full control over his or her behaviour. Visions or hallucinations may be experienced. Sometimes, the personality appears to be changed. Much has been written by anthropologists such as I.M. Lewis, author of the authoritative *Ecstatic Religion*, on the linked phenomena of spirit possession, shamanism (when a human controller is deemed to be directing spirits), healing through exorcism, and mystical experience. These often take a florid institutional form.

It has been suggested that the biological basis of trance states is the release in the brain of endorphins, which enhance resistance to pain, and/or oxytocin, which facilitates feelings of attachment and affiliation. There is nothing necessarily exotic or otherworldly about trance states. They can be induced by hypnotic, ritual or meditative practices, but also by narcotics and alcohol, sexual activity, over-breathing or hyperventilation, music and dance.

For our present purpose, it is enough to note, with Lewis, that new religions herald their advent with a 'flourish of ecstatic effervescence', but those which become successfully 'ensconced at the centre of public morality' proceed to lose their inspirational savour:

> Inspiration then becomes an institutionalized property of the religious establishment which, as the divinely appointed church, incarnates god; the inspired truth is then mediated to the masses through rituals performed by its duly accredited officers. In these circumstances individual possession experiences are discouraged and where necessary discredited. Possession in fact becomes an aberration, even a satanic heresy. This certainly is the pattern which is clearly and deeply inscribed in the long history of Christianity.

One example is the 'speaking in tongues' (glossolalia) recorded in the *Acts of the Apostles* (2:4–13) as a gift of the Holy Spirit; another is the history of the Quaker movement, which gradually became less possession-oriented as the movement became more established.

To suggest a possible neurochemical basis for trance states is not intended as a move to reduce their rich manifestations in diverse cultures to a 'mere' materialist explanation. The relationship between the human subject and the natural chemicals in the brain is a product of evolution, which connects us intimately with the pre-human and indeed the primordial world. Contemplating these scientific and at the same time impenetrable facts is surely as valid an exercise of the imagination as that offered by any mystical system that floats free of science. It is also not incompatible with some kinds of religious sensibility, and as suggested above we may regard the Asiatic doctrine of reincarnation as a kind of metaphor for evolutionary memory.

However widespread trance states may be in the world's religious cultures, since they are actually disapproved of by many religious authorities they can hardly be regarded as an essential criterion for definition of the religious.

18. From the Local to the Transnational

Graduation from the local to the transnational is a firm feature of religious activity. Many ethno-religious groups – such as the Jews, the Sikhs, the Jains – have established their diasporas. Some religious groups are so small that they have never tried to extend their influence beyond a small ethnic group. But even the Free Church of Scotland – the 'Wee Free' – has conducted missionary activity and spread its Presbyterian doctrine to Australia.

The world's most prominent religious traditions all originated during the millennium following 500 BCE, which has been called the 'Axial Age': Christianity, Islam, the Hindu–Buddhist nexus in south Asia, and the amalgam of Confucianism, Taoism and Buddhism in east Asia. It has been suggested that – replacing both the divine kingship of Mesopotamia and Egypt, and military coercion – a new kind of secular rule emerged whose power was legitimated by an intelligentsia of religious specialists. According to William Herbrechtsmeier, the rise of these missionary world-views was intimately connected with transcultural imperialism:

> Having concluded that there is a second-order truth, more abstract, more universally applicable, and therefore truer than localized cultural expressions, they perceived also a correlate imperative that such truth be spread and that more people be brought under its sway. ... Such systems were transcendent over ethnicity and class (i.e. they applied to all people regardless of class or ethnicity). To the degree that such people would be convinced of the truths articulated by Axial intelligentsia, rulers could find legitimacy by advancing this cause.

Episodes of fleeing from one area to another seem to be widespread in narratives of the origins of religions. The Israelites, according to *Exodus*, were delivered from their slavery under the Egyptians and led by God through the wilderness to Mount Sinai. In *Matthew* 3, Joseph, the baby Jesus's foster-father in Bethlehem, obeys an instruction given him by an angel in a dream, to flee with Mary and Jesus to Egypt in order to save the baby from being killed by king Herod. And the first Muslims, led by the Prophet Muhammad, fled from Mecca, having lost the protection of his powerful uncle, to take refuge in Yathrib, an oasis later known as Medina.

Such a narrative of enforced flight is not a universal feature of religions, but some later parallels may be noted. Many of the seventeenth century English settlers in what was to become the United States were Puritans escaping from discrimination and looking in America for the 'new Jerusalem'. Quakers found a sanctuary in Philadelphia. The Mormons (members of the Church of Jesus Christ of Latter-Day Saints) installed themselves in Utah after their founder Joseph Smith – who had founded communities in the States of New York, Ohio, Missouri and Illinois – met a martyr's death by lynching in 1844 in Carthage, Illinois, along with other leaders of the sect. The history of persecution of Jews in Europe, dating back to the early Christian interpretations of the biblical texts and resulting both in a worldwide intensification of the diaspora and in the Zionist movement, needs no underlining.

19. Patina
To become widely accepted, religions need to be old, and though I have listed this last, it is one of the most important criteria. Religions are a special case of cultural heritage property rights, which are required to have patina. This is the opposite of so-called Intellectual Property Rights, one of whose constituents is the opposite principle: that they are supposed to embody innovation. The statement has been attributed to Ron Hubbard, founder of Dianetics and its successor Scientology, that there is no quicker way of making money than founding a new religion. However, Scientology's acceptance as an authentic religion is so far patchy. Its astuteness in offering its ideology as compatible with modern science has worked for it in gaining a reputation for relevance and contemporaneity, but against it in that these qualities are incompatible with patina. New Religious Movements whose founders become conspicuously wealthy are regarded with deep suspicion – and yet this can be visited almost equally on those whose founders appear to be ascetic and unmaterialistic. It is a rational consequence of hyper-consumerist capitalism that some entrepreneurs will try to take advantage of the 'religious imperative' by founding simulacra of religion on business lines, and this may well be true of Scientology. It does not follow that all New Religious Movements are motivated by economic self-interest alone.

Some New Religious Movements present themselves as old with a view to acquiring instant reverence, like mirrors that have been 'antiqued'. An example is the neo-pagan movement, which has had similar difficulties in Britain in gaining recognition from the Charity Commission. We shall review this movement in more detail in our chapter on the environmental movement.

Conclusion

In this chapter, we have set out the criteria for deciding that given social movements have a common 'family resemblance' which may be called religious or parareligious. In the next chapter, we will consider: first, how we can make use of this list of criteria to illuminate the topic of parareligion, by proposing an analytical spectrum from a strong to a weak religious field; second, how the religious field relates to other social fields in a continuous process of renegotiation; and third, some specific examples of parareligious movements.

3

THE RELIGIOUS FIELD AND ITS SHIFTING NEIGHBOURHOOD

The Religious Field: Strong, Medium and Weak

Nineteen criteria for religion or parareligion were suggested in the last chapter. The detailed criteria are not presented as unassailable: the argument depends for its success less on the exact definition of the criteria than on the process of identifying a range of possibilities for discussion. For instance, a further criterion might be added – the institution of spiritual office-holders, often distinguished by special clothes – which has been subsumed here under 'ceremonies and rituals'. An intriguing characteristic of many religions is the prohibition on eating various kinds of food, which was not mentioned specifically among the criteria. I have suggested 'ontology or an explanation of human beings' place in nature' and 'identity politics' as two criteria; but another list, that compiled by Bron Taylor, mentions more specifically 'beliefs and practices which divide humans (and/or other living things) into hierarchical classifications', i.e. as quasi-divine, ordinary or sub-human. This has indeed some merits as it opens up the whole topic of classification of the natural world, to which anthropologists have given much attention. It would be difficult and time-consuming, though not perhaps impossible in principle, to arrive at a list of criteria that would satisfy everyone, regardless of their personal biases.

This chapter will explore how we may identify particular social movements as belonging to a strong, medium or weak religious field by means of the 'cornucopia model', and also how the religious field interacts with and overlaps with others. It will then go on to consider briefly how two kind of social phenomena fit into this pattern: first, political ideologies, and second, movements in the arts. Hence this chapter is intended as a transition between the first two chapters, which advance some general principles, and the three chapters that follow, which explore some other kinds of social movement in greater depth and detail. But first, some words on the need to try to optimize one's objectivity in dealing with sensitive and contentious issues of this kind. Not that complete objectivity is ever remotely attainable, but we will reject here the school of social research that makes a virtue of brandishing one's own prejudices. Where expressions of personal opinion are to be found in this book, I hope it will be clear from the context that they are merely opinions rather than assertions deduced from evidence.

Allowing for one's Prejudices

It is essential for this exercise to try to make allowances for one's own taken-for-granted assumptions. To take my own case, as a conventional Anglican by upbringing after a childhood partly spent in India under the British Raj, I have great respect for the ethics of Jesus's Sermon on the Mount, and for much of the liturgy, visual art, architecture, music and literature inspired by Christianity in its mainstream forms, as well as a more eclectic appreciation of some non-Christian religious art-forms; and I have a visceral suspicion both of new-fangled movements such as Scientology or neo-paganism, and of anything that smacks of 'fundamentalism' or 'brain-washing' of the emotionally vulnerable. However, as a social researcher it is incumbent on me to try to discount these personal preferences. Mary Douglas has convincingly argued that what we dignify by the term 'gut-reaction' – as if it were somehow closer to nature than civilized reasoning, and hence imparting a specially reliable message – usually, on the contrary, represents a pole in a system of classification induced by our social position. (Thus, for instance, we may experience a 'gut-reaction' of distaste when we encounter a helpless beggar in the street, but this is because we classify the beggar as an outcast from society, social 'rubbish', whereas reason reminds us that he or she is a human being whose experience of life we might, in certain circumstances of disaster, come to share ourselves.) Some writers on the subject of political religion are quick to incorporate their own opinions into their analysis. For instance, Michael Burleigh, a brilliant historian of nazism, mounts a spirited defence of 'cultural Christianity' and articulates a deep-seated suspicion both of Islam and of the 'New Age'. This can make for provocative and pungent social criticism, but I prefer to emulate a model of scholarship that tries to be as objective, or indeed scientific, as possible through minimizing personal bias. Cultural anthropology and history are, in this view, the two great modes of comparative analysis, forcing us to be conscious of our own provinciality – in space and time respectively.

Here we need to remember two things with regard to religion. First, most of the old religions have not only inspired great imaginative creativity but also legitimated persecutions and oppressions. And second, 'fundamentalism' is a pejorative and heavily loaded term. It is difficult for a non-Catholic to see how the Roman Catholic Church escapes the charge of fundamentalism in a more neutral sense when it forbids the use of a condom by a married couple, even if one of them is HIV-positive, on the grounds that such a practice contradicts the finality of sexual intercourse. The same goes for the doctrine of mainstream Islam that every word of the Qur'an was directly dictated by God as His final revelation to humanity.

The word fundamentalism has a technical sense within the history of Protestant Christianity – alluding to movements based in the United States since the early 1900s which set out to defend what were declared to be the 'fundamentals' of Christianity, such as the Virgin Birth and the total inerrancy of scripture. It has a wider sense too, applied within all religious traditions. A number of traits have been suggested as polythetically defining fundamentalism. Some of these are doctrinal: such as reactivity to the marginalization of religion, selectivity with regard to religious traditions, absolutism and millennialism. Other traits are organizational: an elect membership, sharp boundaries, charismatic and authoritarian leadership.

Fundamentalist movements may justly be likened to a machine that offers to answer questions. The question is keyed in, there is a clanking of gears, and the answer is printed out – always much the same. (The term has been adapted to characterize dogmatic wings within ideological movements such as Marxist-Leninism, behaviourist psychology and free-market economics, as well as religions.) As a pattern of religious movements, fundamentalism has been described as

> [a] strategy, or set of strategies, by which beleaguered believers attempt to preserve their distinctive identity as a people or group. Feeling this identity to be at risk in the contemporary era, these believers fortify it by a selective retrieval of doctrines, beliefs, and practices from a sacred past. These retrieved 'fundamentals' are refined, modified, and sanctioned in a spirit of pragmatism: they are to serve as a bulwark against the encroachment of outsiders who threaten to draw them into a syncretistic, areligious, or irreligious cultural milieu. Moreover, fundamentalists present the retrieved fundamentals alongside unprecedented claims and doctrinal innovations. These innovations and supporting doctrines lend the retrieved and updated fundamentals an urgency and charismatic intensity reminiscent of the religious experiences that originally forged communal identity.

The problem, though, in designating any contemporary movement as fundamentalist is that early Christianity, early Islam, early Buddhism and numerous other historical movements shared these characteristics precisely. The historian William H. McNeill has made a valiant attempt to argue that religiously inspired reform movements in our day are qualitatively different from these. His argument is that population growth and new communication media result today in a more widespread perception of social suffering than previously, and hence in the mushrooming of new reform movements. One variety of fundamentalist movement derives its energy from the breakdown of rural economies and migration to cities: examples of these are Pentecostalism in Guatemala or Hindu militancy in India. Another variety is rooted in urban affluence, especially in the United States as a reaction against the individualized pursuit of happiness, which can notoriously lead to personal dissatisfaction. The second variety meets the first through Christian evangelical missionary activity. McNeill concludes that interaction between the United States styles of evangelical piety and the religious life of poor immigrants to cities could present an effective institutional expression for solidarity between Euro-American prosperity and the poverty of the South, thus facilitating a worldwide exchange economy to maximize wealth for humanity as a whole. But such a movement, if it were to emerge, would be similar to the Catholic liberation theology of Latin America, which no-one calls fundamentalist because it is in fact a politically sophisticated reinterpretation of Christian doctrine in favour of Jesus's 'option for the poor'. It would seem therefore that the designation of a religious movement as 'fundamentalist' carries a weight of political motivation. It is true that the world population has increased hugely and that the mass media have been a notable force for change, but these are historical changes that affect every sector of life.

Does a religious movement deserve to be called fundamentalist if it lends its name to political violence? However, not only virtually all religions, but virtually all political movements, can be interpreted in such a way as to lead to violence. This excludes of course, those such as Quakers, Jehovah's Witnesses, Gandhians or followers of late Tolstoy, who actively espouse non-violence. Islam is often accused of being inherently more violent than Christianity, but it has been objected that this is 'no more than ancient holy-war propaganda':

> The teachings of both Muhammad and Jesus place the love and mercy of God at the front of the models of life that they propose. Because Muhammad saw that he could not carry out the divine commands that were transmitted to him without resort to arms, the resort to arms was incorporated in the society that he founded, although only as a last resort against moral impiety (fitna). In Christian terms the result was as though the [Roman] Emperor Domitian had adopted Christianity at the end of the first century,

instead of the Emperor Constantine having done so in the fourth. The society inspired by Jesus was unarmed for almost three centuries, and subsequently armed. The society inspired by Muhammad was armed almost from the beginning.

It is true that the survival in some Islamic States of cruel (as they seem to everyone else) practices of corporal and capital punishment gives weight to the view that Muslim reform movements have not yet found the institutional momentum needed to counteract conservative authorities. Thus in an important respect there is a historical time-lag between Islam, on the one hand, and Christianity and Judaism on the other hand, both of which have experienced institutional reform movements over a long period – five centuries for Christianity, two centuries for Judaism. This theory of a time lag is highly controversial, but it is endorsed by many Muslims of a questioning persuasion, as well as by some non-Muslim students of Islam.

Fundamentalism is justly associated with literalism, a refusal to engage in creative interpretation. Many of the theological positions generally labelled 'fundamentalist' do not encourage debate and freedom of thought, and discourage imaginative metaphorical thinking. Of course, all reading of a text is an interpretation. No reading of the Bible or the Qur'an can be other than highly selective, so that the difference is between conscious and unconscious selection. Some selections, emphases, cross-references and glosses have become institutionally crystallized. Liberalizing theologians sometimes argue that religious traditions such as the Eucharist for Christians, or praying in the direction of Mecca for Muslims, are essentially metaphors beautifully expressing solidarity and inclusiveness. Such theologians may be called anti-fundamentalist. They are disparaged by conservative theologians, who insist on a 'bottom line' of objective truth that is non-negotiable. Whether conservative theologians argue a position with philosophical sophistication or by bluntly laying down the law may be mainly to do with the level of education of themselves and their followers. Both 'conservative' and 'fundamentalist' religious movements draw their energy from what Liogier calls 'symbolic frustration'.

The truth is that religion is indeed like a dangerously slippery weapon of defence and offence. Russell McCutcheon has argued that the modern nation-state has attempted to break the teeth of religion by relegating it to the subordinate sphere of individual choice, where each confessional group is granted the right to express itself provided that it does not interfere with the rights of others. The religious sphere thus becomes, according to him, 'an idealistic phantom devoid of all behavioural content and what belongs to the State are all matters material, empirical, social, economic, and political'. However, he argues, this leads to the paradox that it is permissible in the multi-cultural nation-state to hold one's religious views strongly, but not to act on them. This is indeed the liberal consensus, which enjoys wide support, especially from those who have reflected on the divisive potential of religion.

But the religious imperative does not always conduce to the acceptance of toothlessness. It also makes for the development of theological laagers of every confessional variety, some of them inimical to the idea of religious toleration. To call some of these fundamentalist and others not is to risk imposing arbitrary value judgments – inevitable as part of daily living, but to be avoided in the field of social research.

The Cornucopia Model

Taking our 19 criteria, we may imagine them as scattering by gravity from a cornucopia, or horn of plenty, from heaven to earth as it were (*see Illustration*). The conical space in which they are more or less densely clustered represents the religious field, strong at the top and weak at the bottom.

Clearly the world religions belong at the top, each satisfying most of the criteria – which is inevitable, as this is an admittedly circular argument. The Baha'i or the Mormons, dating back only to the nineteenth century, satisfy most of the criteria for occupying the strong religious field. Less obviously, here we can put newer movements such as Scientology that as yet have no patina, and may never have: indeed, it might be the strategy of future Scientology leaders to act so that it never acquires patina but tries to stay, on the contrary, up to date with the latest idioms of science. It remains, for better or worse, one of the more original of the New Religious Movements in that it sprouted from the mind of its founder, with some inspiration from science fiction, psychoanalysis and Asian religions.

As the traits scatter to the bottom, so the field get weaker. At the very weak base of the field, almost any social group, however secular, may embody some scattered elements of the religious. We may imagine for instance a local organization whose aims are to maintain the amenities of an English village. It provides status, dignity and self-respect for the individuals who manage it; a history is constructed; local notables who have contributed to the village's well-being in the past are honoured; a pub sign commemorates a local World War hero; threats such as property developers, government officials and burglars from a neighbouring village are mobilized against or neutralized; a bring-and-buy sale or coffee morning may be organized to raise funds for a cricket pavilion or for poor people overseas, and so forth. To say that such an organization has a weakly parareligious aspect is true, but only trivially so.

A little above the weak base, we could place a major organization such as Rotary International, founded in Chicago in 1905. The name was chosen because its members originally rotated their meetings in one another's offices. Rotary's Four-Way Test for professional ethics – 'Is it the truth? Is it fair to all concerned? Will it build goodwill and better friendships? Will it be beneficial to all concerned' – and its motto 'Service above Self', were clearly devised to find a highest common factor that would unite practically oriented and ethically committed professional men (and women too since 1989) despite their differing positions on religious matters, so that existential issues are systematically excluded from its aims. Nonetheless, the Rotary logo of a spoked cogwheel, originally a wagon wheel, now displayed in so many of the world's hotels, has arguably become itself an object of adoration.

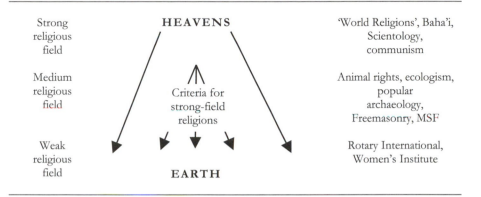

Strong religious field	HEAVENS	'World Religions', Baha'i, Scientology, communism
Medium religious field	Criteria for strong-field religions	Animal rights, ecologism, popular archaeology, Freemasonry, MSF
Weak religious field	EARTH	Rotary International, Women's Institute

The Cornucopia Model

Indeed all logos, whether designed for non-profit or for commercial purposes, may be thought of as deriving historically from basic graphic signs – including hieroglyphs and alphabetic letters – that originally had a ceremonial function. Much has been written about the modern logo as a specific form of communication, representing 'image' rather than conveying a logical message, the corporate personality rather than merely its specific products or services, a life-style that one can buy into, spirituality on the cheap. Since purchasing is not always necessary to 'consume' the logo, it has been described by Malcolm Quinn as 'a miraculous visitation from another world, the world of the "free gift" ' – which brings us back to Gell's analysis of magic as the provision of 'something for nothing'.

The logo seeks to satisfy the consumer's thirst for a meaningful and ordered world. Discussion of its 'tautological' role of the logo has dwelt on the commercial and political varieties. These may indeed be seen as a modern example of the idolatry against which the Jewish and Muslim prophets railed. But if we consider also non-profit logos – the Rotary wheel, the red poppy of the Earl Haig Fund for war veterans, the red cross and red crescent – it is clear that the phenomenon is much older. It dates back to the semiotics of the cross (much older than Christianity, which originally used different symbols), the star, the mandala, the Islamic arabesque, the pharaonic cartouche, plants such as the acanthus in Egypt and the rose in England, animals such as the dragon in China. Heraldic arms and national flags adopted many of these ancient symbols.

Our interest here is in the middle ground, the medium-strong religious field where we will argue that a number of ostensibly secular movements cannot be properly understood without consideration of their parareligious aspects. Rotary International does not quite qualify, nor does the Women's Institute, founded a few years later – despite its choice of an official anthem in William Blake's lyric 'Jerusalem', which recalls the legend that Jesus visited England during his lifetime.

Interlocking Fields or Spheres

It may be objected that by labelling a movement as religioid when it clearly belongs to the sphere of, say, the arts or sport or commerce, we are spreading confusion about words, muddying the waters of language. Let us try to clarify matters with the help of the French sociologist Pierre Bourdieu.

It is true that Western industrial society is characterized by fairly sharp 'vertical' division into fields – vertical in the sense that they cut across both stratification by class or status and differences of age. Let us take the law, for instance. There are eminent Supreme Court judges and there are 'junkyard dogs' or 'ambulance-chasers' sniffing around for speculative accident claims, there are oldsters attending their last memorial service for a colleague and youngsters studying for their exams; but all share to some extent in the 'habitus' of law – ways of thinking, posture, dress, predispositions, jokes – which is reproduced through procedures of recruitment and promotion. The most crucial conflicts in society take place, according to Bourdieu, not between the top dogs and the bottom dogs, but between the top dogs in different 'fields' who compete across the only field that is horizontal rather than vertical, the field of power. (The bottom dogs in each field are needed by the top dogs however, and can benefit or suffer from their fortunes.) Each of the vertical fields is correlated with its own variety of symbolic, informational or cultural capital, which is convertible into economic capital – but at differing exchange rates that are continuously being negotiated. Thus the 'fields' are not fixed but the subject of unceasing contention as regards boundaries and hierarchies – such contention being indeed part of the definition of Bourdieu's 'field'.

We do not have to accept every detail of Bourdieu's rather bleak model. However, his aim in presenting it is not to preach determinism, but to help his readers to avoid the self-deception that is endemic in every 'field', to which its adherents invariably attribute a special prestige, a mystery, pure and sacred values. Bourdieu aptly quotes Pascal: '[…]the weakness of Man appears more in those who do not recognize it than in those who recognize it'; in modern terms, lucidity of thought depends on recognizing the power of social determination. The model is hard to refute in today's world of apparently increasing rather than decreasing inequalities.

'Fields' may rise or decline in prominence at different times. By and large, it appears that the religious field was pushed to the background towards the end of the twentieth century, but has now renewed some of its strength. Much is written about the 'return of the sacred' or the 'spiritual', but we argue here that the religious field has never gone away, but has merely undergone transformations, swelling up in unexpected places and forms. The social science field enjoyed a heyday during the 1950s and 1960s but has now probably receded – with some of its prestige transferred to the biological sciences. Sport and entertainment ride high. But it is the rise of the field of the communication media that has been most salient in the late twentieth century – penetrating almost every other field and exerting an ever more powerful grip. This has been reflected in the world of social studies. A sharp difference may be discerned between texts in social studies before and after the innovatory analyses of media by Marshall McLuhan, Raymond Williams, Edward Said, John Berger and a few others during the 1960s and 1970s, so that older texts often seem media-naïve.

We need not simply the two-dimensional image of a flat field, but a multi-dimensional model of variegated spheroids to understand how fields interpenetrate. Thus the field of religion is penetrated most obviously by the fields of music, art and architecture, but also by those of humanitarianism, law (for instance over issues such as abortion and euthanasia), party politics, the military and numerous others – including in particular the field of the media and journalism.

Conversely, the field of religion is able to penetrate many other fields. This is obvious in such institutions as temple architecture, military chaplaincy or prisons. However, it is the argument of this book that such penetration can also occur subliminally, without the actual label of religion being applied.

Political Parareligions: Communism

Relatively little space will be devoted to political parareligions in this book, for the simple reason that the point is widely recognized already thanks to the insights of writers as diverse as Carl Schmitt (the author of *Politische Theologie*, 1922, who lent his services to nazism), Bertrand Russell, Richard Crossman, T.S. Eliot and Raymond Aron. The dangers of overarching political ideologies with parareligious aspects are not confined to the grandiose aberrations of the twentieth century, but, as argued by John Gray and others, extend to the advocates of universal liberal democracy.

Marxism was a messianic movement answering to almost all the criteria in Chapter 2 –Marx, Lenin and Stalin being in effect deified. This is in itself a paradox because they considered themselves to be entirely rational and were opposed to religion. (The embalmed bodies of Lenin, Mao, Ho Chi Minh and Kim Il Sung are still on display in their respective mausoleums.) The proletarian revolution was believed to be ushering in a new, transnational Golden Age. Salvation was to be secured through merging of the worker's individual interest in that of his class. Capitalists, bourgeois intellectuals, rich peasants, and, at times, priests were demonized. Historical materialism, a totalizing scripture with pretensions to science, claimed to explain all aspects of human life and experience, including the origins of civilization and all the creative arts. Martyrs were not lacking – Rosa Luxemburg, the Polish-born revolutionary murdered by German troops in 1919, or the victims on the Odessa Steps in Eisenstein's film *The Battleship Potemkin* – and heresy thrived, both on a grand scale with the rise and fall of Trotskyism in Russia, and in the proliferation of a myriad splinter groups, some of which survive to this day.

Trance states were induced by such means as huge military parades, or Mao's Little Red Book which succeeded in stirring mass hysteria during the Cultural Revolution in China. Mao himself is on record as saying: 'The question is not whether or not there should be a cult of the individual, but rather whether or not the individual concerned represents the truth. If he does, then he should be worshipped'. In a four-part ritual inaugurated in 1967, the female workers in the Beijing General Knitting Mill started every day by 'asking for instructions' from Chairman Mao's portrait, then studied his words on the factory wall 'quotation board', then exchanged Mao-quotes with fellow-workers when changing shifts, and finally, at the end of the working day, turned once more to Mao's portrait to 'report back' to him with a critical appraisal of their thoughts and work during the day. This and much more elaborate rituals practised by millions all over China were endorsed and approved by Mao himself.

The aspect of conversion experience has been rather less well covered to date in the analysis of communism as a parareligion. One of the most striking examples is the concept of *fanshen* introduced during the earlier period of the Chinese revolution. The American Maoist writer William Hinton used the word as the title for his once widely read 'documentary of revolution in a Chinese village', and explained that *fanshen* had the same connotations – 'turning the body' or 'turning over' – as the European word 'revolution':

> To China's hundreds of millions of landless and land-poor peasants it meant to stand up, to throw off the landlord yoke, to gain land, stock, implements, and houses. But it meant much more than this. It meant to throw off superstition and study science, to abolish 'word blindness' and learn to read, to cease considering women as chattels

and establish equality between the sexes, to do away with appointed village magistrates and replace them with elected councils. It meant to enter a new world.

Hinton's partisan account is challenged today on grounds of historical accuracy but typifies the blind faith of early Maoists. He describes ideological tensions as arising in the late 1940s (the period of his field research) between an ultra-leftist tendency that demanded absolute egalitarianism, based on the mere division of existing wealth and productive resources, and the approach of the Chinese Communist Party, which Hinton claimed to be not only more practical but also more dialectical and hence more theoretically sound. According to Mao, the continuous development of consciousness must proceed from the scattered views of the masses. These views had to be coordinated by the Party, then explained and popularized to the masses to be acted on and tested, so that the cyclical process could begin again. *Fanshen* operated not only on individuals but also on collectivities – though at different rates because, in Hinton's words, 'in real life one had to depend on the more advanced to lead the less advanced and on the less advanced to lead the backward'. However,

> Just as one could speak of the *fanshen* of the individual and the *fanshen* of the community, one could also speak of the *fanshen* of the nation, that process by which a whole people 'turned over,' that process by which a whole continent stood up.

Today this bottom-up aspect of Maoist ideology survives only in a few opposition movements – such as India and the Philippines, with an electoral victory in Nepal in 2008 – and the overall historical benefits to China of Maoism are, to say the least, disputed. But the notion of *fanshen* shows clearly how a political movement actively opposed to religion and founded on a materialist world-view could draw on religious precedents in consciousness-raising.

Maoism succumbed to a thirst for persecution of deviant views less reminiscent of early Christianity than of the Inquisition. The most testing challenge for any political religion – perhaps for all other religions too – is to find a way of dealing with suffering and disappointment. Chinese communism groped towards a way of grappling with setbacks through the concept of 'self-and-mutual criticism', which also served as an effective method of control; but the less demanding strategy of demonizing enemies prevailed until the fall of the Gang of Four in 1976.

Marcuse wrote of the 'magical character' of Soviet Marxism, preserving the original content of Marxist theory 'as a truth that must be believed and enacted against all evidence to the contrary'. Ernest Gellner considered communism to be a religion in the strict sense. As a rationalist himself with regard to religion, he declined to join the received wisdom that the problem with the Soviet ideological system was its rejection of the notion of the sacred. On the contrary, he argued, the great problem was that all the material aspects of life – tractors, production schedules, queuing for chocolate – were sacralized, leaving no space for the profane.

Despite nationalist tensions within the communist world, the international communist system held together with remarkable coherence until 1989, till which year it had been generally accepted that no State which had undergone a communist revolution would be allowed to revert to capitalism. But it was the failure of the Soviet economic system to deliver that caused the sudden collapse of the ideology as well.

The collapse of communist certainties has caused the standard of living in parts of the forested north of Russia to deteriorate. Some villagers, who had already suffered the rigours of collectivization and famine and are now forced to revert to a subsistence economy, look back nonetheless with nostalgia – so the anthropologist Margaret Paxson reports – on the Stalinist era as a happy time. There was a mood of togetherness and a faith in the guiding hand of the dictator – the idealized past being conflated with the idealized future.

Political Parareligions: Nazism

Whereas some historians of the Third Reich are satisfied by materialist explanations of the nazis' rise to power and continued grip on the loyalty of the German people, others have found the historical facts unintelligible – especially the authority that Hitler still maintained within his circle while facing manifest disaster at the end – without an analysis of the nazi ideology as parareligions – indeed, like Marxism-Leninism, occupying what we have called a 'strong' position in the religious field..

According to one of the most recent and eloquent supporters of this view, Michael Burleigh, there are two side issues that must be got out of the way before we understand the true nature of nazism as political religion. First, the attempt to nazify Christianity. For instance, in July 1933, Hitler decided to support the 'German Christians', a group of about 600,000 Protestants who set out to recreate their church as a community of race and blood, and the nazi propaganda machine enabled them to capture two-thirds of the ecclesiastical offices in church elections. A Protestant 'Reich Bishop' was appointed. In the same year Hitler, nominally a Catholic himself, negotiated a concordat with Pope Pius XI, thus gaining international recognition for his regime and allowing the Catholic Church the freedom to continue its worship and charitable works in Germany. However, these moves were merely tactical. Hitler was fundamentally anti-clerical and determined to replace Christianity by a new, homegrown system of beliefs purged of Jewish aspects and of the ethic of humility and compassion. The result was a consistent attack on the clergy, who varied in their responses between courageous defence of their principles and support of nazism as a supposed bastion against bolshevism and amorality. This is not to deny that some elements in historical Christianity – such as the long tradition of anti-Judaism, and Catholic authoritarianism – were incorporated in the nazi blender. Himmler forbade atheism as a declared option for members of the SS, and the Jesuit order was one of the models for its organization.

A second side issue is the luxuriance of 'neo-pagan' ideas and practices that characterized nazism. The swastika itself had been an emblem of folkish mysticism since the late nineteenth century, and some opponents of nazism saw the swastika as a terrible perversion of the Cross. The National Socialist German Workers' Party (NSDAP) was formed from the minuscule German Workers' Party, which Hitler had been sent to as a military spy in September 1919; and the German Workers' Party was itself a splinter-group from the Thule Society, which was a folkish group with esoteric, Masonic and neo-Aryan antecedents. However, Hitler and his partisans later disowned all connections with neo-paganism. The swastika as used by theosophist groups and the neo-Aryan orders had generally been leftward turning with curved arms. Hitler's swastika was straight-armed and rightward turning, which has been interpreted as expressing the doctrine of *Lebensraum* as opposed to a search for inner depth.

Like neo-paganism, the 'blood and soil' doctrine disseminated by the agriculturist Walther Darré had only temporary and marginal influence. Darré's folkishness was not so much mystical as an endeavour to preserve what he saw as priceless racial characteristics in an increasingly urban world alienated from nature. The health of a racial aristocracy depended on the health of the peasantry and their deep connection with the Earth. Darré was minister of agriculture and Peasant Leader between 1933 and 1942, and implemented policies to improve the position of small farmers. However, he predicted that aggressive war would be catastrophic for the peasantry, and as Germany moved into war production mode he lost influence and never recovered it.

Burleigh is surely correct in arguing that Hitler himself had little time for the mystical and ecological notions of some of his subordinates, even for the mystical racism of Alfred Rosenberg's *Myth of the Twentieth Century*. The core doctrine of nazism as a political religion was a sanctification of allegedly scientific facts concerning blood, race and nature, with Hitler himself as a messiah, coupled with an apocalyptic view of providence as bearing either national salvation or – if the German people were to prove unworthy of their destiny – perdition. Nazism, like communism, made plentiful use of spectacular ceremony. But State communism seldom envisaged the possibility of defeat until it stared in the face.

Where one may differ slightly from Michael Burleigh is in the axiomatic distinction he assumes between true and false religion. Writing of those such as the German Catholic intellectual Eric Voegelin (1901–85) who originated the diagnosis of nazism as a political religion as early as the late 1930s, Burleigh writes:

> These men were not arguing that fascism, National Socialism or Communism were the exact counterparts of a religion, for each lacked the depth of Buddhism, Christianity, Islam or Judaism, and was not primarily focused on the transcendent. A puddle contains water, but it is not an ocean. Voegelin regarded all these political movements as by-products of an absence of religion in a world he regarded as decadent, where ideologies akin to Christian heresies of redemption in the here and now had fused with post-Enlightenment doctrines of social transformation.

Hence these ideologies were merely caricatures of religion, or its 'illegitimate brothers'. For Voegelin, nazism was a 'latterday immanentist heresy'.

Condemnation as heresy is a consistent position if one starts from a position of adherence to a religious magisterium. 'Hard cases make good law', however, and if a social science perspective insists on our refraining from judgment, if only for the purpose of analysis, as to the truth values of Buddhism or Christianity, we must observe the same discipline in thinking sociologically about the historical acceptance of nazism by large populations. If Hitler resembles an Anti-Christ, as Burleigh rightly notes, nazism was not merely a 'puddle' to be ridiculed in retrospect, but a tsunami.

Nazism does not appear to have been brought down by its internal ideological contradictions: we have seen in Chapter 2 that a very common feature of religion or parareligion is a high toleration of ambiguity and inconsistency. What primarily brought it down was, in 1941, the entry into the Second World War of the Soviet Union, after Hitler's invasion in June, and of the United States, after the Japanese attack on Pearl Harbour in December – thus making his eventual defeat seem immediately almost certain to many contemporary observers. No doubt if Hitler had succeeded in subjugating the whole of Europe, as he intended, libertarian movements would have emerged to destroy the German hegemony; but this would not necessarily have happened immediately, or without sacrifice and violence on an even greater scale than that of the war itself.

Burleigh notes that Hitler's ceremonial persona at nazi rallies, such as the swearing in of SS recruits, alternated 'manly sincerity, flashes of rage and that simpering smile which passed for contentment, like a tubby matron after devouring a pile of pastries'. It is true that from the beginning of the Second World War, Hitler was treated as a figure of fun by the British media, and also by Chaplin in his film *The Great Dictator*. More recently he has enjoyed a posthumous career as a comedian. But George Steiner has argued that Hitler unearthed in the German language itself a rasping capacity for evoking pre-articulate hysteria and 'hypnotic trance'. To scorn nazism retrospectively as merely a pitiful caricature of religion is to trivialize the hold that it exerted – and hence to underestimate the risk of such an ideology's gaining power again. In particular, the doctrine of sacrifice for the Führer seems to have sustained the German nation through its tribulations until almost the end of the Reich. The emotional power of Albert Speer's pharaonic architecture and light-shows, Leni Riefenstahl's documentary films, performances of Wagner operas at Bayreuth and of Beethoven symphonies in Berlin, cannot be dismissed – except with easy hindsight – as merely contemptible.

It may be objected – by those with a rose-tinted view of the role of religions in history – that Hitler's treatment of the Jews, Slavs, Gypsies and some other categories of human being as sub-human disqualifies nazism from being considered sociologically as a parareligion. However, it is clear from the early histories of Christianity and Islam that both religions originally accepted the institution of slavery, and this was not completely rejected in the Christian West until the second half of the nineteenth century. Many Christian settler communities in the Americas, Africa and Australasia treated the indigenous tribal peoples as sub-human at various times – though none with the industrialized single-mindedness of the nazis.

Unconditional opponents of all religions should certainly be faced with the clinching argument that the worst atrocities of the twentieth century were committed by those hostile to established religions: Hitler, Stalin, Mao, Pol Pot. However, we cannot properly understand the ascendance of these men unless we take them seriously as founders of parareligions. It is logical for a believer in any of the established religions to assert that these parareligions are simply brutal aberrations. But if we suspend judgment methodologically as to the truth of any religion, we must try to be consistent and hence to concentrate our analysis on their power to convince and retain adherents.

It happens that most of the intransigent political ideologies today are neither derivatives, like Marxism, from the atheism of the French Revolution, nor thoroughgoing attempts to challenge established religions, like nazism. They are, on the contrary, ideologies that have piggybacked onto or mutated from established religions, as the Dutch Reformed Churches in South Africa did under apartheid, as Northern Irish Protestantism and Serbian Orthodoxy did in the recent past, and as some of the Israeli religious parties, the Indian BJP, and Japanese nationalist movements still do today – all as a result of symbolic frustration. Al-Qaida style global Islamist radicalism is merely the most prominent and disturbing example, aggravated by the absence in Islam of firmly institutionalized moderate movements that could speak out authoritatively against the appeal of extremism. Some branches of American Protestantism raise the banner of Jesus with an almost comparable political fervour, but with two major differences. First, there is a constant tension with opposing forces in the political and intellectual culture of the United States that have been a mainstay of Enlightenment values for more than two centuries. Second, there is no equivalent within the Judaeo-Christian West to the broad extent of symbolic frustration that is felt in the Muslim world and cunningly fanned by Al-Qaida.

Communism hangs on flamboyantly in North Korea, and a peculiar form of nationalism with Buddhist characteristics in Burma – both supported politically by China, where some lip service is still paid to communism. It may well be that new political ideologies will emerge independently of established religions in future, to gain an acceptance similar to that of Marxist-Leninism or nazism. If the world has to endure serious political and economic upheavals, environmental crises or mortal epidemic diseases, it is likely that some of the new religions – on the lines of Scientology, Candomblé, Cao Dai or Falun Gong – will flourish. Nor, in a world that seems to be backtracking on some of what were once considered to be decisive signs of moral progress – the condemnation of capital punishment and of torture – is it at all inconceivable that another Antichrist movement might gather power.

Nationalism and Resistance Movements

It is sometimes contended that nationalism in itself can become a political religion, and it can certainly be powerfully mobilized for political ends – especially to promote the interests of a minority community against a dominant political entity (as in the case of the Welsh or the Basques), or to protect rule by an elite over a heterogenous nation (as in the case of Iraq under Saddam Hussain or contemporary Syria). In the cases of Turkey and India, an overarching but fragile secular nationalism was installed precisely to dampen religious ardour. Rebellion against widely perceived injustice can unite factions of varying political complexions: as in the case of France under the nazi occupation, or dissident South Africans under apartheid. However, sustained nationalist movements tend to attach themselves to positive ideological structures that are often religious in the conventional sense but may also be based on a theory of political change.

Nationalist propaganda frequently has recourse to symbols drawn from indigenous popular culture – for instance those of the Czechs or the Hungarians in the late nineteenth and early twentieth centuries, or again today when a former European settler community such as Canada pays tribute to the specificity of its indigenous populations. They can also focus purely negatively on differentiating themselves from their neighbours. But I suggest that these are weak supports in themselves. We shall revert in our last chapter to the question of what may happen to nationalist movements when, for one reason or another, they become starved of the sustenance of both religion in the conventional sense and a widely accepted political ideology – taking the specific case of China.

Ideological Movements and the Arts

All ideological movements set out to harness the media of communication in one way or other in order to enhance their legitimacy. The skills of artists are pressed into service in order to satisfy a need that political movements in themselves, because they address abstract ideals and probabilistic aims, can only weakly satisfy: the individual's need for face-to-face reassurance that life and in particular suffering have a purpose. Hence the visual images of pharaohs, redeemers and monarchs that have survived the centuries, the epics and praise-poems, Coronation Masses and funeral marches.

Islam, trying to convey a mystery in the Oneness of God beyond mere visual imagery, embraced geometry to connect the individual worshipper in each mosque to this mystery, and worshippers all over the world to the focal point of Mecca. Some Islamic sects see the Meccan sanctuary as a metaphor for the development of life, a kind of womb – the Arabic words for 'community' and 'mother' having the same root (*amm*). This is the same thought as Joyce's in *Ulysses*: 'The cords of all link back, strandentwining cable of all flesh'. The Qur'an insists at various points that it is not poetry but direct Revelation, yet its majestic evocations of nature and the cosmos have won the aesthetic admiration of many sceptics. The reputedly inimitable quality of the Qur'an has resulted in the classical Arabic language's retaining its unity as a written lingua franca despite the fragmentation of the oral language into a medley of regional dialects.

Artists have always found ways to elude the role of mere ideological message-bearer. During the hegemony of Christian painting, penitent Magdalens and arrow-pierced St Sebastians provided outlets for the sensuality that the bishops tried to banish from their churches. Orthodox Islam bans the visual artist from aspiring to 'create' – which is the prerogative of God – or from representing the divine or human form: all representation must pass through the medium of the sacred text. Thus the *bismillah* –'in the name of God, the Merciful, the Compassionate' – can be inscribed calligraphically to represent a bird, a tiger or a ship, or to compose a rhythmical arabesque integrating geometric and floral elements. If the post-Romantic glorification of artists as vehicles of the divine Spirit belongs more to the Christian tradition than the Islamic, this has not excluded the recognition in the Islamic world that extraordinary talents can transform an artistic tradition and save it from repetitious banality. Despite the absence of any theory of art independent of the worship of Allah, full scope was permitted to calligraphers to exercise their God-given talents. Thus in the history of Arabic calligraphy we are told of a legendary Persian innovator, Ibn Muqla (886–940). He codified the system, with rules of proportion for each letter of the alphabet based on the size of the dot, and he laid down guidance for cutting and manipulation of the pen to achieve the most harmonious effect. This 'prophet of calligraphy' is said to have had his right hand severed and his tongue cut out at the bidding of a jealous vizier, and to have died in jail, and his work survives only indirectly in the tributes paid to his talent and in its eventual scholarly appreciation, which came to fruition only in the late twentieth century.

Examples abound in the history of Western visual art of individual creativity refreshing a tired convention. For instance, a few inspired painters – Jan van Eyck, Rogier van der Weyden and one or two others – developed a new form of naturalistic painting in the Netherlands between 1420 and 1440 that rapidly supplanted the existing 'international style' of late-Gothic stylization. Paintings were commissioned almost exclusively for purposes of Christian devotion until the sixteenth century, when they were also chosen for purposes of decoration in a process that has been called the 'secularization of taste'. 'As the element of enjoyment gained ground', writes Michael North, 'the choice of artistic themes also began to develop, with allegorical and mythological themes first appearing alongside and then gradually displacing religious scenes'. These were in turn replaced in the art market by landscape and genre scenes in the eighteenth century. From the sixteenth century onwards, the 'field' of art began to splinter off from that of religion, until with the Romantic Movement it began to compete with religion as a primary source of spiritual transcendence.

Parareligious Social Movements in the Arts

Cézanne wrote in his letters: 'Art is a religion; its goal is the elevation of truth' and again 'the most intimate manifestation of ourselves'. In his later years, he became almost obsessively attracted by the Montagne Sainte-Victoire, near his home in Aix-en-Provence in southern France, and his series of paintings of the mountain, executed between 1902 and 1906 (the year of his death), are considered among his most heroic and spiritual achievements. 'I work obstinately; he wrote in 1902, 'I glimpse the Promised Land…I've made some progress. Why so late and so painfully? Is Art, then, a priesthood demanding pure beings who belong to it completely?' One leading authority on Cézanne, Theodore Reff, has written of this series:

[A]s the variants succeed each other, they become more passionate in execution and more spiritual in content, the peak seeming to embody that striving upward from the darkness of the valley toward the luminous sky in which Cézanne's own religious aspiration can be felt…

Another, Meyer Schapiro, has written of 'ecstatic release…a stormy rhapsody in which earth, mountain, and sky are united in a common paean, an upsurge of colour, of rich tones on a vast scale'. This commitment to the motif of the mountain was the culmination of the work of the most influential painter of his age, and mountains are associated with the gods in so many religious traditions. The image of the Montagne Sainte-Victoire may be taken as a paradigm of the process whereby the arts, which had always developed in the service of religion, have taken over many of its functions.

This is true of music as well as the visual arts, for as George Steiner has written, 'Music has long been, it continues to be, the unwritten theology of those who lack or reject any formal creed'. A number of writers on music have suggested that the mark of the truly great, as opposed to merely emotionally intense, musical compositions is that they evoke fundamental mysteries of human existence. Moreover Wagner in the nineteenth century, and possibly Stockhausen in the late twentieth, set out to found what were in effect musical religions devoted to their own creative geniuses. Art critics and music critics fill the vital role of theologians and textual interpreters, developing specialized 'support languages' that connoisseurs have to learn.

Perhaps the quasi-religious power of music, and by extension the other arts, has never been more eloquently explained than by Proust. He writes that the field open to the musician (epitomized by the 'little phrase' in a sonata)

is not a miserable stave of seven notes, but an immeasurable keyboard (still, almost all of it, unknown), on which, here and there only, separated by the gross darkness of its unexplored tracts, some few among the millions of keys, keys of tenderness, of passion, of courage, of serenity, which compose it, each one differing from all the rest as one universe differs from another, have been discovered by certain great artists who do us the service, when they awaken in us what corresponds to the theme which they have found, of showing us what richness, what variety lies hidden, unknown to us, in that great black impenetrable night, discouraging exploration, of our soul, which we take for void and nothingness. … Perhaps it is nothingness that is the true state, and all our dream of life is non-existent; but, if so, we feel that it must be that these phrases of music, these notions which exist in relation to our dream, are nothing either. We shall perish, but we have for our hostages these divine captives who will follow and share our fate. And death in their company is something less bitter, less inglorious, perhaps even less certain.

These generalizations about the spiritual power of individual artists would command wide assent. But can we advance the argument more precisely in terms of the arts considered as social movements?

We must be specially sensitive in approaching the arts as social movements because, in the West at least, a high value is set on personal originality, which by definition tends to elude all sociological analysis. Movements in the arts tend to be given somewhat arbitrary names – such as 'the pre-Raphaelites' in painting or 'serialism' in music – which invariably come to be seen as distortions of the unique innovativeness of their individual members. Whereas it is acceptable for ordinary art amateurs and critics to be labelled as elements swept along in a social movement, the true artist is hailed as an avatar of the divine creative spirit and so as relatively immune to sociological analysis. One of the strongest arguments against out-and-out scientific rationalism and materialism is indeed the existence of extraordinary human creativity. An infinite concatenation of quasi-random evolutionary events might have resulted eventually in the paintings of Sir Peter Lely, but could it credibly have led to Velázquez?

A number of fraternities of a quasi-religious hue, indeed explicitly piggy-backing on established Christianity, were formed by artists during the nineteenth century, and at least three made their mark on art history. First, active between 1818 till the 1840s, were the Nazarenes, originally part of a small group of artists based in Vienna known as the Lukasbrüder, or brotherhood of St Luke, formed to promote a romantic version of Christian art and revive the spirit of Italian painters such as Fra Angelico. They acquired new members and adopted a strict monastic regime in San Isidoro, an abandoned monastery in Rome, wearing wide trailing cloaks and their hair long. As in a number of similar cases, this group, whose more prominent members included Friedrich Overbeck and Franz Pforr, is remembered by an originally mocking nickname. Second, the Pre-Raphaelite Brotherhood was active in Britain between 1848 and 1853, founded by Holman Hunt, Millais and D.G. Rossetti and later joined by other painters, Though these artists often chose Christian themes, they were united more by an aesthetic emphasizing colour and precise detail, and by a sacramental view of art influenced by the writings of Ruskin. Third, Les Nabis (from the Semitic word for 'prophet') was the name of a secret brotherhood active in France between 1888 and 1900, devoted to pursuing the example of Gauguin and generally opposed to academicism and the bourgeoisie, but with no particular group style. Some of their members – Paul Sérusier, Maurice Denis and Paul Ranson – were attracted by theosophy, the New-Age-like spiritual movement. All these three fraternities were conscious initiatives to develop the potential of a sect, both internally for encouraging a sense of mission and commitment and externally for attracting the attention of the public. It is as if they did not yet have confidence in the potential of art as a source of transcendence independent of the substructure of religion.

The International Style in Architecture

Turning to the twentieth century, it is possible to see the International Style in architecture which blossomed in the 1930s – its best-known exponents being Le Corbusier, Gropius and Mies van der Rohe, its common principles a 'machine aesthetic' and the edict that form should follow function – as having strongly religioid features. Such at least was the argument put forward in 1977 in a polemical book by David Watkin, *Morality and Architecture*, which was essentially a barbed and Oedipal critique of his mentor, the influential architectural historian Nikolaus Pevsner, whom he mischievously caricatured as standing in the same relation to the twentieth century as the Catholic neo-Gothic architect Pugin did to the nineteenth century. According to Watkin, Pevsner was committed to the idea of a determining *Zeitgeist* and believed that any deviation from the International Modern movement would be 'anti-social and immoral'. 'This quasi-religious commitment to a secular ideal', wrote Watkin, 'acquires a particular emphasis in men who have abandoned formal religious belief themselves': it was an attempt to 'cling to some objectively existing truth in a godless world'. Watkin concluded that in truth architecture was fundamentally a matter of taste and style. The book was condemned by one reviewer as 'stupid and obscene ... wallowing in a cultural sewer ... shit, vomit and spittle', though Charles Jencks, another writer on architecture, wrote later: 'David Watkin charges out on to the field ... finds an enemy, with perfect aim delivers a mortal blow. But lo, the enemy is already dead'. Also in 1977, Jencks himself, having previously written favourably about the Modern Movement and in particular about Le Corbusier, began to criticize it severely and to promote new styles under the umbrella heading of post-modernism. The high idealism of the Modern Movement had degenerated into 'consumer temples and churches of distraction'.

A reaction away from the International Style did indeed set in, with more attention being given to vernacular traditions, to ornament and fantasy, to the human scale, and to the social needs that architecture set out to satisfy. The International Style was criticized for its rigidity and insensitivity to local context, compared to Frank Lloyd Wright's more complex aesthetic. The values of Gropius and the Bauhaus were revived in a new form with the high-tech movement, represented by Rogers, Foster, Piano and others, which in the first decade of the twenty-first century is still in the ascendant.

However, the architectural profession has become intellectually eclectic, and true believers in the International Style died out at the end of the 1970s.

Charles Jencks, a tireless chronicler of contemporary architectural movements, has suggested that, with the waning of religious belief, a new spiritual aesthetic is emerging, based on a recognition of the miraculous balance of the forces of expansion and gravity in the evolution of the cosmos, of the mass extinctions that have occurred in the history of the Earth, and of human beings' continuity with nature. Prefiguring this sensibility are architectural masterpieces such as Le Corbusier's Ronchamp Chapel in western France (1950–55) with its animal and alchemical motifs, Jörn Utzon's Sydney Opera House (1956–73) with its petal shapes that evoke natural growth, Emilio Ambasz's Fukuoka Prefectural International Hall, Japan (1990) with its hanging gardens, and Frank Gehry's New Guggenheim in Bilbao (1993–97) which celebrates the sun. It is the essence of the landmark building today to be an 'enigmatic signifier'. Jencks concludes that this story 'might sublate the world religions and philosophies until it is more or less accepted as *the* global orientation'. The aesthetic that Jencks describes as 'cosmogenesis' – borrowed presumably from Teilhard de Chardin, whose theories we will summarize in Chapter 6 – is mirrored by some trends in the environmental movement that we will consider in Chapter 5.

Abstract Expressionism

The American Abstract Expressionist movement in painting (also known at one time as 'action painting'), which displaced Paris in favour of New York as the centre of modern art after the Second World War, is an even clearer case of parareligion. Harold Rosenberg, one of the principal critics associated with it, said that it was 'based on the phenomenon of conversion', and 'with the majority of the painters, essentially a religious movement'. He and his rival, Clement Greenberg, did much to promote the movement but, as well as hating each other personally, offered completely different interpretations of what it was all about. For Rosenberg, the essence of the movement was 'the creation of private myths':

> The tension of the private myth is the content of every painting of this vanguard. The act on the canvas springs from an attempt to resurrect the saving moment in his 'story' when the painter first felt himself released from Value-myth of past self-recognition. Or it attempts to initiate a new moment in which the painter will realize his total personality-myth of future self-recognition.

The artist was seen as locked into a lonely war with paint and canvas that became the public trace of their agony. Greenberg, however, interpreted

Abstract Expressionism as asserting the flatness of the picture plane, and as the logical development of cubism. Three of the most charismatic figures in this movement were Pollock, Newman and Rothko.

Jackson Pollock (1912–56), the leading figure in the movement and probably the first American painter to gain a truly international reputation during his own lifetime, is the clearest example of a private myth, the 'hero in the studio'. Though probably influenced by Navajo Indian sand painting, he invented a radically new way of painting by using his whole body to pour and drip paint onto a horizontal canvas, producing an 'all-over' result distinct from conventional composition. This technique of his anticipated later developments in 'performance art'. He was the wild man of the West, shamanic, anti-intellectual, tortured, irascible, alcoholic, a 'noble savage engaged in a ritual'. 'When I am in my painting', he said to interviewers, 'I'm not aware of what I'm doing'. His life ended prematurely in a car accident, like the legendary film actor James Dean's. The art market today rates his work extremely highly. However, it is clear that something has to step in when important elements in traditional painting – namely, draughtsmanship, composition and (except for vestigial hints) iconography – are evacuated: Otherwise the painting might slip into being 'merely' decorative – which no painter of this school would have accepted. And that something added is the biographical myth, fostered during Jackson Pollock's lifetime by critics and journalists, and enhanced by his tragic, though alcoholically self-induced, death. 'For the modern consciousness' wrote Susan Sontag in 1966, 'the artist (replacing the saint) is the exemplary sufferer'.

Barnett Newman (1905–70) could not be a greater contrast from Pollock in personality: he was the 'Renaissance Man Old Master' of the movement (in the words of one contemporary critic, Barbara Reise), and he was explicit in presenting his work as deeply spiritual in content, often with religious allusions expressed in the titles of his canvases. The trademark of his mature style was the 'zip', a thin vertical line of colour separating fields of bright homogeneous colour – all on a scale that demands a large gallery space and makes an impact that cannot be conveyed in reproductions. His series of fourteen paintings entitled 'Stations of the Cross' (1958–66) used only black and white colours and unprimed canvas. Yet the first of these paintings, subtitled with Jesus's words 'Lama Sabachthani' ['Why hast Thou forsaken me?'], conveyed an emotional power that prompted the same critic to write:

> ...the skinny un-primed zip at the right seems to screech like fingernails up and down a blackboard of dry-brushed edges, as if in terror of the solid vertical band which seems to move with ominous slowness into the painting's space. This painting almost shrieks vital terror in the face of death as an inevitable absolute: which is the

essence of the cry of Jesus, the sacrifice of Abraham, the timeless tragedy of humanity begun with Adam…

Greenberg, however, wrote in a catalogue for a Newman exhibition in 1959, 'If you are color-deaf, you will focus on the stripes' and argued that he was the inheritor of French Impressionism.

Historians of the Abstract Expressionist movement have noted the political context of the Cold War, during which modernist art was promoted in the West, sometimes with subsidies from the CIA, as a symbol of free enterprise in opposition to the propagandist stagnancy of totalitarian art. Newman's political sympathies were with anarchism and he was, compared with artists of the early twenty-first century, extremely ambitious as regards the political import of his work, saying in an interview shortly before his death:

> Some twenty-two years ago in a gathering, I was asked what my painting really means in terms of society, in terms of the world. . . . And my answer then was that if my work were properly understood, it would be the end of state capitalism and totalitarianism. Because to the extent that my painting was not an arrangement of objects, not an arrangement of spaces, not an arrangement of graphic elements, was [instead] an open painting . . . to that extent I thought, and I still believe, that my work in terms of its social impact does denote the possibility of an open society.

In retrospect, Newman's intellectual ambitions, and his skill as a writer as well as a painter, enabled him to become a private myth on a more verbally articulate level than the other painters of this school.

Like Newman, Mark Rothko (1903–70) was a self-consciously spiritual and meditative artist, and one whose mature style of large-scale paintings that envelop the viewer is instantly recognizable. Rothko's mature style consists of shapes ('hedges') of shimmering colour with blurred edges, hovering against a contrastive background. Like Pollock, Rothko was an alcoholic and died violently – in his case, by suicide. Pollock's and Rothko's martyrdoms to art both revived the nineteenth century trope of the *artiste maudit* (accursed). The private myth of Rothko's life was enhanced by the legal scandal that erupted after his death when certain directors of the Marlborough Gallery were convicted of defrauding his heirs. His posthumous reputation is now as high as Pollock's, his market valuation almost as high.

The National Gallery of Art in Washington, DC, presents on its ground floor seven Rothko paintings from his late, relatively sombre years, some originally designed for Harvard University and some, rather paradoxically, for a New York restaurant. Rothko hoped that his paintings would arouse a quasi-mystical experience in those who looked at them, and in neutral spaces they can indeed exercise a peculiar power. However, the architectural grandiosity of I.M. Pei's modernist extension to the Gallery competes vigorously with the Rothkos, whose quiet contemplativeness is challenged by echoing voices from the foyer and a noisy escalator.

The major memorial to Rothko, commissioned from him by the Menil Foundation in Houston but not completed and opened till shortly after his death, is the Rothko Chapel in Houston, Texas, intentionally a place of pilgrimage, where it stands next to Barnett Newman's most famous sculpture, 'Broken Obelisk'. It has ignited controversy, largely because the architecture of the octagonal building, and the lighting in particular, are thought by many to be unworthy of the paintings. Though Rothko was a secular Jew, it was originally conceived as a Roman Catholic place of worship, yet it was eventually dedicated as an ecumenical chapel. It contains fourteen large monochrome, apparently black canvases that subtly reveal purple and oxblood colours as the eye accustoms itself to them – a compelling sensory experience. It has been written of them that they are

> ...a testimony to Rothko's faith in the power of art – 'imageless' art – to meet, create, and transform an audience one by one, to place each person in contact with a tragic idea made urgent by the contemplation of death. ... That is their myth, nourished in the absence of mythic subjects.

We might add to these three the name of another major American painter associated with Abstract Expressionism, Mark Tobey (1890–1976), who developed an 'all-over' pictorial style before Pollock and may have been an influence on him. Tobey was a committed member of the Baha'i faith and also influenced by Buddhism. But as one of the most cosmopolitan painters of the twentieth century, he was never closely identified with New York – which is probably why his fame grew only towards the end of his career.

The same may be said of the leaders of Abstract Expressionism as what David Watkin wrote of Pevsnerian modernism: that they were clinging to a substitute for religion in a godless world. Taken as a holistic movement rather than a set of individuals, it seems to fulfil many of the criteria we have identified with parareligion. Money already played a major part, in relationships with museums and collectors, but without prejudice to the principles of the sacredness of the art, its power to alter states of mind, and the struggle against philistinism and aesthetic conservatism. Clement Greenberg and Harold Rosenberg were the rival theologians, and the atmosphere was electrified by harsh polemics.

For a time, Abstract Expressionism spread its influence to Britain and elsewhere, under such labels as 'post-painterly abstraction', but it was not long before the Western visual art world splintered into a wide variety of movements, some of them highly self-conscious and self-referential – with financial speculation on artists' reputations becoming larger in scale and more overt. Though 'minimalism' came near it, none of the subsequent movements seems to have acquired quite the momentum that Abstract Expressionism had for two decades or so. But whereas it was a movement that interested at the time only a small avant-garde elite of modernist enthusiasts, the whole field of the arts has since then expanded to provide, for a much wider range of secular people, some of the sense of meaning in life that organized religions offer to believers. The art museum, originally conceived and architecturally designed as a temple or large-scale reliquary to be visited with veneration, has extended its reach to an unlimited public through the new communication media.

Spirituality and Morality in the Arts

We have noted earlier that one of the polythetic criteria for religion is 'moral imperatives based on altruism'. It is true that some visual artists and musicians have contended that their role is merely to divert and entertain – a role mirrored in times past, in European and some other traditions, by their low social status relative to that of their patrons. Others have contended that their art belongs to a realm of pure aesthetics quite distinct from, indeed higher than, that of everyday life and morality – and ultimately more 'real'. One of Nabokov's characters writes that '... "reality" is neither the subject nor the object of true art which creates its own special reality having nothing to do with the average "reality" perceived by the communal eye'. This derives from the Romantic image of the artist as an autonomous creative genius, penetrating to a sphere of universal truth; but we must remember that some of the most important originators of this image, particularly the English Romantic poets such as Wordsworth, Blake, Coleridge and Shelley, were closely engaged with the political and social issues of their day. The extreme doctrine of 'art for art's sake' was developed by the 'aesthetic movement' of the 1880s and 1890s but was fairly short-lived.

The high prestige of the arts today results from the belief in their power to help individuals develop spiritually and morally, and sometimes as well from ambitions to modify social norms – as in the traditions of documentary photography or Pop Art, both of which in different ways challenged conventional hierarchies of taste. It would be stretching language to claim that altruism is a feature of the arts today. Artists may perform altruistic acts, such as donating their works to charity auctions or giving benefit concerts for earthquake victims, but competition through marketing and the media necessitates an approach to their careers that is the reverse of anonymous. Artists characteristically claim a longer-term altruism than that of the charity worker, in that they are, at least, helping to change sensibility for the better and to alert their public to depths of experience that only the arts have access to. They would tend to sympathize with Proust's view that 'all the altruisms in nature that are fertile develop in an egoistic manner, and any human altruism that is not egoistic is sterile: that of the writer who interrupts his work to welcome an unhappy friend, to accept a public position, to write propagandistic articles'. However, a special niche in the artistic pantheon is reserved today for a few such as Daniel Barenboim, probably the world's most admired living classical musician, who apart from being a supreme pianist and conductor has also co-founded, with the late Edward Said, the West–Eastern Divan Workshop and Orchestra, in which young Jewish and Arab musicians work together – so that he has been aptly called a one-man peace process.

At certain crises in history, visual artists have been in a position to make specific political statements that may have had a real impact on political developments: the anti-nazi art of Dix, Grosz, Beckman, Heartfield and Kokoschka is a good example. Today, however, the art market in time-honoured capitalist fashion has succeeded in turning even the most apparently subversive art into collectibles. And neither Picasso's masterpiece condemning aerial bombardment, 'Guernica', nor Don McCullin's searing photography of famine, has done much to abate the horrors that they document.

It is natural, in secularizing societies, for us to search for the divine in the product of human hands or the human voice. For many, this is an adequate substitute for religious observance. The arts originated with religion, and still retain the aura of 'enthusiasm' in the original Greek sense of possession by the gods. Lévi-Strauss contends that, whereas the European nineteenth century represented the artist, first as a romantic genius and later as persecuted and damned, the Plains Indians of northern America had the same notions but expressed literally rather than figuratively. The Plains Indian embroideress, working with porcupine spines, was inspired in a dream or a vision by a two-faced divinity, the mother of the arts, and the dream gave her the status of an exceptional, unpredictable person. She would laugh impulsively, drive men who approached her out of their minds, sleep with anyone – and produce superlative works of art. Lévi-Strauss also observes that in other north American Indian cultures, highly ambitious and elaborate mechanical spectacles were devised by religious artists of great reputation, but their public showed no pity towards them if they failed. This, he says, is because such a failure ruined the conviction of continuity between the human and the supernatural world, on which the whole hierarchic social order depended. So in the Western contemporary arts, though we do not put artists to death when they are deemed to have failed, they are frequently shunned and humiliated. For Lévi-Strauss, as for many others today, works of art created over the centuries and by different cultures are the truest, least replaceable of all human achievements, giving birth to other works of art and so achieving a kind of perpetuity. He goes so far as to say that human beings only exist through their works of art. Clearly this view of art is a surrogate for religion. Proust writes of composers being reincarnate in their music, and of the unique 'accent' of a great musician as 'proof of the irreducibly individual existence of the soul'.

The above section has focussed on the visual arts and music, rather than literature. There have been many identifiable movements in literature, such as French symbolist poetry, the Celtic Literary Renaissance, the Bloomsbury Group, existentialism, the Beat Generation. One movement, not in literature itself but in literary criticism, calls for our attention here. This is the Cambridge English School associated particularly with F.R. Leavis (1895–1978), which once spread its deeply moralizing influence in schools and universities throughout Britain and the Commonwealth. Leavis argued that 'Discrimination is life, indiscrimination is death', that the act of reading and interpreting a literary text was inseparable from the act of evaluating it, and that the great writers all have in common a religious, by which he meant life-affirming and moral, approach to their subject-matter. The English language and its literature, while not unique in their importance compared to other peoples', were a priceless educational and spiritual asset, a bastion against the coming age of technocracy and consumerism. Literature attained a 'third realm' of human experience through the creative collaboration of writers and readers. But the canon was a restricted one, giving prominence to what Leavis called the Great Tradition of English novelists – particularly Jane Austen, George Eliot, Conrad, Henry James and D.H. Lawrence – while certain other writers of note, such as Sterne, Thackeray and Trollope were downgraded. Perhaps the exemplary novelist of this tradition was George Eliot, with her inspired animations in fictional form of fulfilled and wasted human relationships, without recourse to doctrinal rules or transcendental rewards and punishments.

Leavis was surely justified philosophically in his refusal to separate judgment from analysis in the study of literature, but his insistence on dogmatically distinguishing sheep from goats, coupled with an increasing cultural conservatism towards the end of his career, resulted in his going abruptly out of fashion. His passion for 'seriousness' in responding to literature struck a sympathetic chord with religious people; but I can testify, having attended his seminars in the early 1960s in Cambridge, that devotion to his charismatic teaching also became a psychological safety-net for undergraduates who had recently come to reject the religious faiths in which they had been brought up. There was an element of nonconformist opposition to hierarchy and to the Establishment in his critical sensibility. In the analytical terms introduced by Mary Douglas (which we will consider in detail later) Leavis was clearly, in retrospect, the inspired leader of an 'enclavist' sect.

Some experts on the arts continue to believe in 'objective' standards of merit. It is safer to say, with Leavis, that the essence of creativity in any domain lies in the fine distinctions that separate the exceptional from the run-of-the-mill. But it is hard not to admit that aesthetic judgments are ultimately matters of taste, and that appreciation of particular art-forms is correlated with particular life-style assumptions and choices. Here we would have to move away from the study of art itself as a process of creation, into so-called 'reception studies'. An admirer of Henry James's novels or Bartók's chamber music will find fellow-admirers all over the world to participate in the worship of the Master – but so, on a much more industrial scale, will admirers of J.K. Rowling or Andrew Lloyd Webber. Both the elite minority persuasions and the mass movements are oriented towards an individual creative spirit as the primary source of inspiration. Both are sustained by a support system of promoters, commentators and biographers.

Difficult as it may be for the adherents of any religion or parareligion to accept, there is a strong element of aesthetic choice in all such adherence, correlated with life-style and social position. The arts and literature are for many people a large part of what makes their life worth living. How much they can protect a society from falling into disaster is an open question. Günter Grass recalls in his memoir *Peeling the Onion* that as a boy he had read and was moved by Erich Maria Remarque's pacifist novel about the First World War, *All Quiet on the Western Front*, but he volunteered for nazi Germany's armed forces all the same, and as an old man he ponders 'how limited an effect literature may have'. A similar though more nuanced thought appears in W.H. Auden's elegy for Yeats in 1939: 'Poetry makes nothing happen: it survives / In the valley of its making…'. George Steiner writes of the 'Cordelia paradox':

> The outcry of tortured Lear over Cordelia blots out the world. We do not hear the cry in the street, or if we do hear it, we do not listen to it, let alone act in response. …Whether it is feasible to study, to internalise and echo the agony of Cordelia so as to strengthen, to render more concentrate our moral and civic resources, is a question to which I have no answer.

And the protagonist of Saul Bellow's novel *Herzog* reflects, after witnessing a sordid criminal court trial in New York, 'I fail to understand … but this is the difficulty with people who spend their lives in humane studies and therefore imagine once cruelty has been described in books, it is ended'. Fortunately, a few twentieth century creative writers such as Orwell and Solzhenitsyn can be adduced as powerful counter-examples.

Conclusion

This has been a transitional chapter between the opening Chapters 1 and 2, which set out some broad explanatory principles, and the more detailed case studies examined in Chapters 4, 5 and 6. At the risk of superficiality, I have kept the discussion, first of political ideologies and then of art movements, rather brief, because their religioid features have already been delineated by a number of other writers.

Political ideologies and art movements clearly belong to two different spheres or levels of analysis. They join together however when we consider how the arts are used to sustain political ideologies. The films of Eisenstein have always been accepted as transcending the political ideology of Soviet communism that they were glorifying; the documentary films of Riefenstahl and the neo-classical sculpture of Arno Breker still seem irremediably tainted by their ideological content.

The arts are ever more explicitly used today to further official political objectives: in particular, a multiculturalism to which museums in Britain or the USA are obliged to subscribe as a condition for public funding. This can help an institution such as the British Museum to exert a powerful influence towards civic integration in a society threatened by many divisions – with its collections assembled from all the world's cultures, making possible a sustained comparative approach. Indeed its policy is to achieve a global presence and thereby, as it were, to redeem the colonial conditions in which some of the best known of its collections were acquired. Under the British Museum's current widely acclaimed leadership in 2008, one of the central displays was the Wellcome Trust Gallery, which displayed 'different approaches to our shared challenges as human beings, focussing on how diverse cultures seek to maintain health and well-being'. In the USA, the Metropolitan Museum of Art consciously set out after 11 September 2001 to provide a haven of tranquil contemplation for the traumatized citizens of ethnically diverse New York. But officially sponsored multiculturalism can often lead to blandness.

Another increasing trend – not political in a narrow sense, but with some adverse implications for the autonomy of the arts – is the subsidy of exhibitions, concerts and operas by the public relations and client relations departments of large financial institutions and other corporations. However, we may say of the arts as Liogier has said of religion when it is used as a political tool (see p.51): 'The handle of the knife adapts to just about every hand, but never completely: the weapon is slippery'.

4

THE HUMANITARIAN MOVEMENT

Humanitarianism and Charity

If the coverage of political ideologies and artistic movements in the last chapter may seem to have gone over some trodden ground, the connections between the humanitarian movement and the religious and parareligious field have not yet been much explored.

This chapter will show that the humanitarian movement emerged historically from religious sources, but was strongly influenced by the secular values of the Enlightenment – especially by the belief in a common humanity. The movement today appears to be dominated by secular values, but Faith Based Organizations, as they are officially called, have a continuing and perhaps increasing importance. Moreover, some major secular organizations in this field have markedly religioid features, as will be argued in an extended case study of Médecins Sans Frontières.

We must define the 'humanitarian', or rather, make explicit the word's many different nuances. In colloquial speech it can mean nothing more specific than 'compassionate'. More technically, the term 'humanitarian' is sometimes used as a synonym for 'relief', in the sense of helping people recover from a state of immediate need, whether resulting from natural or 'man-made' disaster. Humanitarian relief is often contrasted today with 'development', or programmes designed to improve the life-chances of disadvantaged people over a longer term, though the distinction is increasingly blurred. (The distinction between natural and man-made disasters is also blurred today, since it is realized that suffering caused by natural disasters is, more often than not, aggravated by political ill-will.) But 'humanitarian' also has a technical meaning in the context of International Humanitarian Law (Geneva law), which sets out to define the responsibilities of parties engaged in armed conflicts. Recently the term 'humanitarian space' has become popular: it refers primarily to safe zones and corridors, and by extension to the scope for action, based on impartial and independent principles, to bring relief to affected populations. This may be seen as deriving originally from the institution of 'cities of asylum' in the Hebrew Bible (*Joshua* 20:1–20) and the acceptance of churches as places of sanctuary during the Middle Ages. (Even today, churches are sometimes used in this way.) Another kind of humanitarian initiative aims to promote reconciliation between parties in conflict. More controversially, the right of 'humanitarian intervention' (*droit d'ingérence*), or armed intervention in response to grave violations of the laws of humanity, has been partially accepted by lawyers. Here we will use the word in a wide, inclusive sense.

A semantically linked term is 'charity'. In English and some other languages since the sixteenth century, confusion has been caused within Christianity by two senses of the word 'charity' – spiritual love or (in Greek) *agapē*, and almsgiving or donating to the disadvantaged. Some Christian theologians have argued that they are the same, but in non-European languages such as Hebrew and Arabic they are distinct concepts. Charity in the broadest, not exclusively Christian, sense means a gift freely offered without expectation of reciprocity – though with some expectation of spiritual benefit for the donor and/or a measure of worldly recognition. Charity as a cornerstone of social order has come under severe fire since the nineteenth century both from social critics (for instance in Dickens's novels and Emerson's essays), and from Marxists and other socialists who claim that it merely addresses symptoms of poverty and distress while allowing the root causes to be obfuscated. Progressive social thinkers strove to replace it by the principle that the disadvantaged have inalienable rights to health, shelter, food and the like, which should be satisfied through redistributive taxation rather than voluntary donations. Many professionals working in the field of aid and development contend that what they do has nothing to do with charity. However, this is an illusion. Even humanitarian aid given through governmental agencies can for the most part be seen as an act of charity – collective rather than individual – since, except in the case of certain treaties, such aid is not enforceable through any form of contractual relationship. Development professionals tend to repress, in the psychoanalytic sense, the element of charity in their work.

Until recently, Western historians largely underestimated non-Western traditions of humanitarianism. But the importance of, for instance, the institution of *waqf* in the history of Islam is now widely recognized. The *waqf*, equivalent to the charitable trust or foundation (*hubs* in North Africa), dates back virtually to the founding of Islam. It spread over almost the whole of the Islamic world except sub-Saharan Africa, so that, for example, between a half and two thirds of the lands of the huge Ottoman Empire were *waqf* at the start of the nineteenth century. Since the nineteenth century, most centralizing States nationalized their *waqf* properties; but since the 1960s the institution has been given new life in some countries, partly as an Islamic response to the worldwide upsurge of voluntary organizations, but sometimes with a strong admixture of political motivation.

Another example is the 'Confucian' paternalism that sustained the Manchu dynasty for centuries in China from the seventeenth century until its decline and eventual collapse in 1911. Confucianism dictated respect to superiors, who in turn were expected to protect their inferiors. Admittedly, the Chinese imperial State was sharply stratified, with no active role allowed to the masses in the organization of the State. The measures taken to prevent and alleviate famines were no doubt primarily taken to ensure a stable political order. This however is a universal feature of humanitarianism.

A third example is the Indian tradition of mendicancy or begging, which used to be a major resource for the survival of people who were holy, old, handicapped, poor or socially excluded. Giving alms to anyone in need brought merit to the donor, and refusal to do so was supposed to bring terrible consequences in the next birth:

> A pandit [brahmin] not coming forward with help for the unfortunate fellow-beings during a famine, he would be reborn as a crying bird flying from one tree to another in the dark; any rich man who refrained from giving grain and clothes to the needy and who committed the sin of hiding his wealth inside a pit by digging the ground, his next birth as a serpent would be spent guarding the hidden wealth for thousands of years.

But under British rule, official relief aid came to favour the deserving poor, that is to say those willing to work. The Indian middle classes gradually absorbed this attitude, so that in modern India, giving alms to beggars and vagabonds is actively discouraged by the State.

Overseas humanitarian relief in Europe may be dated back at least to the period of the Crusades and the foundation of sovereign orders of knighthood with mixed military and 'hospitaller' aims, such as the Templars. One of these, the Order of Malta, founded in Jerusalem in the eleventh century, still survives with some 12,000 Roman Catholic members worldwide and extraterritorial diplomatic status. The Catholic Church was the principal provider in Europe of charitable services of every kind, until its virtual monopoly was broken first by the Protestant Reformation and then by the Enlightenment.

One of the innovations of the Enlightenment was a determination that neither the suffering of the wounded or defeated in battle nor natural disasters need be accepted with fatalism. The Dutch jurist Grotius laid the foundations for International Humanitarian Law with his *On the Law of War and Peace*, published in 1625, distinguishing the concept of justice in resorting to war from the concept of justice in the conduct of a war: the latter, he argued, should apply whether or not the original recourse to war was just. Voltaire lambasted the obscurantist response of the authorities to the earthquake that destroyed two-thirds of Lisbon in 1755: the wise men of the country could think of no more effective way of averting total destruction than burning some people ceremonially at the stake – 'an infallible way of preventing earthquakes'. The word 'charity', with its religious connotations, tended to be replaced by words such as 'philanthropy', 'good works' and 'humanity', and these values were aligned with pleas for freedom and the Rights of Man. The initiative passed from the church to private charitable associations, anti-slavery societies, the Quaker movement, subscriptions for insurgents in far-off wars such as the war of Greek Independence (1821–29), nursing and sanitary reform. The second half of the nineteenth century, a period of extensive colonization by the European powers, saw a burst of progress in tropical medicine.

However, the foundation of the Red Cross Movement is rightly regarded as a turning point in the history of relief. History meets myth with the foundation of the International Committee of the Red Cross (ICRC) by Henry Dunant in 1864, as an outcome of his heroic care for the wounded and dead after the battle of Solferino, and with the ratification of the First Geneva Convention. The Movement is and has always been committed to the principle of non-confessionalism, but it was essentially a product of Genevois Calvinism. Dunant himself was a devout Protestant Christian who had travelled in North Africa and was deeply impressed by Muslim hospitality and piety. The choice of the red cross on a white ground as the Movement's emblem, intended as a compliment to Switzerland (whose national flag is a white cross on a red ground), unfortunately created troubles as early as the 1870s, when Turkish soldiers rejected it as reminiscent of the Crusades, with the result that a second emblem, the red crescent, was accepted as an alternative. The difficulties arising from these decisions endured, and persist to some extent to this day. If Dunant and his co-founders of the Movement had chosen a semiotically neutral emblem, such as a red heart, much trouble would have been avoided. As it is, the authorization of the alternative emblem gave unnecessary emphasis to the religious symbolism of the cross. Some thirty National Societies of the International Red Cross and Red Crescent Movement now use the red crescent as their emblem, but in some countries, notably Israel, neither emblem is acceptable. A recent, but only partial solution has been for an optional alternative emblem to be used: the red crystal, diamond-shaped and, it is hoped, free from any obtrusive ideological connotations.

Faith Based Organizations

The relationship between the Christian churches and present-day humanitarianism has not yet been adequately studied. International NGOs concerned with overseas aid began to be recognized as a growing force in the 1950s, but at that time they were still almost exclusively Christian and, to a minor extent, Jewish. Christian missions of the nineteenth century had developed the strategy of mobilizing mass subscriptions through the publicity media of their day, and thus reducing dependence on rich patrons. The churches continued to play a prominent (and controversial) role in relief aid during such episodes as the Nigerian civil war (1967–70), when they were the major suppliers of emergency food aid to the isolated Biafran enclave. It might seem now that non-confessional NGOs such as CARE, Oxfam and Save the Children are the undisputed leaders of the sector. Yet the evangelical World Vision has become the largest US-based agency, with annual revenues of around $2 billion. Protestant organizations, especially the Baptists, wield great political influence in the United States. Internationally the Catholic Church remains energetically active: through its federation of development agencies, Caritas; through its many and diverse religious communities, from the Order of Malta to the Franciscans; through numerous pro-South lobbying groups; and through independent bodies such as the Italian community of Sant'Egidio, specially well-known for its projects in conflict resolution, or the international Emmaüs movement, devoted to combating poverty and homelessness, originally founded by the Abbé Pierre, an iconic figure in French public life who died in 2007. The World Alliance of YMCAs, which dates back to the foundation in 1844 of the original Young Men's Christian Association in London and was co-sponsored by Henry Dunant, now has 45 million members in 122 countries and boasts a history of pioneering in many fields such as ecumenism, interfaith dialogue, youth work and refugee counselling.

Faith Based Organizations (FBOs) within Christianity may be seen as a special case of what Wuthnow has called alternative forms of religious organization, or Special Purpose Groups. Religious organizations outside the churches and denominations have a long history in contributing to the restructuring of Christianity. These included in the nineteenth century the (Anglo-Catholic) Oxford Movement, missionary organizations and Bible societies, the YMCA and the Salvation Army. But since the 1960s, in parallel with a growth in all kinds of associative activity, Special Purpose Groups have mushroomed. Many of these may be aligned with the New Age, but others are in reaction against it. Wuthnow notes that in the USA even grass-roots movements have tended to evolve into formalized bureaucracies that add to the already weighty bureaucracies of the churches.

One tendency has been for Christian NGOs to place more emphasis than their parent churches on an agenda of individual salvation and to concentrate on material aid and economic development, recalling the 'option for the poor' manifested in the Gospels which is now entrenched in the 'social justice agenda' of the World Council of Churches. Agencies such as the British-based Christian Aid and World Vision, both of them pioneers in media campaigns, owe much of their success to the breadth of their appeal to Christians of various denominations as well as to donors who may not be active Christians at all but who respect Christianity as a system of practical ethics.

Some of the influence of Christianity is evidently migrating from traditional church bureaucracies to the new-style NGO administrations. The management and financial systems of World Vision have been integrated internationally. Christian groups have adapted the potential of the universality of their faith, previously expressed in missionary organizations, to legitimize international promotional strategies of a new kind. They have also negotiated new relationships with governmental and inter-governmental agencies.

An analytical distinction may be made between 'confessional' NGOs – those formally belonging to particular religious groups – and 'faith-inspired' NGOs which depend on a looser commitment to Christian ethics and values. The borderline with 'secular' is blurred. NGOs such as Oxfam, Amnesty International and Greenpeace might seem wholly secular; and yet, members of a small and previously persecuted sect, the Quakers, have played a disproportionate role in inspiring these major organizations, which therefore might be termed 'faith-inspired'. Save the Children, though non-confessional, was founded by Christians and reflects the emphasis on children in the Christian Gospels.

Similarly, there are NGOs founded by people who happen to be Muslims but are entirely secular. By scholarly convention, the adjective 'Muslim' is used to refer to people who call themselves or are regarded as Muslims, while 'Islamic' is reserved for policies or actions that set out to put Islamic teaching into practice. Islamic NGOs, which I have studied myself, emerged in their modern form since the 1970s as a result of the confluence of two movements: the rise of NGOs in general, and the 'Islamic resurgence'. The tradition of charitable giving in Islam is strong, dating back to the foundation of the religion with the institutions of *zakat* (mandatory alms), *sadaqa* (voluntary charity) and *waqf* (the Islamic charitable trust). But there are other strong historical continuities, expressed in such concepts as *dawa* (missionary action or militancy) and *jihad* – a term that sometimes has a military connotation but can also refer to following the 'way of God' by other means, including humanitarian action.

On the one hand, Islamic charities have established what is almost a parallel system of Islamic aid. It has radiated from major Muslim States such as Saudi-Arabia, Kuwait and Sudan, where the Islamic charities have had close links with governments, and has been marked by competition not only with non-Muslim humanitarian agencies but also between different Muslim States with divergent interpretations of Islam. The programmes of these charities were until recently almost entirely excluded from the analysis of international aid flows: one reason being that they are only recently becoming committed to principles of transparency and accountability. These networks of Islamic aid were still functioning in 2007, but they had been severely hampered by obstacles put in their way as a result of political measures taken after 11 September 2001 with a view to countering international 'terrorism'. Many observers in 2007 considered that there had been a serious overreaction against Islamic charities.

Another type of Islamic charity in the Middle East is linked with opposition movements, and these have hitherto had little two-way contact with the international aid system, apart from receiving occasional donations. Charities affiliated – whether closely through control, or loosely, or merely by repute or imputation – with militant organizations such as Hizbullah, the Shia opposition movement in Lebanon, or Hamas in Palestine, an offshoot of the Muslim Brothers of Egypt, have become extremely controversial, though they often command a high degree of local popular trust.

On the other hand, especially in the United Kingdom, where the charity regulation regime has been especially cooperative, Islamic relief and development agencies have developed in a way analogous to Christian agencies such as Christian Aid and CAFOD (the British arm of Caritas): that is to say, distinguishing their aims completely from those of proselytizing organizations and embracing international principles of non-discrimination. This enabled Islamic Relief Worldwide, for instance, to grow in twenty years into the largest Islamic aid charity in the world, drawing financial support from governments and forming collegial relations with non-Muslim aid agencies. This development has been supported by liberally minded *ulama*, though it is contested by some conservative Muslims who still prefer to see Islam as a seamless whole in which it is mistaken to try to separate religion, politics and 'good works'. Charities of this type are able both to draw funds from the international aid system and to use religious tradition as a fund-raising and campaigning resource: for instance, they publish tables enabling devout Muslims to calculate their liability to pay *zakat*, and allow donors to set up earmarked funds under the name of *waqf* (but governed by British charity law). This process of absorption of several Europe-based and North American Islamic charities into the international aid system would no doubt be more rapid but for the political turbulence that has ensued since 2001.

In 2007, the Islamic charities based in oil-rich Middle Eastern States were engaged in tentative negotiations to extend and 'normalize' their relationship with the international aid system. Some of the charities associated with opposition movements in the Middle East were setting out to dissociate themselves gradually from political affiliations, real or presumed, and so acquire a legitimacy that until now has often been disputed.

There are also well-established confessional NGOs belonging to other religious groups. The Church of Scientology has founded a small empire of NGOs, including the Way to Happiness Foundation International, which operates a range of social welfare programmes in many countries, the detoxification agency Narconon, and Criminon, whose aim is 'ending the revolving door of crime'. Soka Gakkei, the Japanese Buddhist network, also runs an international foundation, largely devoted to promoting peace. The originally Indian meditative movement of the Brahma Kumaris was awarded consultative status at the United Nations in 1984 and has since coordinated a number of inter-faith peace projects. The Baha'i faith, originally a reform movement in nineteenth century Islam but long since established as an independent religion, has established a sustained relationship with the United Nations since as far back as 1948, with a special commitment to sustainable development and to human rights.

In order to understand the relationship between religions and civil society, we have to recognize the existence of many forms of associative life that have deep cultural roots but are not NGOs in the usual sense. One example of these is the Hindu caste and community associations, which bring together diaspora communities and their fellow-members in India. Another is the *ton* in Mali – traditional rural associations with both economic and ludic aspects.

A number of different theoretical models have been proposed for interpreting confessional NGOs. One is Raphaël Liogier's 'individuo-globalism', which sees the cult of spirituality and 'personal growth' (or *le narcissisme éclaté*) on the one hand, and a concern for the whole cosmos on the other hand, not as in opposition to each other, but rather as mutually reinforcing. According to this model, what gives ground are established religious hierarchies and national boundaries as reinforcers of personal identity; and we will explore the model in more detail later. Individuo-globalism, according to him, is a widespread movement of ideas, correlated both with Western affluence and with the urge to develop forms of religion compatible with modern science. His sociological model enables us to consider confessional NGOs such as World Vision, as distinct from old-style missionary organizations, in the same comparative bracket as the New Religious Movements – Soka Gakkei, Scientology, Baha'i and many others. Liogier's is not a starry-eyed way of looking at the confessional NGOs: on the contrary, it sees them as playing down any strictly religious character but emphasizing a loose form of spiritual values, supported by the principle of the freely offered gift, the unalloyed purity of charity, which facilitates the fiction that they are lacking in an economic dimension. Rather than constituting an alternative to global capitalism, confessional NGOs are (according to him) engaged in exporting spiritual values that are systematically modulated to conform to the living standards of dominated populations. Moreover, certain neo-evangelical NGOs may actually be exporting an ideology of immediate well-being through faith, as opposed to one of deferring consumption in order to build up capital. Such an 'export' policy could have the effect of helping to maintain such populations in a state of 'unproductive inertia' while they also become dependent on consumer goods imported from the North.

There are similarities with the more historical model advanced by Terje Tvedt. Tvedt sees the world religions as developing in *longue durée*, a time-scale to be measured in centuries, whereas the modern international aid system dates back only to about 1945 and is essentially secular. The religions have found ways of adapting to the international aid system by means of confessional NGOs, possibly (and here Tvedt is in agreement with Liogier) playing down their religious aims in order to gain acceptability and funding.

Both models have merit as frameworks for interpretation, but we need to beware of sweeping statements. A confessional NGO such as Christian Aid sees itself very much as an advocate for the interests of the South, in much the same way as its sister organization, Oxfam, and rigorously avoids any form of proselytism. Liogier's contention that 'religion' is played down in favour of 'spirituality' in Western industrial societies does not yet apply to Muslim organizations such as Islamic Relief Worldwide, though with increasing interaction between Muslim and non-Muslim institutions, and the growing Western interest in Sufism, it is more than possible that a trend will emerge in that direction.

Faith Based Organizations have recently become a topic for comparative social research. Attempts have been made to draw up typologies that apply across the various faiths – though this runs into a number of problems, such as the fact that the very concept of religion is Eurocentric, or the fact that some charities, in the Palestinian Territories and elsewhere, have their status as bona fide charities refused them by the US authorities. It is probably a mistake to regard Faith Based Organizations as a species distinct from secular NGOs On the contrary, secular NGOs are guided by values and ideologies that can be analysed comparatively – as must also be the interactions between values and practice. In other words, even the most secular NGOs can be seen as, in a sense, Faith Based Organizations. Here I am relying on the argument presented earlier in this book that the concept of religion or faith is much more fluid and open to interrogation than is usually assumed.

One might take Oxfam or Save the Children as a subject for a detailed case study, but I have chosen Médecins Sans Frontières.

A Case-study: the Secular Sanctity of Médecins Sans Frontières
At first sight, Médecins Sans Frontières (MSF – also known as Doctors
Without Borders) might seem to have nothing to do with religion. It is true
that one of its principal founders in France, Max Récamier, was a Christian
conservative, and that the Catholic youth movement post-1968 was also
influential in France at that time. But MSF resulted mainly from an alliance
of medicine, journalism and the Left. I contend however that in a wider
sense MSF is indeed a kind of Faith Based Organization. It has successfully
propagated a myth.

Some historical distinctions must be made. MSF was founded in France in
1971, and despite its border-busting name was for many years a
mononational rather than an international institution. New sections of MSF
were founded in other European countries as early as 1980, but until the
early 1990s they were still conceived, at least from Paris, as extensions of the
founding French organization. It is now a mature and increasingly important
organization, with an international headquarters and nineteen national
sections, and an annual turnover of around € 460 million.

I had been interested in the evolution of MSF since the early 1990s, but
was drawn into studying it more closely when invited to submit a discussion
paper to their strategy review in 2005. The decisions facing its international
board might seem extremely down-to-earth. These include: whether to rely
on a specialized mandate of 'crisis medicine' or to continue to diverge into
the territory of more multi-purpose agencies, for instance in the fight against
HIV/AIDS and other epidemics; how to balance an overarching global
identity against the autonomy of national sections and 'subsidiarity' (taking
decisions at the lowest possible level); and whether recruiting expatriate
volunteers on short contracts is still a relevant way of operating, at a time
when many other agencies consider local training and 'capacity-building' to
be more important. Ever since its foundation, there has been debate within
MSF about the tension between emergency relief and longer-term
development and health issues. The French insistence on robust *témoignage*, or
'speaking out' against local abuses of human rights, is still strongly associated
with MSF as a whole and seen by some as almost its most distinctive quality,
but the sections differ as to how to do it most effectively. MSF also takes a
lead in chiding the huge intergovernmental organizations such as the World
Bank for their neglect of issues such as HIV/AIDS, and multinational
pharmaceutical companies for hanging onto the patents of life-saving drugs.

The current international leadership looks back with a wry detachment on
the theatricalities of the past. This has been a classic case of routinization of
charisma, fiercely resisted at various points because many successive leaders
of MSF–France have been sociologically well informed about bureaucracies.
To apply Mary Douglas's model of cultural analysis, which we will explore
further in Chapter 5, MSF–France started with a high level of group

coherence but a low level of role prescription, hence tending towards the egalitarian and sectarian – what in the Douglas system would be termed as high-group, low-grid. MSF as whole is now resisting the inevitable pressure to become high-group, high-grid: that is, towards becoming (in the Troeltschian terms set out in Chapter 2) a hierarchic 'church' rather than a 'sect'. It still retains the sense of a strong boundary that is characteristic of sects, and, in its staunch commitment to independence, it is sometimes criticized for standing apart from other humanitarian agencies rather than expressing solidarity and facilitating coordination. For instance, it is not a member of the Disasters Emergency Committee in Britain, which raises funds collectively for relief agencies, nor of the recently established Humanitarian Accountability Partnership in Geneva.

Though the original swashbuckling romanticism of MSF is a dead letter today, I suggest that an analysis of MSF places it fairly high in our imaginary cornucopia described in Chapter 3, that is to say in the medium-strong field of parareligion. Myth making, in the sense of the fabrication of a carefully embroidered narrative as a charter for legitimacy, was explicit in its early history but, as we shall see, became a competitive sport. Bernard Kouchner, the best known of its co-founders, wrote of the 'aristocracy of risk', and Xavier Emmanuelli, another of its leaders, of 'glorious mythological conquerors under the immodest eye of cameras the world over', while a French *grand reporter* subtitled his book on the movement 'The great epic of humanitarian medicine'. There was the occasion in 1978 when Kouchner persuaded the two grand old men of Paris intellectual life, Jean-Paul Sartre and Raymond Aron, to shake hands in public after a thirty-year personal rift, in support of a hospital boat, named the *Île de Lumière*, that Kouchner and some associates had decided to send to the China Sea to pick up the Vietnamese refugees known as Boat People. This provoked Emmanuelli to publish a stinging attack entitled 'A boat for Saint-Germain-des-Prés' – that is to say, Paris's intellectual Latin Quarter – and resulted in Kouchner's leaving MSF and founding a new organization, Médecins du Monde.

The principal history of MSF to date, by Anne Vallaeys, relates ironically what she calls the 'official version of the emergence of MSF' during the Nigerian civil war of 1967–70, when the [Biafran] Ibo were being pitilessly massacred by the Federal death-machine based in Lagos. (On her lively history this chapter will draw for evidence though it is not in every detail reliable, and is also deeply biased in favour of the French contribution.)

> Discovering the inhumanity of this war and dismayed by the ravages
> of famine, the French broke for the first time the golden rule of
> silence enjoined by the International Committee of the Red Cross.
> The young medics denounced the Nigerian massacres and unveiled
> the ICRC's diplomatic dumbness. They tried too to mobilize French

and international public opinion by playing the game of the media. They ended by founding an association that proclaimed the 'right of intervention' [*droit d'ingérence*] while collecting testimony [of breaches of human rights, *témoignage*] and denouncing barbaric behaviour.

This narrative, strongly endorsed by Bernard Kouchner, is revised by Vallaeys. For instance, she points out that the French government under de Gaulle was delivering arms to the secessionist Biafrans with one hand and with the other supporting the French Red Cross's medical mission to which Kouchner belonged. European mercenaries, recruited with the help of the French secret services, were fighting on the secessionist side. The Nigerian Federal government was hence able to insinuate that the French Red Cross was an active participant in the rebellion, sponsored by the French government. Kouchner's role in denouncing the ICRC's silence was exaggerated in retrospect, and in any case its role in seeking to preserve its neutrality was arguably more consistent than the French government's role in helping to promote a media spectacle of starving Biafran babies – which had the actual effect of prolonging the war through appealing successfully to international sympathy. The Nigerian civil war is now recognized as prefiguring many of the geopolitical dilemmas facing humanitarianism today.

Biafra was one of the first warring parties to engage a commercial Public Relations service. Kouchner was a self-proclaimed enthusiast of what he called the *loi du tapage* (law of hype) and turned himself into a heroic figure of imaginative fiction. His objective courage and dynamism are not in doubt, and his place in the history of humanitarianism is assured. However, the early years of MSF were marked by schism. In its origins, it stood to the ICRC as Luther and Calvin once stood to the Roman Catholic Church. Then there were the later split with Médecins du Monde in 1980, and subsequent bitter disputes over ideology and policy, including a lawsuit in 1985 when MSF–France unsuccessfully sued MSF–Belgium in Brussels to try to prevent it from using the MSF trademark and logo. For many years, Rony Brauman declined to use the word MSF–France, of which he became the head, on the grounds that 'When I go to the cinema, I don't say that I am going to the talking cinema'. Another dispute arose over the launching in 1985 of a research centre associated with MSF under the name of Liberté sans Frontières, designed to offer a critique of facile third-worldism, which lasted for only four years.

A characteristically Parisian polemical style used to dominate the activities of MSF–France. Emmanuelli followed up his attack in 1978 on the *Île de Lumière* hospital ship project with another savage attack, entitled *Les Prédateurs de l'Action Humanitaire*. Two former MSF leaders, Claude Malhuret and Kouchner, had allegedly betrayed the humanitarian cause by successively accepting ministerial office – with responsibilities for human rights and humanitarian action respectively. Authentic humanitarianism, he argued (in accordance with MSF orthodoxy) could never be undertaken by governments, only by NGOs. Not long afterwards, Emmanuelli accepted government office himself as minister for humanitarian action in succession to Kouchner.

MSF's name and inspiration derive from medicine, which is the paradigm of science and technology devoted to salvatory human ends, and whose practitioners form a hierarchic caste comparable to that of priesthoods. MSF's secular sanctity derived from that of the Red Cross, with which it once had an Oedipal relationship, for it is common ground among all historians of humanitarianism that the Red Cross in the 1960s and 1970s was an excessively conservative and cautious organization that needed to be revitalized. At one time, MSF's logo used to be a red cross that sloped forward and was half erased by a red squiggle, no doubt to take advantage of the red cross's visibility, but it also had the effect of saying 'not the Red Cross'; and the ICRC was not amused. This has been replaced by a less provocative design.

Furthermore, MSF is associated with extreme medicine, such as field surgery, and the presence of death in wars and disasters. One of the functions of the religious sensibility is always to combat, and make sense of, the fact of death: eschatology, the 'last things'. If suffering in life is a foreshadowing of and preparation for death, coming to terms with suffering and death is near the core of the religious sensibility.

In alleviating suffering and saving lives, MSF fieldworkers risk their own lives. On the night of 27 April 1990, a group of three masked and armed men, probably young *mujahidin*, broke into a little MSF hospital in Afghanistan and shot Dr Frédéric Galland, aged 28, in the head. MSF withdrew after a ten-year commitment. It went back two years later in 1992, after the fall of President Najibullah. In June 2004 two Afghan staff and three expatriates were killed in the province of Badghis. Their vehicle had been attacked by unidentified armed men. *Le Monde* reported (2 June 2004) that at least 26 members of humanitarian NGOs had been killed in similar incidents over the last eighteen months. MSF pulled out of Afghanistan – with its staff of about 80 expatriates and about 1,400 employees – at the end of July. This is the reality of humanitarian action in countries such as Afghanistan and Iraq today. It has been calculated by an independent source that MSF suffered twelve separate incidents of major violence (defined as killings, kidnappings or hostage-takings, gunshot wounds and landmine explosions) between 1997 and 2005 – the highest of any NGO, though not quite as high as the total for the Red Cross or the World Food Programme.

This is a form of martyrdom though without an explicit martyrology. I happened to be present at a meeting of MSF in Brussels on the day in June 2004 when the news came through of their loss of five staff in Afghanistan.

Though many of the participants were under shock, the meeting went ahead with just a few restrained words of mourning and solidarity. As far as I know, NGOs that work in conflict zones do not commemorate their dead in ceremonial ways other than private funerals. It seems that, set up as they are to relieve suffering on an immense scale, these NGOs find themselves restrained by tact and good taste in not dwelling on the tribulations and deaths of their own volunteers and staff. These, however, are fully aware of the risks that face them in the field.

There are also records of conversion experiences of a kind, owing to MSF's long-standing practice – especially favoured by MSF–France – of drawing on the temporary services of doctors and other health workers who are committed to conventional careers in the State health service. There is an element here of the rite of passage that middle class young Europeans voluntarily undergo when they travel to far-off, sometimes dangerous places in search of spiritual experience before shackling themselves to careers and mortgages. Older recruits may experience the same wanderlust. Vallaeys tells of two of these. One was Geneviève, a 30-year-old paediatrician, with a grey flannel skirt, pearl necklace on a silk blouse. She dropped everything to spend a year in a village in Gabon. 'Perhaps for love of adventure', she said. 'In fact, for fear of getting bogged down in a linear life, set out in advance. To get away! No matter where, but to get away!' Again, Michel, a 50-year-old country doctor, father of five: 'I had had enough of my role as a local worthy, a sorting-machine, a service station'.

Gilles, another of Vallaeys' interviewees, was a logistic specialist (for not only doctors and nurses are recruited), who came into contact with MSF when he was 23 in the 1980s and had already spent some months working on an abortive scheme to find precious stones in Madagascar. 'Nothing to do with the idea of going to look after people in distress! … That ambition comes only later, when one has seen and taken note of suffering, when one has seen difficult situations in the field. My ambition was quite different. But I behaved like any would-be volunteer: I hid it, I didn't want to be failed at the recruiting stage.' He was sent to Malawi, which turned out to be one of MSF–France's main programmes. At that time, there were some half a million refugees from the civil war in Mozambique, and Gilles' job was to help build hospitals and handle every aspect of drinking water supplies, control of epidemics, nutrition, hygiene and public health. On his arrival at the airport in Malawi, Gilles was met in a four-by-four but had to walk 25 kilometres, as the roads leading to the camp they were making for had been flooded. He arrived with his feet bloody and his torso and arms roasted by the sun. He immediately had to install an isolation centre for a cholera epidemic and rebuild water standpipes and latrines. In his 40s, Gilles was still undertaking missions for MSF, but said of the Malawi experience: 'For the first time, I had the feeling of being really responsible. I was free to take what initiatives I wanted'.

Another documented experience, this time from the USA, is that of Barry Gutwein, a farmer and agricultural engineer from Indiana, who joined MSF at the age of 53 after his four children had grown up and he became separated from his wife. He had previous experience of Africa while studying for a doctorate. He sold up in 2004 and joined MSF full-time as an emergency water and sanitation specialist. After a few days of training, he was sent to Kalma refugee camp in Sudan, which accommodated some 125,000 displaced Sudanese people in minimal conditions for survival, with temperatures up to 48 degrees Celsius in the dry season. In a six-month assignment stretched to eight, Gutwein

> dug new wells and fixed old ones, chlorinated murky waters, hauled medical supplies in helicopters and boats that were little more than bundles of sticks strapped to empty steel drums. He built a hospital operating room out of mud, assisted doctors who lost more patients in a week than they had in their entire careers prior to coming to Africa, and did any of a thousand daily duties to deny death a little longer.

Service on behalf of MSF became a spiritual experience for Gutwein, who confided to a journalist from his old university: 'To observe people surviving on virtually nothing at this most remote and timeless of places was overwhelming'. He certainly never expected to thrive under such circumstances.

> The endless blanket of darkness overhead, broken only by the stars and the streaking satellites, bathed Gutwein in a calm he had never experienced stateside. 'This is where I am supposed to be,' he thought. 'This is what I am supposed to be doing, my life's mission.'

MSF's commitment to *témoignage*, ethics, impartiality, independence and neutrality amount to a credo to which all involved with it are expected to adhere. Though argument has always smouldered within MSF about policy and in particular interpretation of the founding principles set out in its charter, there is no doubt about its strong commitment to non-negotiable principles:

> Médecins Sans Frontières was founded to contribute to the protection of life and the alleviation of suffering out of respect for human dignity. MSF brings care to people in precarious situations

and works towards helping them regain control over their future. ('Principles of Reference', 1997)

Maybe I was unfair in 1993 to write that the very French language 'lends itself to florid expressions of humanitarian intent', but some quotations from Kouchner and Emmanuelli in particular support the contention:

> We are all doctors without borders from the moment we take our [Hippocratic] oath, from the day of defending our thesis. We medical doctors are all concerned by what happens to our brother human beings all over the world.

These principles, though entirely non-confessional and looking back as far in history as the medicine of Ancient Greece, clearly derive also from Judaeo-Christian 'charitable' values. MSF has in common with many other humanitarian NGOs – as argued earlier in this chapter – that it has sought to dissociate itself from the idea of charity, no doubt because many of its early leaders were strongly committed to the Left, which has always tended to disparage charity and philanthropy. For instance, Xavier Emmanuelli said on television in 1978:

> Medical assistance no longer plays any part in charitable or political good works. It is a technique that has to be learnt ... Médecins Sans Frontières do not want to become the Samaritans of crises, or the apostles of charity, but highly trained specialists to do real medical work wherever urgency is the top priority.

Such an argument is at odds with the evidence, that MSF is an outstanding example of a commitment that is charitable – in the sense of providing services free of charge, out of a sense of moral duty, to beneficiaries who have no enforceable entitlement to them. The fact that MSF volunteers are highly specialized is irrelevant, for they are donating services that command a high market value.

As already noted, MSF is now a genuinely transnational organization. It would appear to be intentional that the growth of its national branches has not followed the usual trajectories associated with the colonial period. For instance, MSF–France has a privileged link with Tokyo, New York and Sydney. MSF–UK is a satellite of MSF–Holland, rather than the reverse, though Holland is a much smaller country. 'Only in MSF', wrote a high MSF official in an internal document in 2005, 'could the Japanese be perceived as "French" and the Swedes as "Belgian" '. The analysis offered here is disproportionately concerned with the French entity, which is now no longer the largest – and English has displaced French as the MSF lingua franca. I will revert later to the transnational aspect.

I come now to MSF's use of publicity and the media, Gell's 'technology of enchantment'. It can be argued that twentieth century NGOs have done no more than adapt with modern technologies the promotional methods used by nineteenth Christian missions, which included newsletters, lantern slide lectures and other communication media of the day. However, the use by Oxfam of advertising experts since the early 1950s, the use of public relations companies by warring parties in Africa since the 1960s, and the growing importance of television (and now internet) news, surely mark a historical shift towards dominance of the 'media field', which is indeed noticeable in its encroachment on all the other fields listed in Chapter 3.

Since its foundation, MSF–France has consistently obeyed Kouchner's *loi du tapage*, though with considerable discussions as to the style to be followed and reservations about the self-publicizing that Kouchner is still often accused of. Indeed Kouchner's recent political activities have made him so unpopular within MSF–France as to give him internally the reputation of a heretic, despite his high popularity rating with the public at large. In 2007, when this committed leftist accepted the post of Minister of Foreign Affairs in Nicolas Sarkozy's centre-right administration, MSF felt obliged to publish statements making clear that Kouchner had had no connection with MSF since 1979 and that the unwarranted association of MSF's name with his put their reputation for independence at risk. The French press has always given MSF great support. In 1988, an opinion poll conducted by *L'Express* placed the medical volunteers at the head of the professions that 'make the French fantasize most'. *Sans-frontiérisme* found its way into the French language and inspired aviators, architects, engineers and reporters without borders.

After a faltering start in 1971, MSF–France was adopted by a marketing expert called Jean-Pierre Audour who wanted to create in France 'social communication', which is now known as 'institutional publicity' (and had actually been anticipated in Britain to some extent by Oxfam and Christian Aid). Audour wanted everyone in the world of publicity to be talking about his agency, Havas. In 1977, a 4 by 3 metre poster for MSF was displayed in every French town with more than 20,000 inhabitants, showing a wide-eyed child with a dark skin behind two bars, which could be those of either a cot or a prison cell: the legend read 'Médecins Sans Frontières: in their waiting room, two billion men'. Another legend read: '*Le monde est à tout le monde, même quand il n'est pas beau*' ('the world belongs to all of us, even when it is not nice to look at'). The first part of the sentence took up the familiar slogan of a travel agency. In the political economy of Third World, tourism and humanitarianism have this in common, that they depend to a great extent on visual images of human bodies: healthy and seductive in the case of tourism, helpless and hungry or diseased in the case of humanitarianism. MSF has enjoyed a productive relationship with the documentary photographer Sebastião Salgado. He is undoubtedly an outstanding photographer, though controversial on the grounds that he is apt to turn tragic circumstances into sacred images. MSF–France has recently made a political decision not to use publicity agents as it did in the past, but to compose all the content of its publicity in-house (while out-sourcing some of the distribution function).

In the 1990s MSF paid little attention, unlike most other aid agencies, to the political implications of its visual communications. They reminded one observer of the Crucifixion and the Pietà, with the 'white, bare-chested, cruciform MSF doctor working himself to death over his much more suffering yet depersonalized patient' or the 'clean, white, blond-haired MSF nurse fully framed in the picture with the faceless body of yet another dehydrated black child draped over her lap, its arm flopped over her thigh showing no identity beyond the numbered armband of the feeding centre'. MSF has more recently fallen into line with other agencies, showing a greater sensitivity towards visual imagery.

Some have considered that MSF–France's principal achievement has been to mobilize the media not only for its own promotion but to exert public pressure. This is somewhat resented by the new transnational generation of MSF leaders, who point to many other achievements. In any case, MSF was awarded the Nobel Prize for Peace in 1999.

If we now tick off the various criteria in my cornucopia model, all those except 'appeal to an ideal world' and 'appeal to supernatural entities' are satisfied for MSF to be considered a parareligious NGO. By definition, as a non-confessional organization it could not be expected that those particular criteria would apply narrowly. At the same time, MSF–France in the early days seems to have sometimes tried to make up for the absence of belief in an eternal realm, with deities to worship, by creating its own myth of conquering heroes and by idealizing the redemptive role of medicine. Even today, Brauman – who was head of MSF–France for many years and a prolific writer, and is still a highly influential figure – says that the two 'ideal types' of humanitarianism are Oxfam and MSF. This applies both to their public relations and also to the priority attached by Oxfam to development and local capacity building as well as external emergency relief. Whereas Oxfam dwells in its campaigning on the state of victims, MSF identifies with the medical doctor as hero. Brauman justifies this choice, saying that everyone knows what a doctor is, but it is hard to envisage how to solve problems of famine.

Alternatively, from a Durkheimian point of view – that a given society's object of worship is itself – it is the MSF logo itself that becomes deified; or, in other words, it is like other logos (as was suggested in Chapter 3) 'a miraculous visitation from another world, the world of the "free gift" ' –

identifying the donors and volunteers with 'life-style values' that they can 'buy into'.

So where should we put MSF on the continuum of the strong–medium–weak religious field? Certainly at the stronger end of the medium zone, since virtually all the criteria for the religious field are satisfied. It is true that, unlike Faith Based Organizations more strictly defined, it offers no thesis on fundamental questions of being. However, Brauman has averred that there is indeed a philosophy of humanitarianism: 'To the question "What is man?", humanitarian philosophy replies simply "He is not made to suffer" '. This leads to a problem at the heart of all humanitarian endeavour, which is that suffering is all too widespread but unequally distributed among the different classes and nations. Humanitarianism is one way – one of the most practical – in which people who are not cursed by personal deprivation try to maintain a sense of purpose and human dignity in a tormented world. From this fundamental dilemma has arisen a vast body of soul-searching on the ethics and politics of humanitarianism. Among the questions asked are the following. Should a relief organization such as MSF refuse to work in a dictatorial country such as North Korea where to do so is in a sense to prop up the regime, or should the ordinary citizens of such a country be treated with special sympathy and attention because of having no civil rights? Should humanitarian aid be given to the weaker side in a war, when this may inadvertently prolong the conflict? Does the continuous despatch of mainly white medical workers to Third World countries overstate the contribution that expatriates can make? Is neutrality possible when one side in a conflict seems to be clearly the oppressor, and the other the oppressed?

It might be argued: 'Forget about the colourful past of MSF. MSF is a confederation of rational adults with a strong bias towards science. Let us have a debate about rational matters rather than acquiesce in the power of the irrational'. One recalls the confrontation in Camus' classic – and now, in the time of HIV and avian flu, all too topical – novel, *La Peste* [The Plague], published in 1947, which as well as being obliquely concerned with the effects on France of the German Occupation is also a metaphoric meditation on any and all disasters, and on the possibility of sainthood without God. In a key passage, the narrator and principal character of the novel, Dr Rieux, who works indefatigably to save lives and alleviate suffering in a plague-stricken town in French Algeria, rejects all ideas of a heroic role: 'I don't have the taste, I believe, for heroism and sanctity. What interests me is being a man'. And again, 'It's not a matter of heroism, it's a matter of honesty. It's an idea that may seem laughable, but the only way of fighting the plague is honesty'. Thinking particularly of the searching analysis in Camus' novel of how disaster narratives are manipulated by the media, and of the conflict between individual medical care and the statistical morality imposed by emergencies, I used the latter quotation as the last sentence in a book on humanitarianism, as if that clinched the matter.

However, it is easier for a large organization to aim at an unimpeachably 'honest', that is to say rational, approach if it is able to draw on a massive capital endowment such as the Ford Foundation or the Wellcome Trust. Some 95 per cent of MSF–France's revenue derives from the general public, that is, from incessant fund-raising, and the figure for MSF internationally is about 80 per cent. MSF is very careful about which governments it accepts funds from: for instance, the European Community and Nordic governments are considered acceptable donors. But fund-raising is a branch of marketing, and marketing depends on Gell's 'technology of enchantment'. When we respond to a charity appeal – from disposable income, or by bequeathing money in our wills at the expense of our heirs – we are 'buying' identification with the charity brand. MSF is now more than a national charity: it is in competition with other world-scale 'brands' that I have called the parareligious but secular NGOs. The most direct 'competitors' are other humanitarian organizations such as Unicef, Caritas, Save the Children, the Red Cross. But a far wider range of international good causes – Friends of the Earth, Greenpeace, Amnesty International, to name but a few of the secular ones – is also dependent on the disposable income of ordinary people with a sense of public duty, compassion and/or guilt.

MSF has been notably successful in achieving and maintaining an exceptionally high level of independence. Many of the major British relief and development agencies accept a large part of their income from governmental sources. United States agencies seem to be expected by their government to act as 'force-multipliers' for American foreign policy (though they do not all comply). Faith Based Organizations – even when managed with close attention to international codes of non-discrimination, like CAFOD or Islamic Relief – inevitably carry religious baggage. The number of major independent, transnational, non-confessional NGOs is not very high. Their importance is undoubtedly increasing. An indication of this is that MSF has become involved in some major and serious public controversies, and such controversies are likely to increase as its high profile continues to grow.

In other words, MSF answers to most if not all of the criteria for a parareligious movement, while also being acceptable to atheists, agnostics and those who are not specially concerned about the 'spiritual'. It offers a meaningful narrative, a version of faith, an identity. This has not arisen by accident but by highly skilful use of the 'technology of enchantment'. Such an organization on a world scale inevitably takes many decades to build up. It is true that if the narrative deviated too widely from factual achievements, it would soon be exposed as untruthful. This is because it insists on transparency and free debate.

In all NGOs there is a profound ambivalence between the operational side and the public relations side. Fund-raising is to everyday operations as ritual is to everyday action, as rhetoric is to everyday discourse, as merchandising is to everyday goods. Advocacy (or campaigning) is an attempt to bridge the gap between operations and public relations, but the gap always remains. MSF has long and successful, if often turbulent experience in bridging this gap.

MSF's independence is guaranteed by the loyalty of an inner core of volunteers (and professionals willing to work for low salaries) and a very large outer transnational core of individual loyalists. Transnational organizations on this scale are not built in a day. It has taken MSF nearly forty years to reach its present position of influence. Yet it would be hard to overestimate the importance of such organizations for the future. Despite the firm belief of most of those working for MSF that it is simply a down-to-earth, practical organization, I suggest that the quasi-religious aspect of its make-up needs to be recognized, so that observers can appreciate its full significance, and so that its own members can gain a full understanding of the opportunities and challenges that await it.

Conclusion

The strong moral values underpinning the humanitarian movement have always owed much to religion. Explicitly Faith Based Organizations have opened up new forms of relationship between formal religious institutions and humanitarian work. But even an organization such as MSF displays many parareligious features. Thus, though religion may seem to leave by the door, it flies back by the window.

5

ANIMAL RIGHTS AND ENVIRONMENTALISM

Connections

In this chapter I will address the wide field of animal rights and environmentalism, which shade into one another – especially with campaigns to save particular favoured species. The disputed concept of speciesism or anthropocentrism, contrasted with biocentrism or ecocentrism, will be introduced and discussed. Whereas animal rights campaigners do not tend to be particularly wedded to religions, there is a marked crossover between environmentalism and spiritual movements. Because the environmental movement has already been subjected to extensive analysis by social researchers over some thirty years, the opportunity will be taken to summarize some key findings of this research and examine its relevance for the understanding of specific religioid movements.

Animal Liberation and Animal Rights

In the humanitarian movement, discussed in the last chapter, there is no extremist or violent wing. The environmental movement, as we shall see, has a small extremist wing, close to that miscellany of political activists grouped together under the flag of anti-globalization or *altermondialisme*, and vastly outnumbered by associations and networks cutting across all shades of political opinion. But the animal protection movement seems to be deeply fissured, on account of the activities of an extremist wing that is small but highly visible politically.

Opinions are sharply divided in Western industrial societies on the subject of animal liberation, animal rights and associated issues. There is indeed a middle ground of assent to the principle of improving animal welfare and protection, but its implementation is highly selective. Periodically, the British public is alerted with disturbing reports of how animals are treated in abattoirs and factory farms, but most of us prefer not to think too often about how the meat we eat reaches the shops. Though the Royal Society for the Protection of Cruelty to Animals (RSPCA) has declared itself opposed to recreational fishing, no serious attempt has ever been made to restrain the behaviour of Britain's estimated 3.5 million anglers – no doubt because fish do not scream. But the Department of the Environment has been working towards a system of self-regulation for the treatment of animals in the film industry and circuses, which will probably enjoy wide if tacit support. Charities devoted to the care of animals that have a domestic relationship with human beings attract particularly generous donations in Britain.

One cannot help concluding that for most of us, animal welfare belongs more to the field of aesthetics than of ethics. We oppose visible cruelty to animals that are able to dramatize their ordeals, and are embarrassed and upset when such cruelty is exposed through the media. Fur-coats attract a degree of odium, but few of us are prepared to forego leather shoes or become vegetarians. (Disturbingly, this suggests that we may be swayed as much by aesthetics as by ethics in the sphere of humanitarianism as well.) In any case, for most of us, animal welfare is something we vaguely approve of but it is rather low down on our list of priorities.

The animal rights movement opposes the middle ground of 'welfare', and has developed an extremist wing which has specially targeted companies that use animals for experimental purposes. In Britain, the government – strongly committed to encouraging medical and other scientific research – has moved against animal rights extremism. As from 2005, a criminal offence of causing 'economic damage' to companies involved in the animal experimentation supply chain, such as the breeding of laboratory animals, could carry a five-year sentence. A number of activists have been sentenced to substantial prison sentences. An organization called VARE, Victims of Animal Rights Extremism, has been founded to help defend companies and individuals from aggression. But the animal rights extremists in Britain are notably few in numbers, though undoubtedly able to cause considerable personal distress, and it has probably been an overreaction to label them as 'terrorists', that is to say in the same category as Al-Qaida style suicide bombers.

The animal liberation and animal rights movement has two distinctions as opposed to other adversarial movements. The first is that it is one of the few popular movements to have been initiated by a professional philosopher. Admittedly, a few writers such as Brigid Brophy in Britain anticipated him intellectually, but it was a course given by the Australian moral philosopher

Peter Singer at New York University that stimulated the foundation of Animal Rights International in 1974. Singer is a utilitarian philosopher, whose innovation in this field was to assert that the utilitarian quest of 'the greatest happiness for the greatest number' should include non-human animals. His commitment to animal liberation was shortly overtaken by another influential philosopher, Tom Regan, who has favoured a rights-based approach. But according to Regan, animals have rights only if they have enough mental complexity to be 'subjects-of-a-life', which he defines as mammals aged over one year. Much has been written since on these issues, of varying rigour and depth. But it is hard to read a book such as Robert Garner's *Animal Ethics* without concluding that there is a serious debate in progress, and that it ought to be more prominent in the public domain. Attempts, generally falling back on the philosophical classics, to dismiss the whole debate as an intellectual aberration may be over-hasty.

For the second distinction of the movement is that it is a rational response to Darwinism. If the non-human animals are our cousins, how can we easily brush aside the suggestion that we have moral obligations towards them? In reality, our hierarchization of moral obligations is deeply influenced by Christianity, or more precisely by Abrahamic monotheism. According to Christian theology, animals do not have souls. The Abrahamic monotheisms are not the only ideologies to have erected strong boundaries between human beings and other animals: indeed, one of the functions of what anthropologists call 'culture' in many societies, as well as the Abrahamic traditions, is to declare 'we are not animals'. From this imperative originate such manifestations of culture as table manners, clothes, cooking and rites of passage – as well as language itself. (It is true that a contemporary school of anthropologists, led by Tim Ingold and others, has tried to subvert this definition of culture, arguing for the recognition of continuities between culture and nature rather than their opposition, but this may be seen as a corrective to excessive anthropocentrism in the discipline.) Some modern remodellings of Hinduism and Buddhism proclaim a respect for animal life; but whereas it is true that these ancient traditions do not grant human beings any monopoly in having a 'soul', they have also tended to disparage the existential quality of non-human animals.

Darwin wrote that 'the difference in mind between man and the higher animals, great as it is, certainly is one of degree and not of kind'; and modern anthropology has tended to bear out this proposition with regard to such qualities as communication skills, emotional attachment and use of tools. Consequently we experience a strong resistance when reminded of the animal as well as the spiritual aspect to our nature. The fact that we experience this strong 'gut-reaction' against being lumped together with the non-human animals is not a decisive point in favour of the arguments for taking the interests of animals more seriously than most of us do, but it is a point we ought to bear in mind.

In the animal rights movement, though the extremists or activists are probably fewer in number than they may seem, largely consisting of 'micro-gangs' and declining rather than growing in popular support, they have attracted considerable attention. Examples in Britain are the death in prison in 2001, after a hunger strike, of Barry Horne, sentenced to eighteen years' imprisonment for arson and criminal damage against companies involved in vivisection; or the sentencing in 2006 of four activists to imprisonment (four to twelve years) for conspiracy to blackmail the owners of a farm in Staffordshire that bred guinea pigs for medical research. Their campaign against the farm culminated in the theft of the body of Gladys Hammond from her grave the previous year. It is possible that extremist splinter groups help the more mainstream groups by making them seem moderate and sensible. More probably, direct action of this kind has weakened the force of the animal rights movement, turning the public against it and buttressing the position of powerful commercial interests. However, the issues have been set out with admirable judiciousness in the Nuffield Council on Bioethics' report on 'The ethics of research involving animals' (2005).

History of the Animal Rights Movement
There can be little doubt that the mainstream of Western thought has declared Man to be the lord over nature. This is broadly true of both the Greek and the Hebraic traditions. The Hebrew Bible or Old Testament is rich with references to animals, including some injunctions to be kind to them ('A righteous man regardeth the life of his beast', *Proverbs* 12:10) as well as many evocations, in *Job* and elsewhere, of the grandeur of the animal world. But it is surprising how few sympathetic references there are to non-human animals in the Christian New Testament. True, every sparrow that falls is included in God's providence, even though two are sold for a farthing (*Matthew* 11:29), but when St Paul reminds his disciples that the Mosaic law forbids the muzzling of agricultural oxen (*1 Corinthians* 9:9, *Deuteronomy* 25:4) he says it is not for the sake of the oxen but for the sake of the farmer. On one occasion, it is recorded that, during a visit to Gadara, Jesus exorcized some devils that were tormenting one or two crazed men, and transferred the devils to a herd of two thousand swine, so that they rushed down a cliff to drown in a lake (*Matthew* 8:28, *Mark* 5:1, *Luke* 8:26). (The pig was and still is deeply despised in the Middle East.) One has to conclude that Jesus and his followers had hardly any interest in or sympathy for animals.

The standard history of animal protection proceeds from this base line to point out that when St Thomas Aquinas, Locke and Kant recommended kindness towards animals, it was mainly because they thought that those who are cruel towards animals are likely to tend to be cruel towards human beings too. A more sympathetic approach emerged during the Enlightenment. The first patron saint of animal rights must be the utilitarian philosopher Jeremy Bentham, who published in 1789 this much-quoted passage:

> The day has been, I grieve to say in many places it is not yet past, in which the greater part of the species, under the denomination of slaves, have been treated by the law exactly upon the same footing as, in England for example, the inferior races of animals are still. The day *may* come, when the rest of the animal creation may acquire those rights which never could have been withholden from them but by the hand of tyranny. The French have already discovered that the blackness of the skin is no reason why a human being should be abandoned without redress to the caprice of a tormentor. It may come one day to be recognized, that the number of the legs, the villosity of the skin, or the termination of the *os sacrum*, are reasons equally insufficient for abandoning a sensitive being to the same fate. What else is it that should trace the insuperable line? Is it the faculty of reason, or, perhaps, the faculty of discourse? But a full-grown horse or dog is beyond comparison a more rational, as well as a more conversable animal, than an infant of a day, or a week, or even a month, old. But suppose the case were otherwise, what would it avail? the question is not, Can they reason? nor, Can they *talk*? but, Can they *suffer*?

Animal welfare societies were founded in the first half of the nineteenth century, and the anti-vivisection movement in the second half. According to the standard history, a concern for animal welfare is correlated with civilization and progress.

An American historian, Kathleen Kete, has questioned this received idea, arguing that concern for animal welfare has always had a political motivation. When the Puritans in England introduced in 1654 the first legislation in Europe against cruelty to animals, prohibiting cockfighting and similar sports, it was theologically motivated by the thought that animals as well as humans were having to pay for the Original Sin of Adam and Eve, but it was also part of a widespread attack on popular recreations which included dancing round the maypole. In order that a middle class should develop, it was necessary for the lower classes to internalize norms of discipline.

When the animal protection societies were formed in Europe during the early nineteenth century, they were targeted against the practices of urban workers, peasants and southerners. Laws for the protection of game were skewed towards the interests of the landed gentry, and hunting was excluded from animal protection laws. The anti-vivisection movement, according to Kete, was primarily an outburst of disquiet about science and rationality.

Animal rights were also anticipated by the long history of vegetarianism, which has had some association with the Buddhist and Pythagorean doctrine of reincarnation but has also been espoused by many influential figures for other reasons. The second patron saint of animal rights must be Henry Salt, the English humanitarian and vegetarian activist (1851–1939), whose book, *Animals' Rights Considered in Relation to Social Progress*, was published in 1892 and who was a major influence on both George Bernard Shaw and Gandhi; yet his life and work were almost forgotten until the 1970s. The first half of the twentieth century saw a decline in the animal welfare movement, with domestic animals becoming the centre of attention. The breakthrough came with Peter Singer's book *Animal Liberation*, published in 1975, whose essential argument was that if the possession of a higher degree of intelligence does not authorize a human being to use another human being for his own ends, how can it authorize human beings to exploit non-human animals? Animal Rights International was founded in the United States by Henry Spira (1927–98), a Belgian Jewish refugee from the nazis who became a brilliant activist, targeting particularly factory farming and the testing of cosmetics on animals.

Peter Singer, like Henry Spira, has always condemned violence and intimidation in the cause of animal protection, holding that the issues should be settled in the process of democratic debate. Organizations such as the Animal Liberation Front and the Animal Rights Militia derived historically from the hunt sabotage movement in Britain. These movements have been branded as terrorist, but they compare themselves to the anti-nazi resistance or the anti-apartheid movement. The following translated extracts from the policy statement of Collectif Anti-spéciste in France gives a flavour of the ideology of the more moderate, peaceful wing of the movement:

> The anti-speciesist campaign does not replace other campaigns, but rather sets out to extend their scope. We are egalitarian in that we consider all sentient beings, capable of experiencing suffering or pleasure through their nervous systems, as possessing equal rights, whatever their sex, skin colour, age, income level, or species. ... Humanism is built on discrimination against non-human species. We are against the hierarchy of campaigns and against the kind of humanism that advocates 'human beings first' but could just as well have said 'French people first' and that excludes animals automatically because they are different. The difference should be neither a factor for hierarchization nor for exclusion, and still less for exploitation. Let us free ourselves, and free all beings that are

oppressed by capitalism and its dramatic consequences. Animals are not objects for consumption. Eating is a political act. ...

This is the antispeciesism of the Left. By contrast, the extensive animal protection laws introduced in Germany by Hitler in 1933 were not just an expression of sentimentality but, as shrewdly argued by Kathleen Kete, an attack on Judaeo-Christian humanism. She suggests that nazism, which also set out to dehumanize certain categories of humans, produced the worst possible solution to the 'dethronement of humans' effected by European rationalism; but: 'Animal liberation, on the left, is exploring some others. It is a mark of Peter Singer's importance that he has raised for us this most central philosophical issue of our time'.

Antispeciesism has been little studied by researchers, but surely in a neo-Darwinian world we cannot dismiss the position outright. An anthropologist studying the religion of the Jains attempts to enter their life-world and to understand why a Jain *sadhu* avoids hurting any insect, out of his reverence for all life. So we should try to understand the life-world of those who passionately oppose the relative indifference of most people to the suffering of animals, and who try to reduce that suffering.

Nor is Singer a negligible philosopher: indeed he has made influential contributions to debates on other topics such as poverty, euthanasia and *in vitro* fertilization. It is part of his underlying aim to seek to dethrone the principle of the sacredness of human life that has been inherited from Christianity by liberal humanist morality. A regular component in the argument about animal liberation and animal rights is the so-called Arguments from Marginal Cases: our obligations towards, for instance, people suffering from serious incapacities such as acute brain damage or advanced senility. The question is whether they should be accorded more rights – as our Abrahamic codes of morality insist – than, say, a great ape in good health? It is quite clear in Christian ethics that the rights of, say, a patient suffering from severe Alzheimer's remain unimpaired, although his or her potential enjoyment of or contribution to human life may have been reduced to virtually nil. This is not so clear if we try to build a secular ethic from scratch. 'Lifeboat' cases have been devised, wherein philosophers debate whether, in a lifeboat with room for only a limited number of passengers, priority should be given to saving, say, a person in the last stages of Alzheimer's as opposed to a trained guide-dog in perfect health. This line of argument is strongly opposed by Christians, who generally hold that there is an important principle at stake that needs to be defended; and they are supported by a large majority of 'cultural Christians' as well as atheists and agnostics who adhere to the principle. It is particularly opposed by advocates of the rights of handicapped people, who on the whole are probably more constrained in their lives by social restrictions than by their handicaps.

The Great Ape Project is founded on evidence that not only do great apes share DNA that is similar to their human counterparts, but they also experience emotions such as fear, anxiety and happiness, share the capacity to create and use tools and to communicate in a way that approximates human language, and are capable of remembering and planning for the future. The Project claims for our 'nearest living relatives' certain human rights: the right to life, the right to freedom of movement, and the right to protection from torture. It has been objected that the Project, whatever its merits, runs into ethical difficulties when it makes comparisons between the mental capacities of great apes and those of individual human beings with disabilities.

Many cultures have tried to solve the question of the soul's relationship to the body. The Christian solution is merely one. For the Samo of Burkina Faso, every human person is made up of no less than nine constituent entities, whereas for the Algonquian hunter-gatherers in north America, every living being is a centre of agency and consciousness. Christians accept the authoritative doctrine that animals have no souls, yet a kind of personhood is often accorded to domestic animals. The Argument from Marginal Cases leads inexorably to the claim that if human patients so disabled as to be 'human vegetables' nevertheless retain all their human rights, then we should not shrink from treating at least the 'higher' animals as associate members, if not full members, of the club that possesses these rights.

But there is then the risk that, if the idea of 'rights' is extended to animals, a back door can be created by which rights are denied to certain categories of human. One of these categories might be the severely disabled. Another could be distant peoples living in poverty. Since most of us are fairly selfish for most of the time, if excessive demands are made on us to observe the presumed rights of other entities, there is a risk of falling back on what might appear to be the time-honoured certainties of relationships with 'kith and kin'. Quite apart from the extreme example of Hitler, a case closer to our own time is Brigitte Bardot, a steadfast supporter of animal welfare in France, but also a sympathizer with the far Right. Another example is John Aspinall (1926–2000), the British gambler and ground-breaking zoo reformer, who taught that zoo staff should treat animals with respect and try to bond with them, but was also a self-declared misanthrope and reputed plotter of an extremist right-wing plot against Britain's Labour government. To be fair, it must also be said that many passionate advocates of animal rights are also passionate about human rights, and there is evidence that abuse of animals is sociologically interlocked with abuse of vulnerable human beings.

Animal Rights as Parareligion

The point has already been made by others that the animal rights movement has religioid features, summarized by Wesley Jamison et al. as follows, on the basis of comparative research in Switzerland and the United States:

1. intense and memorable conversion experiences;
2. 'communities of significance' – most of the adherents being atheist or agnostic;
3. creeds (compare the anti-speciesiest creed quoted above);
4. well-developed and defined codes of behaviour;
5. cultic practices – such as meetings and demonstrations.

To which I would add:

6. playing on a feeling of guilt for the suffering of other beings;
7. transnationality (according to Jamison et al., the movements in Switzerland and the United States are similar, though the Swiss are more inclined to consensus and make less use of the idiom of 'rights');
8. use of the media to create a martyrology – images of chained monkeys, elephants whipped by circus trainers, cats with their eyes sewn up or electrodes attached, rabbits with ulcerated eyes and faces, and the like;
9. demonizing of offenders;
10. sectarianism: movements of this kind inevitably splinter into small groups which may be visualized as satellites orbiting round mainstream 'churchlike' sects such as, in Britain, the Royal Society for the Protection of Cruelty to Animals.

The implicit ideal world that the movement appeals to is a Garden of Eden, which was vegetarian with no predation. One reason why I would place the movement on the medium-strong level of the religious field is that it conveys a strong ontological message – the message of Darwinism. Because Darwinism – in its modern forms incorporating genetics and biochemistry – does not seem to be losing its supremacy as a biological paradigm, it is highly likely that the animal liberation and animal rights movement will continue to survive. Trying as we should (if we wish to adopt a scientific approach) to enter and appreciate the life-world of its adherents, we must surely acknowledge that if the commitment to animal rights were justifiable, the justification of some forms of direct action branded as 'extremist' might logically follow. Christian tradition does not exclude the possibility of an 'antinomian' option, in which faith removes the obligation to obey the law. Criminal exhumation of an old lady's corpse is seen by mainstream ethics as extremely distasteful, but some animal rights activists would defend such 'direct action' on the grounds that, though it is intended to cause moral distress, it causes no physical harm and is aimed at drawing attention to and so inhibiting the oppression of sentient beings.

A major weakness of the movement, which will undoubtedly limit its growth, is the impossibility of a dialogue with the presumed possessors of the animal rights. A second weakness is its millenarianism. Though some initiatives such as the Great Ape Project have adopted a set of limited and realizable goals – allied to the 'disappearing species' movements, on which more below – there is no agreed definition as to the cut-off point in the zoological hierarchy below which animals have no rights.

There is no doubt that concrete steps have been taken to improve the treatment of animals, – and this is in large measure due to agitation by the movement. The use of animals for testing cosmetics is now prohibited in the UK, as is the use of great apes for laboratory research of any kind. The largest animal rights organization in the world, the US-based PETA (People for the Ethical Treatment of Animals), claims a million members and has stimulated many minor reforms as well as major ones: for instance, in 2002 the National Collegiate Athletic Association agreed to replace leather basketballs in its tournaments by cruelty-free synthetics; likewise the Women's National Basketball Association, but the NBA itself has not yet followed suit.

The animal liberation and animal rights movement is unlikely to become a mainstream political force, because it conflicts with the interests of many important industries and interrelated consumer habits. There is a connection with the environmental movement but there are also tensions. Should moral priority lie with the welfare of the individual animal, or with the survival of a species threatened with extinction, or with the protection of habitats? Then there are the many societies that depend on hunting, fishing and pastoralism. The movement has been a bastion of feminist activism; and it has been suggested that the beginnings of the movement around the end of the Vietnam War allowed it to fill a niche for a radicalism which suddenly after ten years found itself without a cause. Arguably it is the product of an affluent society and would decline if Western societies were suddenly faced with acute economic hardship.

There is no shortage of candidates for demonization in the animal rights movement: zoo keepers, circus animal trainers, and eaters of *foie gras*, as well as research scientists. One of the most extravagantly demonized has been the fur industry and its consumers: especially the archetypal 'rich bitch' attacked in one of the posters published in 1984 by the British anti-fur organization Lynx (which was succeeded by another body, Respect for Animals, after becoming insolvent as a result of a libel action against it).

If I may interject my own opinion, the claims of the animal liberation and rights movement should not be summarily rejected, if only because it is so convenient to our peace of mind for us to reject them. It may assuage one's guilt, however, even if it does not resolve the issue completely, to consider that – according to the influential Estonian biologist and semiotician, Jakob von Uexküll (1864–1944) – every organism has its own *Umwelt*, a mode of interpreting signs specific to each species. To be concerned with 'rights' is itself anthropocentric or speciesist. W.H. Auden writes in his poem 'Musée des Beaux Arts' that the Old Masters never forgot the indifference of non-human life, for in a corner beside a scene of martyrdom

> ...the dogs go on with their doggy life and the torturer's horse
> Scratches its innocent behind on a tree.

Von Uexküll's followers essentially dispose of any sharp analytical distinction between ecosystems and cultural systems. The 'ecosemiotic' argument could conceivably be pushed the other way, speculating that cultural innovations such as the idea of entitlement might be intelligible in non-human systems of meaning. But equally, human societies have their own species-specific systems of meaning, which include ethical values as well as practices of technological aggression that are qualitatively different from the violence seen in the animal world, which is largely oriented towards survival.

Campaigns to Save Charismatic Animal Species

If circus trainers and furriers are demonized by the animal rights movement, the need of a quasi-religious movement for divine entities is satisfied in the campaigns to save certain species. These campaigns are mid-way between animal rights and environmentalism. The choice of endangered species to be singled out is aesthetic, falling on 'charismatic megafauna': pandas, elephants and tigers rather than, say, vultures (except among the Parsees, who traditionally used them to dispose of their dead) or hyenas. I would argue that when a higher than animal status is ascribed to a non-human animal species, this is analogous to the ascription of a higher than human status to certain human beings, that is to say to deification – but of a whole race of gods, not an individual deity. The whale in particular, as argued by Arne Kalland, has become a totem for goodness and respect for nature, since it does not fit easily into our simple categories of mammals and fish, and hence forms an anomalous category which easily becomes the object of myths and taboos.

> Whales are often anthropomorphized by being given human traits as well. They are depicted as living in societies similar to our own. The

super-whale [an amalgam of traits actually found in a number of different species] is endowed with all the qualities we would like to see in our fellow humans: kindness, caring, playfulness. ... The super-whale cares for the sick and dying, baby-sits and runs nurseries. ... It is claimed that their long history gives them special rights to the sea ... The age of whales places them above humans; they become our teachers and might be capable of telling us stories 25 million years old if we only manage to learn their language.

Even more than the whale, the dolphin is interpreted as challenging us to become better humans and to make a world that is more spiritually and ecologically harmonious. The dolphin's legendary affection for human beings has been reciprocated by the foundation of a New Age cult, which was historically linked with the psychedelic universe of the 1960s and its seers, John Lilly (1915–2001) and Timothy Leary (1920–96). Dolphin enthusiasts speculate that, because dolphin brains are larger than humans' and the species is older, if dolphin brains had not been used during the long evolutionary period they would have atrophied. Human beings used their brains to change the planet radically, but dolphins are in total harmony with their environment and probably use their brains to appreciate and enjoy their surroundings. This, some animal behaviourists argue, could make them more intelligent than us – but in a completely different way. 'Total harmony with their environment' – yes, but not if you happened to be a mackerel, hunted by a well-coordinated school of dolphins. Comparison of cetaceans' brains with those of any land mammals is scientifically questionable, for all 'intelligence', including that of humans, is a specialized adaptation.

The cult of the dolphin has been well analysed by an anthropologist, Véronique Servais. She observes that big meetings of the International Cetacean Education Research Centre, based in Australia, 'closely resemble religious ceremonies devoted to the glory of the dolphin. On each page of the programme of one such conference, those attending could read: "may the spirit of the dolphin be with you" '. Solitary dolphins – those that stay for a few months at the same location near a coast, and frequently interact with humans – are known as 'ambassadors' by people who believe that dolphins are sending important messages to humans. Servais argues that the 'rhetoric of revelation' in these enchanted human–dolphin encounters is not (as many social scientists would argue) a mere cultural construct, but results from specific patterns of interaction between the dolphin and human species.

Swimmers who encounter the friendliness of dolphins at sea often report 'uncommon euphoria, happiness, beauty and love', a life transforming experience – though Véronique Servais reports that her own experience of swimming with a friendly dolphin was merely a nice touristic moment. She speculates that the specially heightened experience of interaction with dolphins, which comes only to those who are ready and primed for it, is due to three factors. First, the directness of the dolphin's eye contact: among human beings, a direct stare can be interpreted as aggressive but also, in a friendly context, as expressive of intimacy and courtship:

> Second, the characteristic tilt of the dolphin's head, which is interpreted as an appeasement posture. Third, the impassiveness of a marine-adapted mammal that has no ears, hair or limbs to distract the human observer from projecting thoughts and feelings onto it. Hence the behaviour of the dolphin provokes a meditation or mild trance state in the brain of those who are looking for it and already lulled by contemplation of the sea.

The more scientifically minded environmentalists often make use of emotional campaigns to save certain eye-catching species – with their special appeal to children – having in mind a wider purpose: that of preserving a life-supporting environment for all. For instance, the richer the oceans can remain in plankton, the greater will be the surviving population of the whales that feed on them; but a high density of plankton also assures the survival of many other forms of marine life, which are valuable from multiple points of view: scientific, economic and cultural.

The Environmental Movement

Many environmentalists are indifferent to or hostile to religion, and many religious people are uninterested in environmental matters. Yet the relations between the environmental movement and religion are much richer than most people imagine. The interconnections have begun to be better understood under the auspices of a new interdisciplinary area of study known rather cumbersomely as 'religion and nature', with a strong recent impetus coming from universities in the United States: an area of study wherein fundamental issues are addressed not only by scholars of religion and environmentalists but also by philosophers, anthropologists and historians of ideas. It is not surprising that a great deal of intellectual effort has been put into the study of 'religion and nature', given the importance of the issues at stake.

In earlier chapters of this book, we have attempted to elucidate some of the problems that arise from the term 'religion'. The term 'nature' has stimulated an equal amount of academic controversy, since it has several different meanings that can slide into one another (the origin of anything that is not a human artefact; the principle that gives rise to life and death; the essence of anything; and so forth). Mary Douglas explained in her influential article 'Environments at risk' in 1971 that 'time, money, God and Nature' are four more or less universal weapons for imposing social control, and of these Nature is the ultimate trump card; therefore the utmost caution must be applied when evaluating the use of the term as a counter in arguments that have a political import. A broad working definition is proposed by Bron R. Taylor for our present context: 'Nature is that world which includes – but at the same time is perceived to be largely beyond – our human bodies, and which confronts us daily with its apparent otherness'. The relationship between beliefs and nature in this broad sense is at the core of all cultures studied by anthropologists, so that the store of knowledge we might draw on to further the discussion is virtually unlimited. Here we will confine ourselves to sketching some striking interconnections.

Prehistory of the Modern Environmental Movement

The prehistory of the environmental movement was correlated with the reaction against industrialization that was a feature of Romanticism. One of its first major prophetic figures was Rousseau (1712–78), who came to reject revealed Christianity in favour of a form of 'natural religion' that relied on the experience of order and beauty in the universe as the guarantor of human beings' essential goodness. A second prophetic figure was the poet and artist William Blake (1757–1827), a visionary antinomian Christian who inveighed against materialism and mechanization in favour of an imaginative communion with the natural world. Then in the poetry of Wordsworth (1770–1830) we find both a quest for communion with natural phenomena at their most dramatic, and an account of the poet's imaginative development since childhood. Though linguistically austere, poles apart in literary style from the rhetorical euphoria of the American poet Walt Whitman (1819–92), Wordsworth in his prime might be seen as an even earlier precursor than Whitman of 'individuo-globalism', in that he proclaimed a reciprocal dependence between his own spiritual experience and the well-being of humanity and nature as a whole. This quality of Wordsworth's was satirized by his fellow-poet Keats as the 'egotistical sublime'. These and other literary Romantics of the period greatly influenced Western attitudes to nature; but it is a mistake to try to tease out from them any simple didactic messages. Their works often articulate a tension between faith in progress through human inventiveness, and nostalgia for some earlier state of supposed beatitude; but it is exactly this tension – as old as the history of civilization – which continues to prompt agonized debate today.

The early Romantic reaction against industrialization in Europe was recapitulated and developed in the United States during the second half of the nineteenth century. New England Transcendentalism was an informal religioid movement that flourished in the middle of the century, mainly in Massachusetts, uniting many different individual points of view around general ideas of the primacy of the spiritual, optimism with regard to humanity, and the assertion of American cultural independence. The two leading Transcendentalists were the author and naturalist Thoreau (1817–62) and the essayist Emerson (1803–82), both of whom have been claimed as prophets of environmentalism. Thoreau's interpretive stance, according to Rebecca Kneale Gould, is neither Christian nor secular, neither wholly scientific nor traditionally religious:

> His vision of nature was pursued outside the boundaries of both Christian orthodoxy and liberalism and his contemporaries therefore often criticized his writing (or expurgated it) because of its 'paganistic' tendencies. ... Thoreau's relative self-sufficiency, his concerns about the marketplace and emerging capitalism, and his view of nature as a beneficent source of spiritual transformation all contributed to the dominant themes of contemporary environmentalism: a growing interest in simple, sustainable living, a critique of consumer culture and a view of nature as the source for personal (often spiritual) renewal.

Emerson, though more concerned with the symbolism of nature than with its external reality, inspired not only Thoreau's *Walden* but also many other influential texts whose authors testified to finding a more spiritual life, closer to nature, than the standard experience of an urbanizing nation. Emerson also inspired the early Scottish-born conservationist and nature mystic, John Muir (1838–1914), who had much to do with the creation of American national parks such as Yosemite in northern California, and who founded the Sierra Club. A cult of wilderness areas has long been central to American conservationism, and only quite recently has it come to be realized that the concept is somewhat flawed, since, to name only one of the objections, the creation of national parks has usually, until recently, involved dispossessing the autochthonous human inhabitants.

Muir's commitment to 'nature preservation' ran into conflict with a more utilitarian environmental ethic, focusing on the present and future needs of citizens, adopted by America's first professional forester and pioneer of environmental management, Gifford Pinchot (1865–1946). Both these paradigmatic figures, who clashed over the damming of a valley in Yosemite in 1913, were influenced by new liberalizing theological developments in American Protestantism. This clash, between a spiritual and a utilitarian approach to environmentalism, has often since been recapitulated. Though ecology can be defined as a straight sub-set of biological science, and hence can be practised in a totally materialistic way – for instance, in the quantitative analysis of energy flows in an ecosystem –, it is noteworthy that the first scientist to use the term 'ecology' was the German zoologist Ernst

Haeckel (1834–1919), who combined evolutionary theories with a kind of anti-Christian pantheism which he called 'Monistic Religion'. One cannot sharply distinguish the scientific from the spiritual origins of ecology. It has been suggested that a love of green (chlorophilia) may be a universal aspect of human beings, an emotional response to nature that is largely visual, owing to our perception of colour.

Many of the prophets of twentieth century environmentalism were spiritually motivated. Aldo Leopold (1887–1949) wrote an essay entitled 'The Land Ethic', published posthumously, in which he proclaimed 'biotic' as opposed to anthropocentric values, extending natural rights from human beings to the whole of nature, and identifying a need to deepen the existing conservation movement – largely seen till then as a matter of prudent resource management – into a consideration of the whole relationship between human beings and nature. Though Leopold's professional training was in forestry and wildlife management, his biographer concludes that he was drawn to a kind of pantheism fused with ideas from the Russian mystic, Ouspensky. Again, Rachel Carson (1907–64) – whose *The Silent Spring*, published two years before her death, alerted the public forcefully to the perils of industrial and agricultural chemicals, courageously challenging the interests of large corporations – expressed in two earlier books a religious reverence for the sea as the womb of life.

Unpalatably for Green activists today, some scholars have noted the propensity of extreme right-wing movements to co-opt an environmental rhetoric – one of the most notorious examples being the purist 'blood and soil' ideology identified with Hitler's Minister of Agriculture, Walther Darré, inventor of the term 'organic farming' (see Chapter 3, p.69). Less radically, the cyclical imagery of nature can tend to favour quietist or fatalist views of history and – as sharply observed by Simone de Beauvoir in 1955 – a preference on the part of elites for the transcendent over the demands of one's fellow human beings. In her words, 'Nature is pliable: she tells us the words that we dictate to her'. It is now appreciated, thanks to the work of philosophers and sociologists of science, how hard it is to use biological language free from social and political value judgments.

The environmental movement remains a favoured field for those who believe that science and religion are compatible, drawing on philosophers such as Bergson and Whitehead whose work offers a challenge to scientific materialism. Whereas scientists' views on religion vary widely (as we will note later in this chapter), the majority of scientists probably prefer to think of science and religion as occupying two distinct domain of discourse: science being constantly ready to test and re-examine hypotheses, whereas religion is more a matter of embracing a moral and spiritual code by which life is given a meaning. If this separation of powers is endorsed, the social science of religion must aspire to belong to the domain of science, while trying as part of its research method to enter as far as possible the mind-set and experience of those who take part in religious or parareligious activities, as well as merely observing them from the outside. To some extent science itself can become a parareligion, as we shall see in Chapter 6.

The Religions and Environmentalism

One watershed in the developing debate about religion and the environment was the publication in 1967 of an article by Lynn White, an American medieval historian who had pioneered in demonstrating the effects of technological innovation such as the stirrup and the mechanical clock on medieval society. White's thesis, constantly referred to in the literature on this subject, was that Judaeo-Christian theology appointed Man to have 'dominion over the earth', as set out in *Genesis*, while nature-worship was condemned as pagan and as therefore heretical. He claimed that this assumption caused environmentally harmful applications of technology well before the Industrial Revolution, and was now resulting in the dreadful consequences of pollution, population explosion and the 'carcinoma of planless urbanism'. Religion for White was a potent force in shaping human societies, often working below the level of consciousness: for instance, in the atheist Soviet States that retained the Christian belief in progress through subjugating nature, though at the same time White wanted to exempt Eastern or Greek Christianity from his strictures.

Among the diverse respondents to White's argument were those who looked for alternatives in Asiatic philosophies or religions or in forms of paganism and animism. But a new surge of Christian theology revived an old theme of biblical interpretation that emphasized stewardship. If Man was created in the image of God, as is also taught in *Genesis*, then (despite his Fall into Original Sin) his rule over nature should be like God's and should not be exploitative. And so an alternative tradition within Christianity began to be sketched – looking back not to the anthropocentrism of Aquinas or Calvin but to such Saints as Basil the Great of Caesarea, John Chrystostom and Augustine, who had recognized the intrinsic value of non-human creatures; and above all to Francis of Assisi (c. 1181–1226), whose legacy to Catholicism had largely been through legend and hagiography. Francis's chosen way of life as a world-renouncing itinerant preacher, staying in caves and huts, had given him sustained contact with nature, and he had taught that all creatures are mirrors of God. Some important theologians such as the American Protestant, John R. Cobb, Jr., came to accept the White thesis and to call on the churches to repent for their past anthropocentrism and to embrace a new 'earthism' as a corrective to the dominance of economic models. Another watershed in the encounter between religions and conservation was the convening in 1986 of an inter-faith meeting by the World Wildlife Fund (WWF) in Assisi, Italy, the birthplace of St. Francis.

White's thesis was criticized not only by defensive theologians but by historians. There is no clear evidence that Christian societies were more environmentally destructive than others before the Industrial Revolution, at which point it happened that technological advance took place in societies that were permeated by religious thinking. Moreover, among ordinary people theological doctrine was often at odds with surviving astrological, magical and pagan beliefs. It is indeed unwarranted to assume any direct causality from doctrine to social institutions, and from social institutions to environmental impact. A sceptical note was already sounded in 1968 by a geographer, Yi Fu Tuan, who concluded that 'A culture's published ethos about its environment seldom covers more than a fraction of the total range of its attributes and practices pertaining to that environment'. This view is probably, by and large, supported by subsequent sociological and historical research, though no empirical studies can yet be said to either confirm or falsify the White thesis.

Independently of Lynn White and even a little before him, an Iranian historian of science, Seyyed Hossain Nasr, also attacked the disastrous anthropocentrism of Christianity, warning of impending ecological crisis and arguing that it had spiritual roots. His argument was that in Islam, science never lost its sacred character, and that environmental degradation was a Western export. He is now recognized as the founder of contemporary Islamic environmentalism.

The best academic treatment of Islamic environmentalism to date is by Richard C. Foltz. Two interwoven themes run through the argument. One is theological, as expressed in some of the most glorious passages of the Qur'an: the majesty, logic and diversity of the cosmos, and the cyclical regeneration of life as a sign of God's purposes. Man is not set up as Nature's overlord but as its *khalīfa* or viceroy. The second theme, also reflected in the Qur'an, is more factual, recording the geographical setting in which Islam was founded: an environment where natural resources – especially water, fruit trees and livestock – have always to be conserved to secure human survival. The colour green, adopted by the environmental movement, has a much older association with the Prophet Muhammad, and the Qur'an is full of imagery of fruits and gardens as emblems of paradise, while every carpet can represent a garden.

Foltz has gone further than explaining the environmentalist potential of Islamic doctrine, and has become an advocate for the causes of animal rights and vegetarianism in the Islamic context. Reverence for all animal creation runs right through the Qur'an, but, despite Foltz's pleading, the Islamic tradition of meat sacrifice is so strong as to make vegetarianism seem alien. A leading Fatimid theologian once condemned vegetarianism as a blasphemous attempt to be even more compassionate than God the Merciful, the Compassionate. Foltz takes the breezy view that it is less important which interpretations of Islam are correct than to encourage the articulation and putting into practice of 'eco-friendly, non-hierarchical' ones. Non-Muslims might well agree, but the process of interpretation is rather more complicated than that. Who you are – your training and status – may be almost as important as what you say in the world of Islamic interpretative theology, and outsiders need to adopt a sensitive approach if they are to have any hope of influence.

Few in the West are aware of the existence of Islamic environmentalism in today's Iran – a homegrown movement independent of Western-imported models, enshrined in a 1979 constitution but now also represented by numerous independent environmental organizations. At least three of these have combined women's issues with environmental campaigning. However, more generally it seems that the idea of Islamic environmentalism has gained favour among only a few intellectuals, with the Sufi mystical poet Rumi elevated to the status of Islam's St Francis, but has not been taken up by the mainstream *ulama*. A British-based charity, the Alliance of Religions and Conservation (ARC), which grew out of the Assisi meeting in 1986, supported by WWF and patronized by Britain's Prince Philip, has set itself the tasks of persuading the world's religious leaders to lend their authority to environmentalism, and of initiating practical collaborative projects. ARC has found it more difficult to form practical alliances with Muslim leaders than with some of the other religions, but considers that the potential for cooperation with the Muslim world is promising.

The most persuasive argument in favour of ARC's programme is perhaps in terms of time-scale. Politicians, by and large, are focussed on the next election, and even the most far-sighted industrialists are under pressure by financial analysts for their share price to rise annually. But religious leaders have a longer view, thinking of their adherents' children and grandchildren. To take a pragmatic view, even if religious values do not (as Lynn White and Hossain Nasr claimed) determine a culture's behaviour with regard to its environment, they undoubtedly have some degree of influence. And it is also certain that religious organizations have a rootedness in the popular culture of many nations that secular forms of 'civil society' can only envy.

ARC's philosophy, under the leadership of Martin Palmer, has relied on an assumption that all faith traditions have in common a deep reverence for nature which is ours to draw on, and its approach to the various traditions is egalitarian and even-handed. The consequence is that it does not set out to encourage changes in the various theologies, which would necessitate a degree of controversy, so much as to draw out by amicable consensus what is already there. This approach does effectively contest the charge that some of the great religions are inherently and disastrously anthropocentric, for their eco-friendly internal counter-traditions are by now fairly well known and publicized. There is more difficulty, perhaps, in contesting the charge that a powerful theme in many religious traditions is fatalism, which is inconsistent with all forms of organized purposive action.

An influential component in religious environmentalism has been the proposition that non-Abrahamic traditions are in some way environmentally superior to the Abrahamic faiths. The supposed beneficiaries of this change of heart are the South Asian and Eastern cosmologies – especially Buddhism, which has been singled out for special praise in the West, though Taoism and Jainism have also attracted favourable attention. It is true that the distinctions between the human and the animal, even between the animate and the inanimate, are less marked in these traditions. However, some scholars have cast doubt on the validity of turning Eastern religions into ecocentric religions, and it has been suggested by William Sweetman that this is yet another manifestation of the orientalism diagnosed by Edward Said:

> For Said, Orientalism is characterized by the conviction that the Orient is above all different, that which the West is not. This gives rise to a series of oppositions that configure Orientalist perceptions of both self and other. ... [T]he best evidence for thinking that ecological concern in the West has simply extended this binary logic by adding another series of oppositions to it (where the West is environmentally destructive and polluting, the Orient – and its religions – are environmentally affirming and beneficent) is the uniformity and vehemence of the claims made on behalf of Asian religions.

The evidence that Buddhism and other Asian religions are more ecologically friendly is at best inconclusive. It is probably nearer the truth to assume that all religious traditions have both an anthropocentric and an ecocentric aspect, and that all are shot through with contradictions and ambiguities (just as are non-religious world-views).

A similarly sceptical view needs to be taken of the idealization of indigenous religions, especially those of the Native Americans, which have been the object of imaginative projection on the part of their colonizers as well as of a simultaneous and systematic contempt and disparagement. This is not to deny that there are salutary lessons to be learnt from the inventiveness and resilience of many indigenous peoples, and from world-views such as those of Native Americans and Australian Aborigines which deserve to be respected as, at least, sophisticated human artefacts – sometimes as profound in their reflections on the place of humanity in nature as are any of the great world religions. There are also strong moral grounds for supporting the land claims of indigenous peoples when their traditional ways of life are threatened by the industrial extraction of raw materials. However, wholesale destruction of forests, and hunting to extinction of many animal and bird species in Australasia, were carried out by peoples who would now be regarded as 'close to Nature'. In a much cited critique in 1986 of the 'illusory images of Green primitivism', the social anthropologist Roy Ellen concluded that 'no one human culture has the monopoly of environmental wisdom, and … it seems unlikely that we could ever escape some of the more profound dilemmas of human social life'.

Buddhist Environmentalism

Liogier has distinguished three variants of globalized Buddhism, each of which has adopted an ecological mission. They are as follows:

Humanist Buddhist Ecology

The principal vehicle of this line of thought is Soka Gakkai, literally 'Society for the Creation of Value', an international lay Buddhist movement which was founded in Japan in 1930 and is now said to have some twelve million members dispersed in almost every country of the world. It is based on the teaching of the thirteenth century Japanese monk, Nichiren, and it has received both criticism – the latter focusing particularly on its aggressive proselytism (at least in the 1950s and 1960s, when it was expanding fast in Japan) and on its alleged aim to take over Japanese society – and praise for its efforts to promote world peace and development. Its umbrella body Soka Gakkai International (SGI) is an NGO accredited with the United Nations since 1981. Soka Gakkai is a structured movement, controlled from Japan like a multinational. For instance, the Soka Gakkai Française is vertically organized as a pyramid with a national centre, regional centres, districts, chapters and at the lowest level *zadankai* or discussion groups; and horizontally organized with five departments for women (who are in the majority), men, young men, young women and students, as well as an administrative head office. Unlike other Buddhist movements in France, of a Tibetan or Zen complexion, which have tended to attract the urban well off, Soka Gakkai has been successful in recruiting from more marginal sectors in the suburbs, including French people of North African origin. Whereas other Buddhist movements aim primarily to 'awake' the individual participant through rationally based spiritual exercises, Soka Gakkai gives some priority to integrating its members into groups for discussion and the recitation of mantras, rather on the lines of group psychotherapy and with a pronounced emotional content.

SGI runs an affiliated ecological research centre in Brazil, and the Soka University of America built on a 4,000-acre nature reserve in California; and it has strongly supported the UN's Earth Charter as a common ground that can be shared by all spiritual traditions. It encourages grass-roots activities such as clean-up, energy-saving and tree-planting campaigns, but also engages in high-level international exchanges. The position of Soka Gakkai on the environment is that it should be preserved and managed at a global level, not so much for the protection of other orders of being but because 'without a healthy Nature, humanity can neither survive nor prosper'.

Vitalist Buddhist Ecology

This has been developed particularly by the Dalai Lama and more generally by the Tibetan school of Buddhism – at least its more educated members and its international admirers, for a practical concern for the environment does not seem to have been part of the popular legacy of Tibetan Buddhism. The key principle (also shared by Soka Gakkai) is that of interdependence. But the central proposition is that global conservation should be pursued in order to facilitate the survival of all sentient beings, including human beings: in other words, it is ecocentric rather than anthropocentric. The strategies recommended by the Dalai Lama are top-down, when he criticizes industrialization, and bottom-up, when he calls for individuals to heal themselves and thus to take part in the healing of civilization. Because according to this view there is no such thing as an enduring essence or soul, individuals' concern for themselves becomes extended to the whole cosmos. The Dalai Lama also argues the connections between Buddhism and modern sciences such as molecular biology.

If western Buddhism is the most ideologically coherent and institutionally best organized component – by contrast with the New Age nexus – of the new 'individuo-globalist' religiosity, we must also note the contrast between the Buddhist idea of the self as an transitory illusion to be transcended, by various means including disciplined meditation, and what might be caricatured as the 'Californian' idea of the self as a precious plant to be nurtured by self-love.

To this category of vitalist ecology we may add the engaged Buddhism of Thailand and Cambodia. Thai monks have devised a way of protecting trees by symbolically 'ordaining' them as monks. Some form of engaged Buddhism is indeed now found in nearly all the Buddhist and formerly Buddhist countries of Asia, as well as in Europe and North America.

Radical Buddhist Ecology

This has been developed in the Buddhist context by the influential Vietnamese Zen monk and peace activist Thich Nhat Hanh (1926–). He founded the Order of Interbeing in 1966 and a meditation centre in France, Plum Village, in southern France in 1982. The heart of his teaching is the idea of healing, for the whole of liberal democratic society is deeply corrupted. Somewhat paradoxically, he attaches an almost Confucian importance to family and social order, but also champions civil disobedience and a kind of antinomianism.

The doctrine that the perfection of Buddhahood could be attained by plants and trees was originally developed within Chinese Buddhism: it became an established tenet by the Tang period (618–907 CE) and later influential in Japan. Nonetheless, the majority of Buddhists have retained the more traditional understanding that only members of the human and animal kingdoms can reach enlightenment. In Thich Nhat Hanh's teaching on the environment, he has extended the core precept of Buddhism, that one should avoid destroying life, to include not only animals, but also plants, and even minerals, for inert matter too can possess the nature of the Buddha. Humanity has no precedence: 'we human beings are made entirely of non-human elements, such as plants, minerals, earth, clouds, and sunshine'.

Environments at Risk: Mary Douglas

Teasing out these sub-movements within the broader movement of Buddhist environmentalism gives an indication of the complexity of the larger field of environmentalism as a whole. Fortunately, there is help at hand to make some sense of this complexity.

Unlike the animal rights movement, which has barely attracted the attention of social scientists as opposed to philosophers, the environmental movement has been carefully studied in its various aspects, particularly by Mary Douglas and her associates. Their thinking on the issue has undergone many changes and variations since she first began publishing about it at the beginning of the 1970s; but the basic idea is that people's most fundamental assumptions concern the social and political institutions under which they consent to live, and their 'deepest emotional investment of all is in the assumption that there is a rule-obeying universe'. Douglas's starting point, following on from her well-known book *Purity and Danger*, was to examine the universal concepts of 'risk', 'danger' and 'pollution' – but refusing any automatic privilege to Western environmentalists in the definition of these terms. She argued that even concepts that appear to have the full backing of natural science, and hence often remain unquestioned, have to be mediated through social institutions and thus take on a different form when expressed by, say, a civil servant drafting new technical regulations as opposed to a radical activist. The most up to date variant of Mary Douglas's 'grid–group analysis' (sometimes known as 'cultural theory') has been advanced by Michael Thompson, and the following is a simplified summary blending together Douglas's and Thompson's terminology, which itself results from efforts to distil a long earlier tradition of sociological thought. It is best perhaps to think of the model not as a 'theory' but as a working tool for making the most of wider developments in social science. The 'grid–group' typology has the advantage of distinguishing the two dimensions of (1) regulation of the conduct of individuals ('grid') and (2) social integration ('group'), which were often confused in traditional sociological analysis.

There are (according to the Douglas–Thompson school) four basic types of cultural orientation which coexist in industrialized societies, at every level from global institutions to family and sexual relationships – and no doubt even within the experience and behaviour of individuals. The model was developed as a tool for comparison between all forms of society, not merely within the Western industrial world, but special attention has been given to environmentalism in a recently published collection of essays under the editorship of Verweij and Thompson. The four ways of organizing and thinking are ascribed as follows:

1. *Positionalists* or *hierarchists* (high-group, high-grid: i.e. with both a high level of group coherence and a high level of role prescription). Here the good of the individual is subordinated to the whole, there is a coherent structure of leadership and responsibility, and a high value is placed on loyalty, tradition and continuity. (Douglas's original distinction was between the 'positional family' where roles are determined by age, sex and kinship, and the 'personal family' where roles are continuously negotiable.) Positionalists' lack of interest in transparency and accountability can lead to the snares of bureaucracy which include nepotism, corruption and hostility to innovation. Positionalists believe that Nature is stable within scientifically discoverable limits, and human beings are so flawed that they must be kept in check by systems of authority. They want to rely on accredited experts and regulate the environment from the top down. For them, the problem lies in the absence of an effective world government, and the solution lies in taking a longer-term view than that of the markets and specifically in strengthening science-based intergovernmental treaties such as the Kyoto Protocol. The neo-Christian (and neo-Islamic) idea of environmental stewardship also fits this pattern.

2. *Individualists* or *competitors* (low-group, low-grid). Here the most admired values are independence, cleverness, dynamism, success leading to wealth and power. It is a harsh world, where the weakest go to the wall. But unfettered entrepreneurship self-destructs since it depends on a system of law, inevitably hierarchic in form, that enshrines property rights. Individualists see Nature as essentially resilient, and Man as essentially self-seeking, and they believe that the market can be relied on to find optimal solutions, whereas subsidies and other distortions of the market merely reward inefficiency.

3. *Enclavists*, *sectarians* or *egalitarians* (high-group, low grid). They are committed to groups that are strongly bounded but with weak internal structures, leading to suspicion and envy, a preference for charismatic leadership, and an intolerance of outsiders. Their weaknesses include a lack of mechanism for reaching decisions, and a lack of economic drive, which can lead to impoverishment. They believe that the ecosystem is interconnected and extremely fragile, and favour activism from the bottom up, benefiting from the natural goodness of human beings provided that they are not corrupted by hierarchies or markets. The global ecological crisis is due to the reckless selfishness of the industrialized nations, and the solution is to go ecocentric: back to Nature.

4. *Isolates* or *fatalists* (low-group, high grid). They are not necessarily hermits, separated from others in literal space, but may for instance be marginal or alienated city-dwellers. These are the most vulnerable category in any social system. They think that Nature is arbitrary, conspiracies are everywhere, and concerted action is useless. Though this might appear to be a wholly negative point of view, in fact it is one that can often put a healthy damper on enthusiastic schemes that are prone to backfire with unintended consequences.

Verweij and Thompson conclude that in any public policy debate – environmentalism being just one example – if any of these ways of organizing and perceiving and thinking are excluded, the best-intentioned projects will derail. They call for 'clumsy solutions' as opposed to the 'elegance' that is essentially optimizing around one definition of a problem and silencing other voices. Each of the four modes has its strengths and weaknesses, 'none of which should ever be allowed to gain the upper hand'. We may see each of the four modes as a personal 'aesthetic' deeply intertwined with social position. The model should certainly not be seen as deterministic, since it is open to individuals to resite themselves along the coordinates and indeed to adopt multiple points of view at different times.

The Environmental Movement Today: 'Churches' and 'Sects'
A truly successful environmental movement would therefore, if Verweij and Thompson's advice were followed, integrate some elements of all these 'modes'. We may speculate that an organization such as Soka Gakkai has already gone some way towards doing this, and that a fair amount of sociological thought may well have underpinned its operations. But the 'individualist' mode and the 'isolate' mode are, as the labels suggest, the least likely to exercise vital roles in the galvanization of political movements.

Individualists, while extremely active in commercial corporations, make their contribution to civil society by forming associations such as the Adam Smith Institute in London, which typically argues against the Green Belt policy that has prevented the outward growth of city areas, thus pushing up the value of residential property: they recommend that subsidies for uneconomic farmland should be terminated, and the farmland replaced by housing and woodland. 'Isolates' by definition refrain from forming organizations – or in the case of some extremely marginal groups, such as that of undocumented workers, are legally prevented from doing so; but they sometimes exercise public influence in other ways, for instance as teachers or journalists or by taking advantage of the new opportunities for communication thrown up by the internet.

The main dialectic is between the 'positionalists' and the 'enclavists', and the terms of this relationship are similar to those of 'church' and 'sect', as defined by Troeltsch, which are discussed above in Chapter 2 (p.48). An example of this dynamic may be found in the history of the Sierra Club, which was founded in 1892 in order to protect Californian wildlands, described as a kind of cathedral, and now has a membership of nearly 800,000. John Muir, its founder, wrote 'The clearest way into the Universe is through a forest wilderness', and it soon became famous for offering its members excursions into backcountry areas with a strong element of spiritual therapy as well as adventure; but it has always avoided any formal religious affiliation. It also made its name by vigorous lobbying against dams and timber projects. In the 1950s, under the charismatic leadership of David Brower (1912–2000), it worked to negotiate common strategies and goals with government organizations and other conservation groups. As its influence in United States environmentalism grew, so it came to host some burning internal debates: over the validity of the wilderness ideal (see above), over the interests of Nature as opposed to people, and over the advantages of taking up an adversarial stance as opposed to working 'within the system'. More radical splinter groups were founded: Friends of the Earth in 1969, by David Brower when he was ousted from the Sierra Club by conservatives, and Earth First! in 1980. But as Van Horn and Taylor point out, the formation of the splinter groups inspired internal revitalization movements within the Sierra Club, helping to turn it in a more radical and ecocentric direction, though in 2007 its board of directors was divided between anthropocentric and ecocentric tendencies.

David Brower, deeply influenced by Muir's wilderness aesthetic, was given to using religious imagery to promote the environmental cause, and was once described as an 'environmental Billy Graham'. As executive director of the Sierra Club, he published an advertisement in the *Scientific American* likening the US government's project to build two massive dams in the Grand Canyon to a plan to flood the Sistine Chapel in order to get tourists closer to the ceiling. He is credited with having helped to persuade the US government not to finance a supersonic passenger aircraft, and is regarded in retrospect as one of the most important and effective environmentalists of the twentieth century. Friends of the Earth is a completely secular, non-confessional organization, yet in its origin lay the assumption that God and Nature are synonymous.

Rivalling with Friends of the Earth as the other transnational leader in environmental activism is Greenpeace, which was founded in Vancouver three years later, in 1972. Though lacking any explicit religious affiliation, three of Greenpeace's founders were Quakers and it is indebted to the Quaker tradition of 'bearing witness', that is to say, drawing attention to morally objectionable acts (which is also an essential principle of Médecins Sans Frontières, as we saw in Chapter 4). Greenpeace draws on the non-violent tradition of Gandhi and Martin Luther King, and also from time to time (as Paul Wapner notes) on Native American spirituality. For instance, the name of the flagship vessel of its 'eco-navy', *Rainbow Warrior II* – *Rainbow Warrior* was bombed and sunk by the French Navy in 1985 as a result of Greenpeace actions against its nuclear tests in the South Pacific – was borrowed from a Cree Indian prophecy that Nature can only be saved from the white man's greed when all the peoples of the Earth unite under one banner, that of 'Warriors of the Rainbow'.

Friends of the Earth and Greenpeace have joined the select band of genuinely global NGOs. Inevitably with such organizations, the routinization of charisma sets in, and these organizations with their mass membership and large budgets inevitably become hierarchical and technocratic. Just as they have grown from their origins as enclavist sects, so, as they mature into 'churches', they spawn splinter groups.

Radical Environmentalism

We will not chronicle here in all its variety the growth of radical environmentalism, which is the subject of excellent studies by Bron Taylor in the USA and David Pepper in Britain. Instead, we will highlight some representative currents in a heterogeneous movement.

The Gaia Hypothesis

The Gaia hypothesis was developed by the British scientist James Lovelock (1919–) with the help of the American biologist Lynn Margulis (1938–) as a new way of understanding planet Earth as if it were a single self-regulating superorganism. The hypothesis is not yet accepted by all earth scientists but is now, after initial rejection, increasingly regarded as a valid focus for serious scientific debate, where it is known more prosaically as earth system science.

It is not simply a scientific theory, however, since from its origin in the 1970s it incorporated a strong mythic element – which was partly responsible for its late acceptance by scientists who were suspicious of anything to do with the New Age. The name Gaia, that of the ancient Greek earth-goddess, was suggested by the novelist William Golding, and found a ready resonance with the 'deep ecology' school promoted by the Norwegian philosopher Arne Naess (1912–), where 'shallow' is associated with anthropocentrism and 'deep' with ecocentrism. Lovelock himself, having previously advocated the wholesale release of Chlorofluorocarbons (CFCs) into the atmosphere as a means to avert the imminent Ice Age, has recently become deeply pessimistic about the likely effects of global warming, and has become an advocate for nuclear energy and such 'technological fixes' as the positioning of giant silver sunshades between the Earth and the Sun.

This has disappointed Lovelock's spiritual followers, who look back to ancient beliefs in the Earth Mother. Their 'thealogy' leads into the eco-feminist movement that seeks to promote traditional female values of cooperation and altruism as opposed to male individualism and domination, seen as having raped the world.

Neo-paganism

Neo-paganism, a kind of Christian heresy, is to be sharply distinguished from Satanism. There is an overlap with eco-feminism in that many contemporary Pagans attach special importance to goddesses such as Isis, Diana and Astarte. A widespread idea is that of recovering an understanding of ancient, long suppressed pre-Christian fertility religions, including witchcraft ('Wicca'), and of hermetic orders such as the Rosicrucians. The movement dates back to the middle of the twentieth century, and was inspired in particular by Gerald Gardner (1884–1964), who was a British civil servant. Contemporary Pagans recognize festivals according to both the solar and lunar calendars. Though some Wiccans are interested only in liberating their inner selves rather than having an effect on the external world, the best known practitioner of feminist witchcraft in the United States is Starhawk (1950–), originally Miriam Simos, an activist who has helped organize protests against nuclear energy and logging projects. Wicca is an initiatory religion with secret knowledge and symbols. Druidry is more inclusive and non-feminist, and proclaims a special attachment to ancient sites, landscapes and forests.

Some Pagans are both witches and druids, which illustrates the eclecticism of contemporary spiritual movements in their reinvention of the past. Neo-paganism does not fall easily into the categories of 'church' or 'sect', and some sociologists have applied themselves to trying to understand it as a new form of multicentred network. Paganism is recognized in Britain as a religion by the prison chaplaincy service, but not by the Charity Commission.

Green Anarchism

The mainstream of European anarchism, represented by such figures as Proudhon and Bakunin, was atheistic and anticlerical. Kropotkin, perhaps the most influential anarchist of all, was best known for his emphasis on 'mutual aid' as a reality in nature which has evolutionary value so that human societies are not condemned to the Darwinian 'struggle for survival'. He praised early Christianity for its teaching of solidarity with the oppressed, but condemned its later cooption by a hierarchical church. A more explicitly spiritual tradition in anarchism has also been identified – associated with Blake, Thoreau and in particular the French anarchist and geographical philosopher Elisée Reclus (1830–1905). Reclus – though professing atheism and secularism – wrote in a pantheistic mode of the need for human beings to realize themselves in a dialectical interaction with nature. There is a substantial overlap between neo-paganism and anarchism.

But probably the most prominent Green anarchist of the twentieth century was Murray Bookchin (1921–2006), an American of Russian Jewish stock, who promoted a 'social ecology' with a libertarian and communitarian bias. Though sympathetic to various forms of spirituality in his earlier work, he became an acerbic opponent of what he saw as irrational and anti-humanist elements in the 'deep ecology' movement. Here his opinion is shared by many mainstream scientists who are deeply sceptical of all New Age ecologism, characterizing it as 'woo-woo' or 'eco-la-la', and by political scientists who criticize it for neglecting the interests of the world's poor. The dangers of 'eco-fascism' have also been pointed out: that is to say, a political ideology that forces individuals to subordinate their interests to Nature or the Land. The nazis' enthusiasm for purity of Aryan blood and Aryan land provides a warning of what could happen again if ecocentric forms of environmentalism were to be transformed into a regressive political ideology.

Direct Action Groups

Like the animal rights movement, the environmentalist movement includes a wing dedicated to direct action – but on a very small scale in relation to the size and complexity of the wider movement. The most prominent network promoting direct action in defiance of the law is the Earth Liberation Front (ELF), formed in Britain in 1992 as an offshoot of the more moderate Earth First! Its name was derived from the older Animal Liberation Front. Its activities have included attacks on corporations and on ski resorts. ELF has been classified as a major domestic terrorism group in the USA, and it is alleged to have caused $100 to $200 million dollars' worth of damage, though at the time of writing neither Earth First! nor ELF has yet caused serious injury or death.

The Voluntary Human Extinction Movement

Contrary to any assumption that the 'isolate-fatalist' mode of thought identified in the Douglas–Thompson model is incapable of acquiring the slightest organizational weight, the Voluntary Human Extinction Movement contends that the only way to restore the Earth's biosphere to good health is to phase out the human race by voluntarily ceasing to breed. It is not clear to what extent it is more than a provocative and witty web site.

Environmentalism as Parareligion

The overall aim of this chapter has been to demonstrate that the animal rights and environmentalist movements, which are distinct but with certain important overlaps, belong to the medium-strong religious field.

The animal rights debate may be seen as a subset of the much larger debate concerning environmentalism, which is probably the most serious issue of our time. (As regards the other three major global issues – poverty, disease and conflict – some overall progress has been made in alleviating mass suffering, despite frequent and serious setbacks: the problems seem at least soluble in principle.)

That thorn in the side of the mainstream environmentalists, Bjørn Lomborg, is not wrong in describing the environmentalist warning as an often repeated 'litany'. He says that global warming discussion sounds like the clash of two religions: one looking for the best solutions within the general economic framework of industrial capitalism, the other seeking to promote a change to a decentralized society which is less resource oriented, less industrialized, less commercialized, less production-oriented. And he has a point in reminding us of the exaggerated doomsday predictions of environmentalists in the past. Pessimism, he argues, also has a price-tag: 'if we do not believe in the future we will become more apathetic, indifferent and scared – hiding within ourselves': in other words, taking refuge in the 'isolate' or 'fatalist' mode.

Scientists differ greatly among one another in their views of religion in general. Some believe that religion and science occupy two totally distinct spheres of discourse that should not be confused but are both valid; others believe that they are intimately connected; others that science is in conflict with religion and is intellectually superior; still others that religious doctrines may not be true but are socially desirable – the view taken by the molecular biologist Max Perutz: 'Even if we do not believe in God, we should try to live as though we did'. Questionnaire surveys in the 1990s and earlier tended to suggest that the majority of American scientists rejected belief in a personal God: for instance, only 40 per cent of scientists at the Bachelor of Science level and 10 per cent of 'eminent' scientists said they believed in a personal God, as opposed to 90 per cent of the general population, according to a *Scientific American* poll conducted in 1999. These findings have since been broadly confirmed by more rigorous research. When the term 'religion' or 'God' is replaced by 'spirituality', a much higher proportion of American scientists attest to positive beliefs: more than half, with social scientists rather higher than natural scientists. While all questionnaires of this kind must be treated with scepticism – to deny a belief in 'spirituality' is tantamount to confessing to being a Philistine – it is clear that any stereotype of scientists being implacably opposed to religion, in the manner of Richard Dawkins, is over-simplified. Some environmental scientists believe it is their duty simply to analyse the facts rather than engage with political solutions. But there is a surge of determination that – whereas some possible planetary catastrophes, such as a large asteroid hitting the Earth or the Moon, are probably beyond human control – insofar as environmental risks can be mitigated by concerted human endeavour, this should be mobilized. And almost all strands of the environmentalist movement affirm a sense of the sacred, the spiritual or the aesthetic – however it is defined – in the cosmos.

Many scientists opposed to all religious dogma believe that the verifiable facts of the emergence of life in a tiny planet, and subsequently of human life and civilization, are far more interesting than anything that man-made mythology has ever devised. Some rationalists believe that systems of ethics can be extrapolated from these scientific facts without the need for intervention of religious or spiritual values. The problem is that even if such a system of ethics were to meet with agreement from scientists and philosophers, it would be powerless to assert itself unless it were translated into a popular movement – which would be impossible without the charisma to communicate and 'enchant'. Scientology presents what most scientists would see as a sad simulacrum of what might be achieved in this direction.

In the meantime, many non-religious environmentalists are coming to accept that religious movements – just because of their genius for being extremely malleable while giving the appearance of standing still – present opportunities for spreading essential messages about better management of the planet. But it is the secular environmental movements that have grown up to dominate the field. From a global scale, such as Greenpeace or Friends of the Earth, down to regional, national and local organizations, these have a parareligious aspect. They thus tend to exemplify the dynamics of church-like and sect-like organizations.

Choices of affiliation may appear to be based on reason but also have a pronounced aesthetic aspect. It is indeed hard to disentangle the moral from the aesthetic. Utilitarianism was based on the conceit of Bentham's 'felicific calculus', as if it were possible for human beings to calculate the happiness of other human beings by an objective statistical process. If the felicific calculus has to take into account the well-being of the non-human as well as the human, which is the essence of the 'ecocentric' position, it is shown up as even more unrealistic a solution to the problem of morality than in the days when anthropocentrism was unchallenged. Hence the doctrine of 'clumsy solutions' with checks and balances, as proposed by Verweij and Thompson, is probably the best we can do.

6

SOME HUMANE DISCIPLINES AS
RELIGIOID MOVEMENTS

This chapter will argue that some intellectual disciplines in the humanities, at least at the popular level, belong to the medium-strong religious field. We will take as illustrations psychotherapy (very broadly defined), archaeology (including palaeoanthropology) and cultural anthropology. First we need to clear some ground, for the term 'humanities' is imprecise, and these disciplines abut onto the scientific field and raise some questions we have already touched on.

I think it can be argued that even popular genetics, for example, has religioid features, though it belongs to the domain of 'natural' science. Popular genetics has at various times been transformed into plans to engineer a race of superhumans. At the elite level of science and science-based technology, it is hard not to see the Manhattan Project to build the atomic bomb during the Second World War, and thus defeat nazism, as having a religioid character. On this reading, one of the protagonists, Edward Teller, remained a true believer, while another, J. Robert Oppenheimer, became a mystically oriented apostate. Many have noted, too, that 'scientism' – the inflexible and dogmatic application of supposedly scientific method to issues where a more nuanced approach is appropriate – shares some of the characteristics of religious 'fundamentalism'.

Yet the scientific frame of mind – constantly asking questions, insisting on replicability of findings, exposing unexamined assumptions – is certainly inimical to the religious frame of mind. Steven Jay Gould wrote that science and religion constitute 'non-overlapping magisteria' (NOMA), two systems of rationality and authority each with its own validity. There are however obvious qualitative differences between the two magisteria. The magisterium of science is continually gaining ground over nearly all aspects of life, though when it pretends to be able to explain everything these claims are widely and deservedly rejected. The magisteria of religion strive to hold their ground, drawing credibility and respect from centuries of homage from the arts, but have to contend with scepticism from many sides. Yet each of the individual religious magisteria preserves something that seems like a secret formula protected in a safe, explaining otherwise inexplicable existential questions, a formula on which the success of an immense enterprise depends.

The separation of scientific from religious magisteria did not apply at many earlier stages in history. Muslim astronomers between the eleventh and fifteenth centuries CE built observatories, but in large part were motivated by the need to predict prayer times and the Muslim lunar months, and to find the correct direction in which to pray towards Mecca. Newton firmly believed that only God could have set the solar system in motion and that the discussion of God was part of natural philosophy. However, a strong body of opinion now contends that the two kinds of magisteria are and should be separate.

Ultimately, I suggest that religion has to bow to science, but only if science is defined in the broadest way to include an effort to understand the whole of the universe including religious and parareligious phenomena, both as they are observed as behaviour and (to the extent that this is possible) as they are experienced by individuals. Even within the natural sciences, there is a great variety of methods between the different specialties – controlled experiments, for instance, being basic to chemistry but not to astronomy. The social sciences need to embrace specific techniques, such as participant observation, which are foreign to the natural sciences but not necessarily less scientific. Nor indeed is 'magisterium' an ideal term to associate with religion, since the religious field is so diverse and contentious. But science does make objective intellectual advances. Individuals in the history of scientific discoveries are, at least in principle, replaceable – though the strength of personality of Darwin or Einstein, impressed on the very language of science, also makes it fair to think of them as figures of myth, and the production of science in laboratories and teaching institutions may be treated as a cultural and political system on a par with all other human activities.

From Psychoanalysis to New Age Therapies

Psychoanalysis was fully intended to be a science, and Freud regarded religion as a dangerous illusion. The task of showing that Freudianism is a religioid movement was adequately, if brutally, achieved by Ernest Gellner – though many others, not least Vladimir Nabokov, anticipated him. For Gellner, psychoanalysis is a culture-specific form of thought control, a system into which patients are sucked. The system is maintained by the fundamentally unscientific concept of 'resistance', with the help of which the analyst is able to dismiss the patient's reasoned objections as a subconscious symptom of denial.

In his biography of Freud, the loyalist Ernest Jones describes how Ferenczi, an early member of Freud's circle, meeting with Jones in Vienna in 1912, suggested that a number of men who had been thoroughly analysed by Freud personally should be stationed in different centres or countries. As there seemed to be no prospect of this, Jones proposed that in the meantime they form a small group of trustworthy analysts as a sort of 'Old Guard' round Freud. When Freud heard about the plan, he wrote:

> What took hold of my imagination immediately is your idea of a secret council composed of the best and most trustworthy among our men to take care of the further development of psycho-analysis and defend the cause against personalities and accidents when I am no more.

A committee of six was formed, and Jones describes how when it first met in 1913,

> Freud celebrated the event by presenting each of the circle with an antique Greek intaglio from his collection, which they then got mounted in a gold ring. Freud himself had long carried such a ring, a Greco-Roman intaglio with the head of Jupiter.

True, both Freud and Jones recognized a boyish and romantic aspect to the Committee. Another member of Freud's early inner circle, Max Graf, a musicologist, recalls that its gatherings in Vienna

> followed a definite ritual. First, one of the members would present a paper. Then, black coffee and cakes were served; cigars and cigarettes were on the table and were consumed in great quantities. After a social quarter of an hour, the discussion would begin. The last and the decisive word was always spoken by Freud himself. There was an atmosphere of the foundation of a religion in that room.

Jones, in his own autobiography published in 1959, accepts that like all 'movements', psychoanalysis was driven by an ardent desire to promulgate highly valued beliefs, but he adds (and we must remember in reading him that, like Freud, he was strongly opposed to religion):

> It was this element that gave rise to the general criticism of our would-be scientific activities that they partook rather of the nature of a religious movement, and amusing parallels were drawn. Freud was of course the Pope of the new sect, if not a still higher Personage, to whom all owed obeisance; his writings were the sacred text, credence in which was obligatory on the supposed infallibilists who had undergone the necessary conversion, and there were not lacking the heretics who were expelled from the church. It was a pretty obvious caricature to make, but the minute element of truth in it was made to serve in place of the reality, which was far different.

Freudianism began to be fashionable among the intellectual elite, especially in the United States, as early as the 1920s, and has exerted ever since a deep influence on Western intellectual life, an influence partly due to the awe in which the Master was held. It has been often observed that Freudianism provokes in many of those who contemplate it a failure in their sense of humour – because of the feelings of reverence and solemnity that it inspires.

This is not the place to attempt to describe, let alone attempt to resolve, the intricate controversies surrounding the psychoanalytic movement and within it. Suffice it to say that its scientific aspirations are perhaps increasingly held up to question and placed in their historical context, whereas the social and personal benefits to be derived from psychotherapy in the widest sense – to which psychoanalysis made a vital contribution – are increasingly recognized. As we have seen, Ernest Jones interpreted as a slur any imputation that psychoanalysis might have taken on some of the characteristics of a religion, and recognized in that claim only a 'minute element of truth'. A more nuanced conception of parareligion enables us to see that religioid elements are scattered, as from our imaginary cornucopia, across every kind of organized human activity. A movement such as psychoanalysis that dealt with some of the most profound aspects of human experience – birth and death, sex and kinship, the self and consciousness, love and aggression, dreams and trance states – was likely to locate itself in the medium-strong religious field. This fact should not affect our verdict one way or the other as to the value of psychoanalysis either as a purportedly science-based discipline studying the mind, or as a therapeutic aid.

One outcome of the twentieth century has been a tendency for religion in the strict sense and psychotherapy to get closer together. In Catholic theology, confession is a specific ritual or 'sacrament' that has to be preceded by contrition and may be followed by absolution given by a priest, on condition of penance. Emotional contact between the penitent and the priest is kept to a minimum – as witness the design of the confessional in a Catholic church as an enclosed recess with a grille separating the two parties to the sacrament. Several commentators have drawn a parallel between auricular confession and the procedures of psychoanalysis. However, there are major differences. First, one of the objects of psychoanalysis is to help the patient remove, or at least understand, excessive feelings of guilt that are often induced by religious influences. Feelings of guilt about masturbation, for instance, are confronted differently in the psychoanalyst's consulting-room and in the confessional. Second, an essential feature of psychoanalysis – and perhaps the doctrine that unites most closely all the divergent factions in the wider and more inclusive field of psychotherapy – is the theory of transference, whereby the patient's emotions are transferred from one person, such as a parent or sibling, onto the analyst.

The mirror image of the transference is the counter-transference, the projection of the analyst's own unconscious emotions onto the patient. This is fraught with risks of distorting the therapeutic relationship, and was considered by Freud an insidious danger to be mastered by the analyst, just as historians must try to master their unconscious bias. But some analysts, beginning with Ferenczi, began to adopt a more positive view of the counter-transference, as an opportunity – to be used with the utmost caution – for analysts to deepen their understanding of the analysand's mind at work. For there is a balancing risk that, when the counter-transference is not brought to consciousness, the analyst will merely repress his or her emotions towards the analysand, which may also distort the analytic process. In a 'traumatic counter-transference', the analyst may even experience nightmares or other similar symptoms as a result of the therapeutic encounter. The more positive view of counter-transference as a therapeutic tool has been gaining ground recently in psychoanalytic circles. But among traditional Catholics, counter-transference on the part of the priest towards the penitent is recognized simply as a grave risk to be averted through rigorous self-discipline.

Loyalist Freudian psychoanalysis and the Vatican have not abandoned their respective opposite convictions. However, things are changing fast if we look at the wider relations between psychotherapy and spirituality. Current controversy within the American Episcopal Church may give some useful insight. In 2005, a senior American Episcopal theologian of conservative hue, Philip Turner, complained that his church was placing less emphasis on the doctrine of Jesus Christ's Resurrection, and was unofficially reinterpreting the Holy Eucharist as a sign of acceptance of a churchgoer by God and God's people, and so should be open all whether baptised or not, whether intending to repent of their sins or not. Thus the church's theology was in practice becoming like eighteenth century deism: there is a benevolent God who favours love and justice but does not act to save us from sin or to raise us to new life. Christians should consequently be tolerant and not seek to convert. He went on:

The Episcopal Church's working theology is also congruent with a form of pastoral care designed to help people affirm themselves, face their difficulties, and adjust successfully to their particular circumstances. The primary (though not the sole) pastoral formation offered to the Episcopal Church's prospective clergy has for a number of years been 'Clinical Pastoral Education,' which takes the form of an internship at a hospital or some other care-giving institution. The focus tends to be the expressed needs of a 'client,' the attitudes and contributions of a 'counselor,' and the transference and countertransference that define their relationship. In its early days, the supervisors of Clinical Pastoral Education were heavily influenced by the client-centered therapy of Carl Rogers [an influential American psychotherapist], but the theoretical framework employed today varies widely. A dominant assumption in all forms, however, is that the clients have, within themselves, the answer to their perplexities and conflicts. Access to personal resources and successful adjustment are what the pastor is to seek when offering pastoral care.

The image of God becomes that of the therapist or pastor. The American Association of Pastoral Counselors, 'professionally integrating psychotherapy and spirituality', which began in 1964 in order to provide a service to the Christian community, is now multi-denominational.

New and controversial parareligions that have attempted to combine spirituality and psychotherapy include Scientology but also many others. The most influential of these has probably been the Human Potential Movement, which originated in the 1960s in opposition to mainstream religion and psychology. Though thoroughly eclectic in the sources it drew on, one of its principal intellectual guides was Abraham Maslow (1908–70), whose theory of a 'hierarchy of needs' proposes a pyramid, with survival needs at the base and the need for 'self-actualization' at the summit. One of the earliest institutional expressions of this philosophy was the Esalen Institute, a 'growth centre' founded in California in 1962, which together with other innovations pioneered encounter groups. In an encounter group (or sensitivity training group), a dozen or so people meet under a leader to try to shed their normal masks and express their real feelings. This has mutated into such techniques as assertiveness training (where a group is convened to meet to help each other stand up for their rights without impairing those of others), and the corporate meditation programmes that are specially popular among Japanese companies. The fundamental idea is that the human brain has limitless power in its relationship to universal energy: if this power can only be unleashed, evils such as illness and poverty will disappear. The Brahma Kumaris organized a worldwide campaign in the late 1980s for people of all faiths and none to meditate in favour of the peace of the world – and were rewarded by the fall of the Berlin Wall and the collapse of apartheid in South Africa.

These eclectic fusions are a defining feature of New Age sensibility. They support the thesis that spiritual traditions are tending to converge in the industrialized world as varieties of 'individuo-globalism'. This takes many organizational forms, but is also available in do-it-yourself, off-the-shelf products, such as the books on personal success and growth to be found in airport bookstalls all over the world.

Archaeology and Palaeoanthropology

'The discipline of archaeology is not an unmixed product of post-Enlightenment rational objectivity, but in essential respects is founded on pre-modern habits of thought.' So writes a professor of Greek history about the consequences of the discovery in 1977 of spectacular grave goods in a tomb, alleged to be the burial place of King Philip of Macedon, in the village of Vergina in northern Greece. These included the golden sunburst or 'Vergina sun', whose use as a national symbol on flags and coins has become a focus of contention between Greece and the Former Yugoslav Republic of Macedonia. The mutual dependence of archaeology and national imaginings, to meet the human need for identity, is clearly visible all over the world. But it will be argued here that 'pre-modern habits of thought' infuse archaeology over a much wider range of existential concerns than nationalism.

Professional archaeology is a demanding technical discipline. Its strength is that it is able to study humanity since the emergence of *Homo sapiens* in about 250,000 BCE, through the Neolithic (about 10,000 BCE) and up to the recent past. (If we include palaeoanthropology, the study of human evolution from the fossil record, the time-scale goes back to the emergence of hominids one and a half to two and a half million years ago.) One of its constant challenges is that almost all material objects that result from human activity – whether proud temples or animal excreta – lose their systemic context with time, with the result that interpretation becomes progressively more difficult. Archaeologists can excavate only once, unlike physical scientists who can replicate experiments, and hence they have developed increasingly rigorous methods to minimize error. Many archaeological theories were disproved, for instance, by the introduction of radio-carbon dating in the 1950s.

Contemporary archaeologists occupy a continuum, according to the anthropologist Robin Fox, with the 'Rational Objective Scientific' approach to the past at one extreme, and at the other extreme the view that this approach is itself a culturally relative subjective viewpoint. Most academic archaeologists have adopted a modified objectivism, attempting to take into account the somewhat arcane theoretical debates that have raged within the discipline. Some of the post-modern archaeologists – also called 'post-processual', as following on from and overtaking the idea that archaeologists should study processes of cultural and historical change – have seen the archaeological record as a 'text' to be decoded, giving free rein to the archaeologist as interpreter.

Palaeolithic archaeology, reliant as it is on stone tools, soil samples and geological profiles, has the image of a rigorous objective science. However, the Czech archaeologist Silvia Tomášková has shown that when a small ivory head, some clay figurines and other remains were excavated with much publicity in the 1930s in a classic Palaeolithic site, Dolní Věstonice (c. 27,000 BCE), in the ethnically torn part of former Czechoslovakia known as Moravia, they were interpreted as confirming racial origin myths. These were: first, that of a grand pan-European historical unity; and later, under the nazi occupation of Czechoslovakia, that of an 'Indo-German' racial category which excluded Czechs. During the ensuing communist period, archaeologists played safe: first, by immersing themselves in what excavation could tell them about the natural environment of the site and later, after the 1950s, by assenting to 'historical materialist' doctrines about primitive communism, which led them to the endless documentation and analysis of tools. Tomášková argues that, whereas the history of interpretation of the site may give a seamless impression of rational scientific advance, the questions that the archaeologists have been asking themselves have been widely divergent.

Popular archaeology is able to pick and choose its evidence and indulge in reverie. There is clearly a vast market for books by authors such as Erich von Däniken, who has claimed to find archaeological evidence of visitations to Earth by extra-terrestrial beings (also a tenet of Scientology). Another archaeological hero of the New Age is the late Barry Fell, a marine biologist who held that Irish monks visited North America before Columbus. But there are also more ambiguous figures who bridge the gap between the disreputable and the academic mainstream. One of these was Marija Gimbutas (1921–94), a Lithuanian who became a professor of archaeology at the University of California, Los Angeles. She would have earned merely an undisputed specialist reputation as a director of excavation sites in southeast Europe with imaginative theories on Indo-European migrations during the Bronze Age, had she not reached out to a wider public with seductive books such as *The Civilization of the Goddess: The World of Europe* (1991). She contended (and was not far out of line with some standard academic opinion during her earlier career) that Europe had been dominated by an egalitarian and matrifocal civilization worshipping a Mother Goddess, which was displaced between 4,000 and 3,500 BCE by patriarchal, hierarchical Indo-European invaders. Gimbutas's academic critics, including some feminist archaeologists, claimed that she had become a proselytizer who adduced a mass of material to prop up her own thesis without subjecting it to critical examination. Sustained criticism of the Mother Goddess theory was led in the 1960s by such scholars as Peter Ucko, who set out to debunk alleged goddess figures as merely amulets, ex-votos or toys. Others have pointed out that even if figures of goddesses were prevalent four centuries BCE in southeast Europe, this would not necessarily indicate a matrifocal civilization, any more than do the images of the Virgin Mary that are ubiquitous today in Catholic countries. These criticisms have not prevented Gimbutas from becoming an icon of New Age feminism. 'A daughter-goddess is now being made', according to a grittier feminist archaeologist, Lynn Maskell, 'bearer of a holy spirit in our time, to be set aside the wise mother of old'.

Academic archaeologists of the second half of the twentieth century had fun in exposing 'fringe' or 'cult' archaeology. Stuart Piggott was able to show that little is known about the original Celtic priesthood of druids. English antiquaries in the seventeenth and eighteenth centuries, learning from Greek and Roman sources that the druids had worshipped in forest groves, transformed them into the virtuous sages of ancient Britain. From this 'invention of tradition' ensued the modern cult of Stonehenge and also the revival of the Welsh Eisteddfod, which had a measure of genuine continuity with the Middle Ages but had fallen into abeyance. Piggott concluded that, in the later nineteenth century, antiquaries were becoming archaeologists, exorcizing the druids from their new model of the past, the Ages of Stone, Bronze and Iron:

> With increasing knowledge of prehistory has come the need for other models of greater complexity, but no escape from the essential anonymity of the non-literate past. The ordinary man, finding himself in an arid, unreal world of cultures, periods and typologies, turns with relief to people with a name, and instinctively prefers simplistic explanations of complex problems. The Druids make comfortably comprehensible, historical people like the Roundheads, the Crusaders or the Romans, and to attribute Stonehenge to them makes a sort of sense, as a welcome cliché grasped because it avoids the necessity of thought.

Where Piggott was elegantly condescending about the susceptibility of the 'ordinary man' to cliché, Glyn Daniel, another prominent archaeologist of the day, was vitriolic in his attacks on what he called 'lunatic' or 'bullshit' archaeology. Stephen Williams published a book on 'fantastic archaeology' in 1991, exposing all the wild and amateurish declarations that are made when a new site is North America is uncovered, particularly about connections with

other continents, and the tone of the book is very much that of a warning to
novices.

Actually, nobody knows what Stonehenge was built for: possibly as an
eclipse predictor, possibly for ceremonial reasons, possibly as a massive
demonstration of prestige; probably for more than one purpose, since it was
constructed in at least three phases between 2,500 and 1,500 BCE, after
earlier use as a cemetery. A more egalitarian approach to the interpretation of
sites such a Stonehenge has become acceptable to some archaeologists, at
least. As a leading professional expert on Stonehenge writes, alternative
archaeology is a way of expressing opposition to the values of progress and
reason. It 'can give whatever clear and striking picture of the past is required,
while orthodox archaeologists are held back by the limits of their discipline,
which is necessarily based on a few scraps, dumped rubbish, and ruins that
happen to survive'. Confrontation between the New Age and the British
State became violent in June 1985 with the 'Battle of the Beanfield' at
Stonehenge, when a convoy was forcibly prevented by a large force of police
from setting up a free festival. More recently however, New Age sensibility
has become acceptable to the government appointed custodians of
Stonehenge, who enjoin their visitors to 'Radiate your love to those in need
the world over'.

Another representative of this change of heart was a prizewinning
documentary video, *Incidents of Travel in Chichén Itzá*, about an ancient Maya
site in Yucatán, Mexico, made in 1997 by two anthropologists from
American universities, Jeff Himpele and Quetzil Castañeda. The opening
sequences lead one to expect a travelogue, but the point of the film is that it
treats all the interest groups at the site and their perspectives equally. The site
(originally belonging to the tenth to thirteenth centuries CE) consists to a
great extent of reconstructions of temples by archaeologists in space that has
been cleared of previously intrusive vegetation. The setting is the spring
Equinox when a shadow said to represent the Maya serpent-god Kukulcan
appears on one temple pyramid. More than 40,000 New Age spiritualists and
secular tourists from the United States and Mexico converge to witness this
solar phenomenon, while local Maya vendors and artisans struggle to make a
living there, and officials of the State try to clear them from the tourist zone
in order to maintain its pure antiquity. The film presents the New Agers,
rather than the local Mayas, as exotic ritualists, and asks who has authority to
speak about the Maya of the past and those of the present. One of the
themes in this subtly constructed film is that the archaeologists have become
the high priests of the site, intent on preserving its sacredness.

That film was made by cultural anthropologists rather than archaeologists,
as a comment on archaeological practice. But the influence of the New Age
is trickling into professional archaeological practice itself. The history of one
of the most important and intensively researched Neolithic villages in the

world, Çatalhöyük in southern Anatolia, Turkey, has been marked by controversy over the Mother Goddess interpretations that were still more or less acceptable currency among archaeologists when the site was first excavated in the early 1960s by the British archaeologist James Mellaart. Çatalhöyük, dating back to around 9500 BCE, abounds in female figurines that, according to Mellaart, represented goddesses. Mellaart has frequently been accused of over-enthusiastic embroidering of his data, and is one of the more controversial archaeologists of his time. His efforts to establish a chronological link between the Neolithic wall paintings and modern kilim designs have even been charged by an expert on weaving with inventing a 'complete, fantastic mythological pantheon'. Archaeologists now hesitate to pronounce on whether the figurines are religious icons at all. The Mellaart line is, however, staunchly defended by New Agers and by feminists who search for evidence of an ancient matriarchal civilization.

The current director of the Çatalhöyük project, Ian Hodder, perhaps the best known of the post-processual archaeologists, has resisted any temptation to dismiss or patronize these views. He engaged in a public correspondence with a member of the Goddess Community, the late Anita Louise, writing that the current museum and information facilities in 2000

> certainly has not satisfied some of the Goddess groups that have visited the site. Some have said 'but we are not interested in YOUR interpretations; they are already biased; we want to make our own interpretations'. This is an important challenge to archaeologists. WE cannot assume that that the provision of 'raw data' is enough. This is because the data are never 'raw'. The data are immediately interpreted by the archaeologist. And it is quite possible that someone from the Goddess community would interpret the 'primary, raw data' differently.

Hodder accepts that at least one of Anita Louise's suggestions may constructively stimulate the thinking of his team. She wrote to him:

> When I read in a report on the Catal website that the [research] indicated a lack of distinction between 'shrine' and 'non-shrine', I remembered a Native American teacher whose workshop I attended several years ago. One of the participants asked him, 'How can we integrate our spiritual selves with our everyday selves?' His response was, 'You can't integrate them, they are one self.' He told us we were asking the wrong question. The question we should be asking, he explained, is 'how can we make ourselves whole again?' Do you think we are seeing at Catal a culture that did not separate ritual from

domestic functions, that did not separate the spiritual from the secular?

Hodder replied:

> You have put your finger on a very interesting issue. Mellaart had originally thought that the 'Shrines' were separated from domestic houses. But when we used modern scientific techniques to look at the floors in the buildings, we found that all of them, including the 'Shrines' had traces of daily activities in them. Also, we found that in all buildings there was a division of space between a 'clean' area, in which the floors were swept clean but under which burials sometimes occurred, and a 'dirty area' which did not have burials but had hearth and oven, food storage and preparation, and caches (hoards) of obsidian (such as projectile points). The 'art' and 'religious' symbolism tend to concentrate in the 'clean' areas of the houses. What this suggests is that, as you say, there was a close connection between ritual and daily functions. There was a division within the house, but the house made a ritual/domestic whole. I certainly think that life was much more 'holistic' than we understand it today. I do not think that there was a separate religious elite....

Cornelius Holtorf argues that archaeology is mainly about discovering treasures that are buried, with a degree of risk and detective skill in solving 'mysteries', and that it is not a question of needs being satisfied but of deeply felt desires being sustained: the search for the past is the search for ourselves. Archaeology would not come to an end even if we had all the knowledge of the past that we need. As Freud understood, excavation is a way of 'finding oneself'. On similar lines, Gavin Lucas has argued that there is symmetry between individual and collective memory, quoting Freud's remark that 'infantile amnesia ... turns everyone's childhood into something like a prehistoric epoch'. Lucas has also likened archaeology to the attempts of amnesiacs to recall who they are: 'they gaze at photographs, meet people from the past, and hear stories, all in the hope that it might jolt them back into remembrance or provide them with the fragments of a life that they can piece back together'.

As Lucas points out again, archaeology sets out to ask, even if it cannot answer, the question about our prehistoric past, 'who are these people to us? long-lost relatives, or total strangers?' Popular palaeoanthropology goes even further back in time to ask existential questions. Its special features include a continuously revised family tree and global migration narrative, fetishization of dramatic fossil finds, especially skulls, and schisms led by charismatic personalities – such as the colourful Louis Leakey (1903–72), once described as 'that pioneer colonialist, archaeological empire-builder and charismatic philanderer who, through his lovers and offspring, succeeded in founding modern palaeoanthropology'.

Archaeology has traditionally had close associations with nationalist and colonial movements – associations gradually called into question over the last twenty years – and is still deeply linked to the heritage and tourist industries. However, the spiritual aspirations of the New Age are probably increasing their influence on archaeology at the popular level. One of the dominant themes in New Age archaeology, as we have seen, is that of rediscovering feminine power – which allegedly was responsible during an earlier epoch for a more harmonious, compassionate and peaceful world than that bequeathed by patriarchy. Another is the reinterpretation of famous monuments such as the Great Pyramids of Giza, Chichén Itzá or Stonehenge as places of worship, and the discovery that these sacred sites emanate a special 'energy'.

The mainstream archaeological profession, increasingly committed to specialist technologies, is by no means entirely behind Ian Hodder in sharing his hospitable approach to New Agers. However, it is recognized that part of the public's fascination with the subject is a hangover from the heroic days of excavation and discovery, as still extolled in the Indiana Jones films, and concessions are frequently made to tempering science with mystery. For instance, in 2002 the British Museum in London put on an excellent exhibition of Yemeni Bronze Age archaeology, loosely linked to the mysterious biblical and Qur'anic legend of the Queen of Sheba, an icon of eroticism and clairvoyance, the mythical founder of Ethiopian Christianity – although no evidence exists as to her historical existence. Box-office and scholarly goals were thus reconciled.

But if we see popular archaeology today as participating in the evolving *Zeitgeist* of individuo-globalism in its response to the demand for individual spiritual relevance, we should observe also that archaeology has established its relevance to the globe. The collapse of a once thriving civilization on Easter Island (Rapa Nui) in the South Pacific, with its giant statues, has sometimes been taken as a metaphor for the planet as a whole, and archaeologists have debated whether its inhabitants became nearly extinct through over-use of their environmental resources, or (the now favoured view) mainly as a result of disease, slaving and the introduction of destructive animals. Other puzzles explored by archaeologists are the disintegration of the Maya city-states of lowland Mesoamerica during the eighth and ninth centuries CE, and the breaching of the Marib dam in southern Yemen in the late sixth century CE, which made an urban society in the desert no longer viable. Such stories of decline have a lesson for us, for they show the dangers of imposing too heavy a burden on agricultural systems, sometimes compounded by climatic change. We may suspect, writes one archaeologist, that early state societies had the same problem as modern societies in implementing effective policies to deal with long-term risks; phenomena, like global warming today, which appear to threaten not today or tomorrow but with consequences twenty or fifty years hence, are simply too remote in time for the normal span of a human lifetime. Yet in very fragile circumstances, early societies did go to extraordinary lengths to strive for some security, as exemplified by the construction of the Peruvian inter-valley canals. This may be interpreted not as a response to immediate need, but as a measure to anticipate and to counter future droughts such as those which so severely damaged the Moche state [c. 650 CE].

Meanwhile, some palaeobiologists apply their minds to speculation as to which are the other highly adaptable species – rats, spiders and the like – that will inherit the earth when eventually it is no longer inhabitable by humans. Environmental archaeology in many forms has become a flourishing sub-discipline.

Archaeology therefore owes much of its fascination to its ability to ask questions about fundamental issues of existence and survival, both individual and global. Its participation in the forward march of the natural sciences has resulted in a breach between strict scientific professionalism and the confident popularization carried out by academic archaeologists of an earlier generation such as Gordon Childe, who was able to publish successful books entitled simply *What Happened in History* (1942) and *Man Makes Himself* (1936). It is natural that most professional archaeologists should feel the need to hold esoteric or occult interpretations of their data at arm's length. Yet the archaeology of reverie has captured a market on television and in the bookshops, whereas professional archaeology can disappoint the enthusiastic layman with its intellectual cautiousness. The solution implemented by Ian Hodder at Çatalhöyük is to meet the New Age halfway rather than leave the New Age stuck with old science, and to be receptive to stimulus from unconventional sources.

Modern professional archaeology is haunted by discredited fantasies about the past that anticipated, and have been taken up by, the New Age. To take another example, it has been known for nearly two centuries that Egyptian hieroglyphs are a writing system that can be studied like any other dead language. But in Renaissance Europe they were regarded as symbols of mysterious, ineffable knowledge. The view of Ancient Egypt as a repository of ancient wisdom – a view which we now diagnose as symptomatic of 'orientalism' in the pejorative sense – survived in the egyptomania of the nineteenth century decorative arts, and still today in freemasonry, in revivals of the Corpus Hermeticum (revelatory Greek texts of the second and third centuries CE, partly derived from the Egyptian pantheon), and in some new syncretic movements such as the United Nawaubian Nation of Moors, an offshoot of the Black Muslims with premises in Putnam County, Georgia, USA. Even among certain academics of the early twentieth century – though they did not embrace the view of Ancient Egypt as carrying mysterious messages to modernity – there was a tendency to greatly exaggerate its importance as a bearer of civilization: the 'hyperdiffusionists' Sir Grafton Elliot Smith and W.J. Perry held that all megaliths (large stone structures) anywhere in the world were rude imitations of the Egyptian pharaonic monuments.

In Australia, a minor literature on the fringes of the national archaeology has emerged, coexisting with theories of creationism and of extra-terrestrial visitations. Dynastic Egyptian hieroglyphs are alleged to have been identified on sandstone rock faces in New South Wales. Hebrew and Egyptian priests are thought to have explored the world more than 5,000 years ago in search of Mu, the lost Motherland of the Pacific, and to have left engravings that point to earth energies and/or prophecies bequeathed to posterity. Peter Hiscock has written of the dangers to orthodox archaeology of its being swamped in Australia by this kind of alternative archaeology, and he adds sharply that recent trends in post-modern archaeology – being also opposed to the existing political order, relativistic, and opposed to scientism – may make it more difficult than before to dismiss New Age archaeology as mere fantasy.

Professional archaeology may set out to insulate itself from New Ageism, but it is like a scientific laboratory built unwittingly over an ancient pilgrimage site, where spirits roam by moonlight, and pedlars of amulets and elixirs ply their trade by day.

It is not that all present-day academic archaeologists are shy about exploring overarching themes such as time, personhood, the experience of landscape. But they generally reject the oracular role, which has migrated towards the New Age. To conclude this discussion of archaeology and palaeoanthropology, we will consider how two palaeoanthropologists who once belonged to the scientific mainstream have, since their deaths, flowed into independent estuaries of recognition. Both – Pierre Teilhard de Chardin and Loren Eiseley – were remarkable personalities, both were naturalists in a broad sense as well as palaeoanthropologists, and both made heroic efforts to reconcile science and spirituality.

Teilhard de Chardin and Loren Eiseley

Pierre Teilhard de Chardin (1881–1955), a native of Auvergne in southern France, has an honourable place in the history of palaeoanthropology. He played a major part in important expeditions in China and Mongolia, and was one of the first to predict that the Rift Valley in east Africa would be the site of some of the oldest hominid fossils to be discovered. He is also remembered for his determination, as a Jesuit priest, to continue his scientific work despite the firm opposition of the Vatican in his day to all evolutionary studies, resulting in a ban on his publishing during his lifetime, and in the refusal of his superiors in the Society of Jesus to allow him to return from exile in New York to spend his last years in France. He was accused not only of Darwinism but of 'immanent pantheism' and denying the truth of Original Sin. His best-known book, *The Phenomenon of Man*, was published posthumously.

Teilhard's philosophical position is an extension or interpretation of Darwinism, and should not be confused with creationism or 'intelligent design', which positively rejects natural selection. Evolution, according to him, has proceeded from the galaxies to the Earth, then to life and consciousness (the 'noosphere'), reaching progressively new dimensions of complexity, in which the material and the spiritual are fused. Humans participate in the process of 'cosmogenesis', and the awareness of this process that Darwinism made possible opens up new horizons for further evolution towards an eventual Omega Point, which is identified with the God of Christianity.

Despite the difficulties in Teilhard's life – the deaths of two siblings while he was a young man, courageous service as a stretcher-bearer in the blood-soaked trenches of the First World War, continual conflict with Catholic orthodoxy – his overall message is one of sunny optimism and faith in technological progress. Critics accuse him of 'orthogenesis', that is, the theory of a unilinear trend in evolution, which, according to them, is a misunderstanding of the theory of natural selection. Though some eminent scientists such as Sir Julian Huxley supported Teilhard, his reputation among scientists was dealt a heavy blow by a cruel review of *The Phenomenon of Man* published by the British immunologist, Peter Medawar, in 1961 in the philosophical journal *Mind*. Richard Dawkins has called this 'possibly the greatest negative book review of all time'. Among Medawar's conclusions:

> We must not underestimate the size of the market for works of this kind, for philosophy-fiction. Just as compulsory primary education created a market catered for by cheap dailies and weeklies, so the spread of secondary and latterly tertiary education has created a large population of people, often with well-developed literary and scholarly tastes, who have been educated far beyond their capacity to undertake analytical thought.

Teilhard still has an international following, led by Teilhard appreciation societies in France, the United States and Britain. Though his views still conflict with official Roman Catholic theology, many Catholics and other religious people are interested in his work. Yet he has been marginalized from the mainstream of debate. His misfortune was perhaps that of intellectual isolation, which led him to try to speak to two different audiences – the religious and the scientific – without the benefit of informed criticism and feedback. Some of his ideas are finding a renewed vigour, for instance when related to the Gaia hypothesis (see Chapter 5) or to current thinking about the future of the internet and cyberspace as a realization of the noosphere. A continued New Age following seems assured.

With a reputation mainly limited to North America, but in its day considerable, Loren Eiseley (1907–77) also laboured to fuse a commitment to Darwinism with an articulation of spiritual experience, especially that inspired by the natural world. Born in Nebraska, his childhood and youth were troubled, and he even spent a year riding on freight trains in the American West. But he qualified in anthropology and spent most of his career in the anthropology department of the University of Pennsylvania. He was awarded 36 honorary degrees and many other scholarly distinctions.

In the days of Eiseley's prime, American anthropology was noted for its broad coverage of whole study of humanity, and he published on a wide range of topics, ranging from land-tenure among hunters in the northeast of America to the significance of Francis Bacon in the history of science. He published an excellent book on Darwin and his scientific precursors and contemporaries. He also published poetry and attracted the approving attention of W.H. Auden. But bones and fossils were at the core of his work.

Eiseley was best known to the public for a series of occasional essays loosely based on archaeology and biology, and strongly reminiscent of Thoreau's Transcendentalism. A typical one is 'The Angry Winter' (1970), a meditation which opens with the author working by his fireside, 'amid the debris of a far greater winter', on 'the lance points of ice age hunters and the heavy leg bone of a fossil bison', while the windows of his house are shaken by a blizzard. His beloved sheepdog, Wolf, picks up one of the bones in his mouth and begins to defend it with fierce snarls, like the ancestor he is named after, while at the same time imploring his master not to try to force him to give it up. The author distracts Wolf by inviting him to walk in the snow, and Wolf makes up for his aggression by frolicking and then leading him back to the shelter of the house.

The author then reflects on the mystery of human beings' emergence at the end of recurrent glaciations. Urban man still lives at the mercy of giant destructive forces, and has indeed magnified the powers of the natural world himself. 'The explosive force of suns, once safely locked in nature, now lies in the hand that long ago dropped from a tree limb into the upland grass.' We are probably now in the middle of an interglacial summer. Winter is in man's bones: 'try to escape as he might, he would endure an interior ice age'. But it is open to us to discern a universe in a spider's web, or a galaxy in a swarm of summer midges. 'The truly perceptive man must know that where the human eye stops, and hearing terminates, there still vibrates an inconceivable and spectral world, of which we learn only through devised instruments'. There follows an outline of the emergence of *Homo sapiens* in Asia (as many then believed) and the harnessing of fire. The essay ends with another blizzard scene. The author recalls his younger days: he was hiking one evening to an abandoned pioneer cemetery in the High Plains. 'It was as though I, the last living man, stood freezing among the dead'. He exchanged glances with an emaciated jack rabbit, cowering behind a slab. As he began to pick his way home to a fire, he reflected that man is, in essence, a 'belated phantom of the angry winter'.

Eiseley went some way towards contesting anthropocentrism in evolutionary theory, and his work is suffused with a melancholic pessimism: in both these respects, he differs markedly from Teilhard. He saw his life as a 'religious pilgrimage', though in his desire to make this compatible with his scientific commitment he is circumspect in making any reference to a Creator or to first causes except in an oblique way: for instance, writing of God as 'the Dreamer'.

Acerbic reviews of Eiseley's essays by younger scientists began to appear during his lifetime, and now he is almost forgotten in the academic world. Akin to Teilhard's, his self-consciously profound philosophizing style – once presented as exemplary in schools and creative writing courses – became unfashionable. However, the Loren Eiseley Society survives to keep his memory green as 'an oracle reaching out to all of us in troubled times', and it reports considerable interest in his legacy. More convincingly than Teilhard, who too often had recourse to circular reasoning and lacked the stimulus of university colleagues, Eiseley is the model of an 'individuo-globalist' thinker. Following in the tracks of Thoreau's homespun intuitive philosophy, and hovering between a hesitant theism and a near-Buddhist sense of the ubiquity of illusion, Eiseley denies any discontinuity between the inner world and the cosmos:

> The inward skies of man will accompany him across any void upon which he ventures and will be with him to the end of time. There is just one way in which that inward world differs from outer space. It can be more volatile and mobile, more terrible and impoverished, yet withal more ennobling in its self-consciousness, than the universe that gave it birth.

His essays have apparently given some inspiration to the environmental movement, but one may also read them as an exercise in stoical fatalism with regard to the impermanence of our civilizations at the edge of a galaxy, and as poetically expressing the insight of modern science that the scale of the human body is both extremely small and extremely large depending on whether we think of it in an astronomic or a microscopic context.

Both Teilhard and Eiseley, then, had the capacity to enchant the reader; but this dangerous gift has resulted in their being more or less expunged from the canon of serious science. To borrow again from Gell's model, we pick up their books in the hope of painless enlightenment as to ultimate truths. Both write of human suffering. For Teilhard, rephrasing Christ, suffering is a form of energy that can be turned into positive transformations of the Earth. For Eiseley, it is to be grimly accepted as a precondition of life. Pairing them together reminds us how the study of the prehistoric past is inevitably conjoined to suffering. Auden in his poem 'Archaeology' alludes to the discipline's exploration of graves, urban disasters, volcanic eruptions, floods and human hordes 'agog for slaves and glory'. It is true that we have records of the happier aspects of prehistoric life – such as games and sports, music and dancing, intimate family scenes – but mainly from civilizations such as that of Ancient Egypt where much pictorial and carved material has survived. It is deaths of individuals and deaths of cultures that make up the leitmotifs of archaeology.

Cultural Anthropology: Chris Knight Draws Down the Moon

Before considering religioid aspects of the wider field of social and cultural anthropology (terms which, for the sake of simplicity, we will here use interchangeably), one anthropologist deserves special attention because he combines scientific sophistication with conscious myth making. Most cultural anthropologists today – by contrast with earlier, less specialized generations – show little interest in trying to establish the prehistoric origins of humanity. They find enough to interest them in contemporary human societies, brimming not only with data to be collected but also with living people to question and to interact with. Chris Knight, professor of anthropology in the University of East London, is an exception: a cultural anthropologist whose main interest is the evolutionary emergence of language, kinship, art, ritual and religion. He has developed a highly original and imaginative, indeed surprising, model which, though it has not been proved to be valid, has not been refuted. It is an ingenious amalgam of the dialectical materialism of Marx, the social anthropology of Lévi-Strauss and Mary Douglas, intellectual feminism associated with such authors as Donna Haraway, and neo-Darwinism. His major book *Blood Relations*, published in 1991, has required some time to be taken seriously by anthropologists. Its argument may be summarized as the 'sex-strike' model.

One of Knight's starting points is the intriguing convergence in human beings between the lunar month, approximately 28 days, and the menstrual cycle which is on average about the same. It used to be thought that there was a close connection, possibly deriving from our aquatic ancestors, between the rhythm of the tides – which are certainly controlled by the movement of the moon in conjunction with the sun – and that of menstruation. However, this seems unlikely because the duration of the menstrual cycle in our fairly close relative, the chimpanzee, is 37 days rather than the average 28 days. Coincidence is more likely; but many mythological sources assume a close connection. Human females, by contrast with most other species, are distinctive in giving no external signs that they are sexually receptive.

According to Knight's sex-strike model, females capitalized on this convergence to control their own sexuality and use it as a means to negotiate with males to bring home meat from the hunt, which was likely to be most successful by a waxing moon. Every month after the new moon they withdrew from sexual contact, synchronizing their infertile periods, in order to protect one another, procure adequate supplies of high-energy food, and establish the nurturing, stable environment that human infants need in order to survive. Moreover, they used red ochre – which is widely found in archaeological sites – to scramble menstrual signals by painting their bodies, concealing who was imminently fertile and who was not, with the aim of motivating otherwise dominant males to invest in their partners and offspring rather than indulge in opportunistic philandering. Women engaged in ritual dances both to dramatize their solidarity and to remind men of the rewards awaiting them if they returned successfully from the hunt. They dressed up as animals and/or males in an inversion of normal courting rituals. Hence emerged a wide range of ritual behaviours documented in the ethnographic record, and indeed the whole repertoire of human symbolism and language, which is thus intimately linked to deception. Women also took control of cooking through forcing men to hand over meat, dramatizing the distinction which Lévi-Strauss has seen as the epitome of culture dominating nature: the distinction between raw and cooked food.

Knight and his associates have drawn on an impressive body of ethnographic and archaeological evidence, whose result has been to dazzle rather than win over most of their colleagues, for they claim to have set out no less than an integrated model of the origins of kinship, language, religions and art. In Popperian style, they call on colleagues to produce evidence that would falsify the model, such as evidence of pre-hunt, as opposed to post-hunt, rituals prescribing indulgence in marital sex. By contrast, most cultural anthropologists today shy away from advancing falsifiable theories. As a convinced radical socialist, Knight is determined to oppose the conservative contention that human nature, being fixed and prone to aggressive excess, needs to be kept in check by rules and regulations externally imposed. Whereas most archaeologists believe that there was a cognitive revolution at some point in time to make possible such achievements as language and sophisticated tool manufacture, Knight contends that the momentous transition to mind, language and symbolic culture must also have been a political revolution. If there was a benign feminist revolution once at the dawn of prehistory – around 70,000 years ago – there can be one again.

Knight's position is that his work is both objective science, meeting at least as high a standard of explanatory power as that demanded of more orthodox anthropological and archaeological research, and also a salutary narrative or myth. Having absorbed the lesson of Marx and Freud that what presents itself as objective social theory usually conceals unexamined values, he prefers to wear his heart on his sleeve. Whereas social anthropologists, despite their admiration for his ingenuity, often claim that Knight's comparative method is too eclectic, evolutionary biologists have problems with what they see as the 'teleological' aspect of his thinking. As one commentator puts it: '…while Kipling [in *Just So Stories*], in imagining the origins of the alphabet, projects the bourgeois family back into our prehistory, Knight sends the striker, the feminist, and the political militant back into the past'. Others point out that the antinomian counterculture of the 1960s has lost out to rampant hyperconsumerism, so that, in the words of one reviewer of *Blood Relations*, 'the conditions for a sex-strike in late 20th-century America are as remote as a doctors' strike for a rational health care system'. However, Knight ripostes that the coming environmental crisis may well create new conditions for political revolution.

Knight is an atheist but he was brought up as a Catholic and, unlike many others working in his field, never underestimates the power of the religious inclination. While disavowing any New Age credentials, he is a sympathetic witness to annual solstice celebrations at Stonehenge and the nearby Neolithic monuments at Avebury, and he has certainly attracted some degree of New Age following. For he has turned on its head the conventional view that culture was created by males, rearticulating the nineteenth century theory of 'primitive matriarchy' which orthodox twentieth century anthropology claimed to have totally exploded. No wonder his work resonates with contemporary feminist spirituality, goddess worship and eco-druidism. It is a remarkable mixture of erudite science and mythopoeic narrative, mediated by enthusiasm and humour. *Blood Relations* has been aptly called a 'slow-burning classic'. It stands to the early twenty-first century as Teilhard and Eiseley did to the twentieth, in setting out to develop a humanistic ethic compatible with Darwinism rather than parasitic on theological doctrine. It is a convincing and timely expression of individuo-globalism at a sophisticated intellectual level.

Academic Cultural Anthropology

A leading American cultural anthropologist, James Peacock, was asked to fill in a form on being admitted to hospital for surgery, and in the box marked 'Religion' he wrote 'Anthropology'. Another, Sol Tax, who was prominent in the 1950s and 60s, would claim that 'anthropology can save us'. An early twentieth century British anthropologist, C.G. Seligman, used to say that 'fieldwork is to anthropology what the blood of the martyrs is to the church'. Belonging to a relatively small discipline that only achieved professional recognition in the twentieth century, anthropologists characteristically look back reverently to its founders, who initiated a kind of apostolic succession into which new recruits can immediately fit themselves.

If we apply to anthropology itself the analytical tool developed by one of its leading practitioners, we find that it occupies all four niches in the grid–group chart (see Chapter 5). The universities, where most professional anthropologists work, are essentially hierarchic institutions (high grid, high group); the discipline forms an individualist and international market as regards publishing and career status (low grid, low group); it is prone to forming sectarian enclaves (low grid, high group); and some of its dedicated members who do not work in either privileged seats of learning or practical consultancy become economically and professionally marginal and may fall into the 'isolate' category (high grid, low group). To repeat: these Douglasian categories are best seen not as rigid containers but as permeable, and even as negotiable by individuals as conscious decisions for organizing their lives. The sectarian aspect is not peculiar to anthropology but is common to all academic life, and indeed to all communities whose members do not necessarily love one another but are drawn by a charm in common, a specialized desire. We need more robust evidence to ascribe cultural anthropology to the medium-strong religious field, otherwise one might as well include hobby clubs as well.

There are still some public expectations of anthropology as a whole that it will continue to provide grand narratives such as Frazer's *The Golden Bough*. Chris Knight has made a valiant effort to meet this expectation, and he is justified in observing that recent cultural anthropology has disappointed its consumers in turning its back on the quest for human origins in nature.

There is one feature of cultural anthropology that sets it apart from all the other social sciences. This is the continuous battle to try to overcome ethnocentrism, the tendency of all human beings to regard unreflectingly their own ideas and behaviour patterns as 'natural' and right, and thus to downgrade those of others. Debate has raged for decades over how far the battle against ethnocentrism should be extended. On the one hand, some anthropologists push the argument so far as to argue against all rules of objective morality, and thus to condone or defend such practices as bullfighting or female genital cutting, on the grounds that they are deeply embedded in particular local cultures. On the other hand, there are anthropologists who argue that the search for universal structures of meaning is much more important than the identification of differences. But the mainstream of anthropology regards the battle against ethnocentrism as an essential part of the discipline – to be balanced by the recognition that at a deeper level than that of specific beliefs and practices, all human societies share a common heritage that includes language, systems of kinship, and moral and aesthetic codes.

'Culture shock' or disorientation is familiar to every traveller: the clash between formerly acquired and newly imposed values. Indeed, one does not even have to travel to experience it. Most Western children experience it first when they are thrust outside the home into playgroups and schools, which have their own lore and traditions, or among friends who belong to a different 'family culture'. Symptoms of culture shock may include nausea, diarrhoea, irritability, headaches and disturbance of sleeping patterns. Tourists typically reduce this by building a cocoon of familiarity among themselves. Expatriate workers often suffer feelings of inadequacy or depression.

Anthropology has been caustically characterized as the most prestigious form of tourism: for anthropologists go furthest, stay away for longest, and bring back home the most impressive souvenirs – the most prestigious achievement of all being to bring back an informant from far away to address an anthropological conference. Only anthropology turns 'culture shock' into an essential pedagogic tool, an asset rather than an inconvenience. The initial shock of arrival in the fieldwork site is succeeded in due course by the 'reverse culture shock' of return home, equally severe though often less expected, when suddenly previous familiar patterns of behaviour come to seem arbitrary and peculiar. Anthropology turns the recognition of culture shock into a spiritual experience. This was classically described in Laura Bohannan's account of her fieldwork in Nigeria, *Return to Laughter* (1954). It has since been given satirical treatment by Nigel Barley in a number of debunking books such as *The Innocent Anthropologist: Notes from a Mud Hut* (1983), but it remains a principle of induction into anthropology that the experience of fieldwork is likely to change the individual's outlook on life and profoundly inform his or her intellectual work.

Like archaeology, cultural anthropology has had a love–hate relationship with its popularizers. Popular anthropology has tended to hold up a kind of 'tribal mirror' to Western society, in a kind of morality tale. Most often, it has depicted traditional face-to-face groups as possessing virtues of simplicity and innocence that are assumed to have been destroyed by civilization, as in a Garden of Eden. In this respect, popular anthropology has participated in a long tradition of 'cultural primitivism' – looking back to a Golden Age – which dates back to the Ancient Greeks, whose mythology included the

Hyperboreans, people who lived beyond the North Wind, in a land of perpetual sunshine. It is the same idea as the Christian doctrine of the Fall of Man. Giving a twist to this pattern, the anthropologist Colin Turnbull wrote one book, *The Forest People* (1961), romanticizing the Mbuti Pygmies of Congo as untouched by selfishness, and then another on the Ugandan Ik, *The Forest People* (1972), which alleged that every vestige of morality had been destroyed in a society suffering from extreme poverty.

But an evangelical style, proclaiming its salvific virtues for a troubled world as did Sol Tax, is now deeply unfashionable within the discipline itself. Gone are the years when the American anthropologist Margaret Mead (1901–1978) was a household name,

> a particularly forceful personality who was almost always prepared to opine publicly, in an at times very direct manner on matters of general interest. … While prepared to attack values and practices she disagreed with, Mead was ready to shower praise on some behaviours, ones which many Americans held dear, such as caring and friendship, and she liked to reassure her audiences with optimistic messages, such as that failure was only the inability to think positively.

Anthropology in Britain enjoyed an all too brief period of successful popularization during the 1970s and 80s, when a series of outstanding ethnographic films was brought to a large public of television viewers, mainly through the commitment of one company, Granada Television, which influenced the whole industry. And Mead was not the only anthropologist to achieve sanctification by the media. Lévi-Strauss became the Supreme Being of European anthropology, complemented by attendant sub-deities such as Edmund Leach and Mary Douglas, a host of prophets and apostles, and some colourful heretics such as Ernest Gellner, who described himself as an 'Enlightenment fundamentalist'.

We may think of these prominent personalities as like the sculptures on the outer porch of a great cathedral such as Chartres. But as time goes by, some of these images become difficult to identify for the average pilgrim, while the stone begins to crumble. The work of devotion is carried on inside; but the cathedral is too ambitious in scale for modern times, and we find that worshippers are more comfortable in side-chapels that give a sense of intimacy. This is the domain of the indoor cult-figures of present-day anthropology. Their contribution to knowledge has been at least as great as that of the outdoor figures, but is conducted more discreetly. Their particular strength is in getting past the public lineaments of society, its face, which may or may not be masked. They describe society's own back, as it were, which it cannot see itself except in a mirror; or, with even more difficulty and need for sensitivity, the areas of highly charged emotional intimacy. One of anthropology's most impressive achievements in recent years has been to infiltrate almost every branch of medicine and health studies; another, to lead the debate on New Reproductive Technologies and their social and ethical implications. Like the beer, it can reach the parts of society that other social sciences don't reach.

Anthropology's spectrum of interest ranges from the individual – for instance, in studying concepts of the person, the ritual life-cycle, parenting and kinship, sexuality – to the global issues of poverty alleviation, conflict, public health, migration and the environment. No political structures, no religious hierarchies, no national or ethnic ideologies, does it assume as fixed 'givens': it regards them all as constantly shifting phenomena, however confidently they set out to give an impression of fixity. And yet anthropology has so far missed out on its full potential to respond to that movement of thought and feeling which we have summarized as individuo-globalism.

For some anthropologists, the remedy is simply better popularization, and/or the inclusion of anthropology in school curricula. One influential anthropologist, Gustaaf Houtman, an expert on the Burmese meditation movement, has suggested a way forward at a deeper level. For him, there is a similarity between, first, the culture shock which is actively aspired to by the ethnographic fieldworker; second, the 'conversion experience' described by Christian theologians; and third, the Buddhist notions of enlightenment – known to western Buddhists as *satori* and *kensho* in the Zen tradition. What they have in common is that the searcher is able to escape the received paradigms that are maintained by political authority, education, convention, 'habitus' – the 'comfort zone', held in place by fields of power. These experiences can impose passages of pain and distress, but also may result in sensations of happiness and well-being; and they can be cultivated by systematic practices. One of these practices, according to Houtman, is the rite of passage in all its myriad forms; and the ethnographer's journey to do fieldwork, usually in a distant place, resulting in the realization that his or her preconceptions are ethnocentric, is an example of this. Another is the Buddhist practice of *vipassana*, or insight meditation, whose fundamental aim is to dissolve the apparent permanence of objects and bring to awareness the functioning of one's mind and body as a sensorium.

This is following in the steps of Plato, who likened philosophical study to escape by prisoners from inside the cave that represents the restricted horizons of the local culture into which they were born. Socrates had no need to leave Athens to go on his thought-journeys. Some anthropologists today locate the 'culture shock' experience right at the centre of their research – earning the charge of self-indulgence from their more hardheaded colleagues.

We have stressed a confrontation with suffering as one of the most important attributes of the religious or parareligious field. That archaeology is preoccupied with graves and the collapse of civilizations is unlikely to be disputed. Cultural anthropologists today have applied their skills to studying almost every aspect of human life, including its joys and aesthetic fulfilments. Some of the politically marginal peoples traditionally studied by anthropologists have indeed been allowed to maintain their way of life and land rights, or have materially prospered in a wider economic context. Contemporary Australian Aboriginal painters sell their work all over the world and it constitutes a large proportion of the Australian art market. Some Brazilian tribes that happen to be located over gold reserves, such as the Kayapo Gorotire, have negotiated their way to material wealth.

However, progressive immiseration seems to be a more widespread fate for the peoples studied by cultural anthropologists. The Nuer and the Dinka, two pastoralist groups in southern Sudan, both the subjects of classic ethnographies, have been drastically caught up in the Sudanese civil wars that have lasted for nearly a half-century, and have been fighting each other as well as their northern oppressors. While this is an extreme case, there seems little doubt that a globalizing world is increasingly hard on its marginal peoples, exploiting them economically, subjecting them to discrimination and forced assimilation, and often denying them a political voice. Some of the most economically successful are those that consent to become hosts to ethnic tourism – one of the few choices easily open to them, after the collapse of a traditional subsistence economy, other than providing cheap unskilled labour.

Anthropology, taking seriously the values and aspirations of peoples who are generally held of little account, is itself a marginal discipline by contrast with the powerhouses of economics and International Relations. It is haunted by a sense of the tragedy of its traditional subject matter. Anthropologists vary in their responses. Some set out to help the particular indigenous groups that they have worked with, or individual members of those groups, in practical ways. Others support NGOs such as Survival International, Cultural Survival, or the International Work Group for Indigenous Affairs (IWGIA), or the Anthropologists' Fund for Urgent Anthropological Research (which makes possible the documentation of traditional cultures before they are absorbed into larger political entities). Others embark on wider political programmes to call in question globalizing capitalism. Yet others block out the issue, or in some cases develop dexterous theoretical positions to absolve them from caring: such as the view that, because the word 'indigenous' is difficult to define exactly, positive discrimination in favour of indigenous peoples should be opposed.

In the early 1960s, the Minister for Scientific and Cultural Affairs opened a conference in India that resulted in a book called *Anthropology on the March.*

He predicted that, just as physics was gradually incorporating mathematics, chemistry and biology, so anthropology would increasingly include history, philosophy and literature; hence eventually only two disciplines would be left. Whether the Minister's prediction was right, it is perhaps – as Zhou Enlai is supposed to have said when asked about whether the French Revolution had been a success – too early to tell; but the initial indications are to the contrary. However, the Minister also said that all religious literature 'can be said to be works of anthropology, because no religion can survive unless it has a deep understanding of human nature, propensities, customs, and manners'.

It would be foolish to reverse the proposition and say that all anthropological literature is religious in character, because, as was noted at the beginning of this chapter, anthropology aspires to the condition of a science and sometimes attains it. No one today holds the view of Auguste Comte, the nineteenth century French philosopher who coined the word 'sociology', that 'positive science' should be the basis of a new religion worshipping the 'Great Being of Humanity'. However, anthropology is capable of fulfilling the need for a focus of devotion that is experienced by those who have no religion, or who find that religion in the strict definition cannot provide all the answers to the dilemmas of our age. It is a subject that you can be converted to, or fall in love with. In its popular manifestations, it has become a vehicle for the communication of morality tales replete with nostalgia for a vanished past. In its more sophisticated form, it can provide almost everything that philosophy can offer, except that it works with empirical data whereas philosophy is most at home with hypothetical cases.

I am not recommending a kind of drunken anthropology, but a sober and lucid discipline that does full justice to the depth and subtlety of human experience, both the highs and the lows – as explored particularly in the arts and poetry, music and ritual. Such an anthropology would reflect Nietzsche's idea of 'gay science', which sought to resolve the tension between intellectual discipline and a delight in the richness of life.

It has been well exemplified in the work of prophetic writers such as Edmund Leach, who wrote in his 1967 Reith Lectures, *A Runaway World*, '…Art and poetry are the power to transform, the ability to take nature to pieces and recreate it; it is dangerous but it is magical and it has been man's heritage from the beginning. … [D]ivine inventiveness is latent in us all – in you and in me – it is not reserved for genius'.

Another example is the contribution made by anthropologists to recognizing the depth of Australian Aboriginal spiritual sensibility: as one of them writes:

[The Aboriginals'] is a reflection nourished by generations of mental and psychosomatic experience, both individual and collective, depending on an identification with the environment which works a little like a mirror, whereby the body reads the earth by its traces which are reproduced on the body and by the voice in order to give life to the forms and reproduce them.

I suggest, then, that anthropology is well placed to steer the individuo-globalist trend in a more rigorous direction, and merely awaits a revitalization movement.

7

THROW RELIGION OUT OF THE DOOR:

IT FLIES BACK BY THE WINDOW

In this chapter we will examine two diametrically opposite trends, militant atheism and religious conservatism. Finally we will enquire into the prospects for ideological cohesion in mainland China, where a markedly parareligious variant of communism, the cult of Mao, was abruptly withdrawn without any full-blooded substitute being provided – by contrast with the former East Germany, whose continuing cultural atheism may be seen as an exception that tests the rule.

The Dilemma of Militant Atheism

Militant atheism has recently hit the bookshops. Richard Dawkins, the most scientifically qualified of these writers, makes some compelling points. We are all atheists, he says, with regard to gods of the past whose cults have not survived, such as Osiris or Mithras. Religious believers demand a privileged deference and consideration that are not granted to people who profess convictions relating to other domains of life, such as the arts or politics. Scientific progress is historically correlated with the Enlightenment values of free thought and free speech. And so on.

But it is precisely on scientific grounds that the Dawkinsites should be challenged. For social science produces abundant evidence that religious beliefs and practices of some kind, in the broad sense that has been used in this book, are a human universal. Though a struggle has been made in the present book to maintain the strategy of 'methodological agnosticism', it is ultimately hard not to conclude that, just as Gresham's Law tells us about money, 'bad religion drives out good'. Dawkins and those civilized academics who think like him appear not to be sufficiently aware how deeply their liberal humanist morality, inherited from the European Enlightenment, is indebted to implicit Judaeo-Christian values. If no effort is made to provide a convincing substitute for the religious traditions that Dawkins wants to overthrow, can we ignore the risks of lapsing into a Hobbesian state of 'all against all', or more precisely competition along kin and ethnic loyalties, mitigated by mushrooming sects and cults? Whether it is right to deplore all these new-fangled cults, some of which will almost certainly mutate into widely accepted religions, is a problem we have explored already.

For a more subtle approach than that of aggressive atheism we may turn to Mark Lilla's elegantly learned if somewhat confusing book *The Stillborn God*. Lilla accepts that human beings are fundamentally 'theotropic', but argues that the Enlightenment, which emerged historically and uniquely from Christianity, was an experiment in the translation of religious questions into psychological and anthropological questions. He continues with a tortuous claim that the fuzzy modernist theology of the late nineteenth century, both Christian and Jewish, opened the floodgates for messianic and bloody totalitarianisms. Lilla's own conclusion is that the West is engaged in a necessary experiment: to replace political theology by political philosophy. But his narrative, as well as being limited by Eurocentrism, is open to diverse interpretations, one of which might be that social contract theory owes much more historically to its roots in Judaeo-Christianity, for instance to the doctrine of a covenant with God, than its secular proponents allow. Social contract theory in itself is surely too arid to attract huge populations that have little hope of economic inclusion, and hence to offer the protection against political violence that Lilla wishes it to be – especially when wars are fought by the West in the name of spreading democracy and freedom. As one of Lilla's critics, James A.K. Smith, has observed of his effort to make a sharp distinction between political theology and political philosophy, 'It is always already a tension between two faiths, between *competing* theologies, between rival *stories* about the world – neither of which can be "proved" but both of which are affirmed by faith'.

We have seen that political and ideological movements, professions such as psychotherapy, archaeology and anthropology, and movements in the creative arts, and indeed physical sports (many of whose enthusiasts regard them as creative arts) can acquire religioid aspects and partially minister to the universal 'religious imperative' – but only partially. We have located many of these in the medium to medium-strong religious field. However, for a pararelligion to convince large sections of the population it has to acquire an all-encompassing quality, as did in their time communism and nazism – both of which I would place squarely in the strong religious field. It is clear that liberal humanists such as Dawkins would totally oppose a reversion to such movements, but the risk remains.

A possible riposte to their critique of religion is as follows. 'You hold that religions are products of the human mind that have done much harm through dividing people from one another. Will you also concede that they have also done good, through uniting people and through inspiring outstanding creativity? You are not being asked to turn to religion yourself. But if religious symbols are simply that, artefacts of the human mind, and there is no ultimate reality "beyond" them, can you not accept them as ways in which other people choose to order their lives? Natural science has not yet provided a convincing moral order independent of the cultural heritages of religions, and you should by all means go on searching for one. In the meantime, why not support the efforts that religious institutions are making to purge themselves of the exclusive and destructive elements of the past – such as the condemnation of unbelievers, forcible indoctrination of children and students, opposition to natural science, and recourse to blind fatalism – and to develop their toleration of other traditions, including atheism. You may call it an Anglicanization of religion, or soft compromise, but why not?'

The process of soft compromise is well under way, and has been analysed by sociologists. It has also resulted in reactions towards rigorism.

Individuo-globalism and Theologically Conservative Movements

When cultural anthropologists study religion, they tend to dwell on its immense complexity and variety and on the dangers of over-generalization and stereotyping. An important tradition in sociology, on the other hand, sets out to explore convergences. With a broad brush, Raphaël Liogier has argued that the contrast between 'individualism' and the mobilization of a global conscience is sociologically unwarranted. 'Individuo-globalism' is the creeping moral orthodoxy in which personal well-being and a care for the whole of the cosmos mutually reinforce each other. Within this overarching structure of sensibility, all manner of specific religious and parareligious doctrines find their place. Obvious candidates include the New Age movements we have discussed already, including the most intellectually coherent and 'patinated' of them all, western Buddhism, but also neo-paganism and other trends such as 'holistic health'. Reference by some to a 'Next Age' signals the abandonment of the prophetic ideal of the Age of Aquarius, and leaves the movement free to be taken up by corporations that link the 'personal growth' of their employees, through such techniques as yoga, to the sustainable development of the planet.

Liogier's contention is that, despite the apparent variety of belief-systems throughout the industrialized world, there is a marked convergence – just as the apparent variety of choice among branded goods in a supermarket can be an illusion. (One might adduce Hotelling's Law in economics, which holds that in many markets it is rational for suppliers to make their products as similar as possible: thus, in a typical high street, groups of bank branches and fashion boutiques tend to cluster.) New Age practices and the current practices of the established religions are, according to this model, surface manifestations of the 'deep structure' of individuo-globalism. Religious identity becomes a matter of aesthetics more than commitment to a doctrine, and a high value is set on dialogue and toleration. The word 'religion', with its institutional and dogmatic connotations, is often discarded in favour of 'spirituality'. Other channels through which the religious is 'euphemized', according to Liogier, are social work and relief and development aid, providing opportunities for the growth of the Faith Based Organizations. Traditional religious hierarchies and national institutions alike are weakened by individuo-globalism. His thesis suggests that the great-hearted Walt Whitman's 'Song of Myself' has triumphed: 'Whoever degrades another degrades me, / And whatever is done or said returns at last to me'.

Individuo-globalism triggers off, however, conspicuous reactions. The development of a global conscience does not go unchallenged either by traditionalists, whose sincerity we do not need to question, or by vested interests such as national governments, which typically aim to exert a measure of control over religious activity within their borders. Evangelical Protestants, Roman Catholics and Orthodox Christians alike react by pulling up the theological drawbridges of 'fortress Christianity'. If the Vatican under Benedict XVI might seem to represent the fortress at its most conservative, the Eastern Orthodox Church is equally so, but unlike the Roman Catholic Church it hardly has to resist liberalizing tendencies from within as well as without – whereas both liberation theology and feminism have had influence within Catholicism itself. The Orthodox Church agrees on virtually all theological essentials with the Vatican, except on the issue of the primacy of the Bishop of Rome – admitting that he has a 'primacy of honour' but denying him headship over all Christendom and rejecting the dogma of the Pope's infallibility when he speaks *ex cathedra* on doctrinal questions. Eastern Orthodoxy, while being slightly less conservative on family planning than the Vatican (it permits contraceptives that do not terminate an embryo's life), is the more conservative of the two in still following St Paul's emphasis on the primacy of husbands over wives (*1 Corinthians* 11:7–9).

For Bishop Hilarion Alfeyev, a leading Russian Orthodox theologian, three key issues separate the 'traditional' churches, Roman and Orthodox alike, from the 'liberal', post-Reformation Christian communities, which are not, in traditionalist eyes, true churches at all but merely 'ecclesial communities'. These three issues are: inclusive language with reference to God, the ordination of women, and the acceptance of homosexuality. However, Alfeyev sees an even deeper danger in the development of secular humanism. The ideas that he finds questionable are, in particular, 'the affirmation of the right of each individual to his or her own way of life, insofar as this does not cause harm to others' and the repudiation of 'absolute moral norms and the notion of sin'. Some respect he admits to the religions of other, non-Christian civilizations, but militant secularism and New Age cults are, for Alfeyev, clearly beyond the pale.

Unpalatable as it may seem equally to Christians and Muslims alike, a sociological parallel can be drawn between the evolution of the two religions today. The Shia–Sunni split does not of course reproduce exactly the details of the Catholic–Protestant schism that resulted in centuries of religious wars in Europe, but there is a loose analogy to be drawn. Islam has its hard-liners who claim a monopoly on theological truth, such as the influential Sheikh Qaradawi of Qatar, and many *ulama* far to the Right of him. Conservative Islamic *ulama* are willing to join forces with conservative Christians on issues such as the banning of abortion about which they feel strongly. Among the younger generation of Muslims, it should by no means be assumed that all with academic qualifications in medicine, natural sciences, engineering or law have absorbed liberal or progressive interpretations of their religion from contact with Western ideas: often they combine a high level of professional competence with adherence to a hard-line traditional theology.

Let us take the three fault-lines in Christian theology identified by Alfeyev. In Islam, though *Allah* is a masculine noun, some theologians, especially Sufis, hold this to be a limitation of the Arabic language, for Deity is above and beyond gender and is never called 'Father'. Groups of educated women in Malaysia, Indonesia and elsewhere are analysing Qur'anic texts to ask the subversive question: what, if anything, is set down to make it impossible for a properly qualified woman to become an accepted Islamic scholar? As for homosexuality, a 'Muslim gay' identity has recently emerged – partly to resist serious persecution in Egypt and some other Muslim countries.

Many educated Muslims all over the world have adopted what are in effect 'liberal humanist' moralities, with Islam in the background as a cultural heritage but not necessarily a religious discipline – and in this they have much in common with Jews as well as Christians. As with Christians and the Bible, the terrifying threats of Hell described in the Qur'an have been euphemized out of Islam for many. As in the case of Christianity, religious values find a new expression in the formation of confessional NGOs, such as Islamic Relief Worldwide and Muslim Aid, that renounce all proselytizing or missionary aims and concentrate entirely on relief and development aid (see Chapter 4).

There is even a trend towards syncretic religiosity within Islam, deriving from the brotherhoods of traditional popular Sufism but shifting from a commitment to the universal *umma* of believers to a quest for self-development within a brotherhood led by a *sheikh*. Some of these groups, such as the Tijaniyya, founded in north Africa in the nineteenth century, or the much older Naqshbandiyya, which dates back to the Ottoman Empire of the fourteenth century, remain squarely within a cosmopolitan Islam. But others – rejected as heretical by the mainstream *ulama* – aim at a universal message transcending particular religions. There are close parallels to be drawn between western Buddhism and western Sufism. 'Some Sufi orders', writes Olivier Roy,

> once established in the West, function like New Age religions, stressing a general spiritualist approach as opposed to strict compliance with *sharia* [Islamic law], insisting on well-being and happiness, and borrowing paradigms and metaphors from other fields. ('The electromagnetic field is the template in which the body is configured – the cells of the body. Actually the aura of light is a template in which the electromagnetic field is configured. ... Eventually we shall learn to heal with light.' This is a typical 'New Age' Sufi statement.)

The Sufi 'neo-brotherhoods', as Roy calls them, globalize by putting down roots and recruiting outside their countries of origin, working towards a sacred space that transcends nationalism.

In both Christianity and Islam we find an immense variety. But we also find certain trends in common. We find nominal adherents to the faith who may still look to it when the major events in a life-cycle occur – birth, marriage, death – but who do not otherwise comply with the required observances and are guided more by humanist moral values than by religious teaching. We find those who vigorously reject the doctrine they have been brought up in. We find those who have little difficulty in reconciling acceptance of an encompassing world religion with the 'pagan' world view of their local forebears, even though to an outsider the two might appear to be mutually incompatible. We find syncretists and those who opt for a 'pick and choose' approach to spirituality. We find ardent proselytizers, but also those who are quite content for every social group to have its own preferred traditional cult. We find those who see no problem in their religion's adapting fully to a new *Zeitgeist* in which women's equality and wide acceptance of homosexuality are seen as inevitably having an impact on doctrines that were first formulated many centuries ago. Some Catholic priests in the USA encourage members of their congregation to speak in church services about their personal relationships with God, a practice which has no backing in Catholic tradition. And we also find conservatives – some highly sophisticated, but others who place an unquestioning confidence in the inerrancy of their sacred texts.

There are admittedly some momentous points of divergence. Few Christians today still want to establish theocracies, whereas this remains a goal of jihadist–salafist groups within Islam and of some of the networks that derive from the Muslim Brothers of Egypt. Al-Qaida and its offshoots, while relying on an extreme version of Islamic discourse, have much more in common with European fascism and fringe cults than with traditional Islam, though they are skilfully able to muster some support from co-religionists by drawing on their loyalty to the *umma*. Al-Qaida's survival is partly due to the refusal of the Western powers to identify it as a network that could have been politically isolated at all costs, rather than conflated with other adversaries such as Saddam Hussain and the Palestinian resistance. Yet its survival is also partly due to the crisis of authority in the Muslim world. Christian authority structures are today generally strong enough to disown and nip in the bud any movements that try to co-opt Christianity for violent quasi-fascist purposes. However, Christianity had in the past its own long tradition of legitimating violence against heretics.

The Russian Orthodox Church was ferociously persecuted under communism. Between 1917 and 1939 all monasteries and theological schools were shut down, nearly 60,000 pre-revolutionary churches were destroyed or closed, and many tens of thousands of clergy and monks were shot or tortured. After some relaxation by the authorities during the Second World War, new repression began in the 1960s. This must be one reason for its current spectacular resurgence after the collapse of communist institutions in the 1990s. In a comparable way, the Islamic resurgence has been strengthened by the sentiment, following centuries of European, Soviet and more recently American imperialism, that Islam offers an alternative or challenge to political and economic domination.

Conservative Christian and Islamic institutions alike are suspicious of anything that smacks of the New Age. Their theologians' hostility is grounded in centuries of opposition to heresy. Many of their conservative laities are attracted by the aesthetics of sacred architecture and immemorial liturgy, and/or by the satisfactions of belonging to a confident moral community. They are no doubt supported by more pragmatically motivated people who value religion not so much for its truth as for its efficacy as a political bulwark to authority and power. This was essentially the position of the French writer Charles Maurras (1868–1952), whose Action Française movement influenced such diverse figures as the poet T.S. Eliot and the Portuguese dictator Salazar. The view that political authority can only be maintained by means of a 'noble lie' goes back to Plato, and the influential American political philosopher Leo Strauss (1899–1973) probably held this view too.

If the general trend among younger people in industrialized societies is towards some form of secularization and/or pick-and-choose spirituality, reacting against the taken-for-granted religious affiliations of their parents' generation, a considerable proportion of them buck the trend by turning back to more rigid religious doctrines. This is specially true of the Islamic world. The fact that so many young women are attracted by Islam is a challenge to those who believe it to be a system for the oppression of women. But a similar trend can be observed among some Christian movements such as Eastern Orthodoxy and Pentecostalism. Traditionalists on every side claim that this resurgence of a 'hard' version of their religion is a proof of its veracity. This claim cannot be falsified, but we can also look for sociological and psychological reasons for such resurgences.

Moreover, it is part of the genius of great religions to give the impression of standing still, while in fact they are changing quite rapidly. For instance, the Eastern Orthodox churches traditionally adopted the colouring of the various political centres with which they was associated – Constantinople (Istanbul), Jerusalem, Antioch, Alexandria, Moscow and later a number of others – and founded separate churches overseas for each diaspora. These churches tended to become nationalistic and to remain aloof from internationalism, notoriously so in the case of the Serbian church, which had suffered persecution during the Second World War and survived the anti-religious policies of Tito's Yugoslavia. All those that suffered under communism have been preoccupied with their own regional and local problems, and some looked further back still to the Ottoman Empire or the Mongols. 'In the Orthodox world', one commentator wrote in 1998, 'religion sacralizes the nation, and the nation protects religion. ... It is a world martyred by history and hence imprinted with a great rigidity. ... It is a mental universe in which change is equivalent to treason'. Also, amid considerable variations in the theologies of the Orthodox Church, an important strand emphasizes the other-worldly and the mystical, at the expense of practical involvement in the here-and-now.

However, as explained by Lina Molokotos Liederman, one Orthodox interpretation of *diakonia* or social service considers it to be a 'sacramental event ... emancipating humanity and freeing it from poverty, oppression and injustice'. This view has stimulated some sections of the Orthodox Church to move in the direction of a global commitment to humanitarianism, environmentalism and peace-making, led from Istanbul by the Ecumenical Patriarch, Bartholomeos I – whose local Greek congregation in Turkey has been reduced to minute proportions since the exchange of populations between Greece and Turkey following the Treaty of Lausanne in 1923. In 2002, Patriarch Bartholomeos and Pope John Paul II issued a 'common declaration on the environment' in a video hook-up. International Orthodox Christian Charities (IOCC) was founded in 1992 in the United States, and operates programmes mainly in the Balkans, the Americas, the Middle East, Africa and the ex-Soviet Union. It may be predicted that this trend towards the 'deterritorialization' of the Orthodox Church will continue, despite a measure of opposition from its more territorial members. Rowan Williams, the Anglican archbishop, has drawn attention to the contribution that was made after the Soviet revolution by Russian émigrés in Paris towards constructing an Orthodoxy liberated from the 'ethnic particularism' to which it is now, according to Williams, reverting.

The spirituality of Orthodox Christianity is eminently compatible with environmentalism:

> The world in its entirety constitutes the liturgy. God is praised by the trees and by the birds, glorified by the stars and the moon …, worshipped by the sea and the sand. When we reduce religious life to our concerns, we forget the function of the liturgy is to implore God for the renewal of the whole cosmos. Our relationship with this world determines and defines our relationship with heaven.

The divine Incarnation in Jesus is a step towards the deification of humanity and nature. The Orthodox Christian is empowered to participate in the individuo-globalist sensibility, without renouncing the aesthetic splendours of the seamless Orthodox liturgy, whose aim is to create the sense of a Paradise out of earthly time.

We may expect much adaptation in the policies and practice of even the most apparently conservative religious institutions. According to Liogier's model, individuo-globalism is the theological 'grammar' characteristic of affluent Western societies, but even in developing countries it is the ideal to which the growing middle class aspires. In the event of collapse in the living standards of industrialized societies, one would expect a resurgence of political nationalism, economic protectionism and territorial religious movements.

Nationalist Ideologies: the Case of China

Nationalism in itself includes parareligious features; but in order to gain popular adherence it almost invariably needs to be fused with some kind of ideology. Historically these ideologies were religious. Some countries today incorporate religion explicitly in their constitutions: for instance Pakistan, established in 1956 as an Islamic republic, or England, with its Established Church, or Israel, founded as the Jewish homeland. Other nationalisms are supported by a secular political ideology, such as *Liberté, égalité, fraternité* in France, whose national temple is the Panthéon in Paris. France however like many other secular States retains deep cultural roots in religion. The most successful States in terms of scale, power and influence never rely on a nationalism expressed merely in a distinctive language or physical appearance. It may be hard to define exactly the values symbolized by the American flag, the Stars and Stripes, but they are to do with the Manifest Destiny of the American people, freedom and democracy, the Rights of Man, fused with Christianity – as is shown by the reference to God on every dollar bill. Russia has its own national church, to which about 70 per cent of Russians think of themselves as belonging.

China, one of the world's great powers, said to be now the most important motor of the global economy, seems in its post-Maoist phase to be an exception in that despite its pronounced nationalism there is great uncertainty as to what is the ideological 'glue' that can bind the vast population together. Restricting ourselves to Asia, we will briefly contrast the position of some of China's more important neighbours – India, Japan, Thailand and Indonesia – before considering China itself.

In India, no one would contest the importance of religion despite its secular constitution. Granted the long-standing presence of many religious minorities – notably Muslims, Christians, Sikhs, Jains, Parsees and Buddhists – Hindus constitute over two thirds of the population. Though the very word Hinduism is a neologism, and the category of 'religion' superimposed in India from the West, devout Hindus defend its reality as a unified, though extremely diverse spiritual, philosophical, ritual and ethical tradition. Its adherents typically regard it as a kind of default religion for Indians who have no other religious affiliation, and the land itself is sacred. In some contexts, the term 'Hindu' is taken to include Sikhs, Jains and Buddhists. The identification of Hinduism with Indianness is indeed strongly contested, and Hinduism has been extensively exported elsewhere, as well as absorbing Western influences itself. However, it is one of the countries – Israel being another, for very different historical reasons – where the relationship between a religion and a defined territory is closest.

As for Japan, its civilization drew eclectically on Buddhism, Shinto, Confucianism and Taoism. Buddhism was more associated with death and the dead, Shinto with community rites and festivals. Many distinctions familiar in the West such as that between nature and culture, mind and matter, the divine and the human, are less prominent in Japan. The advent of Darwinism in Japan caused less intellectual turbulence in Japan than in the West. One anthropologist, Alan Macfarlane, writes of Japan's diffuse and untheological religiosity which distinguishes it from all the more emphatic religious systems of mainland Europe and Asia – the difference arising from its island history.

A range of religions or sects continues to coexist there, including new ones such as Soka Gakkei that grew at the expense of older traditions discredited by their complicity in the war effort. It has been suggested that as many as a quarter of the Japanese population, some thirty million people, have had some involvement with one or other of these new religions, hundreds in number, which are generally formed around charismatic founding figures. Eclectic rituals and spiritual healing techniques are also widely practised. Japanese spirituality is an elusive topic, closely linked to nationalism, but it is clear that the nation's material prosperity is grounded in a richly laissez-faire religious regime. The penalty for such a high level of religious freedom, as in the West, is the risk of emergence of violent sects such as the Aum Shinrikyo (Aum Supreme Truth Sect) that launched the notorious sarin attack in the Tokyo subway system in 1995.

Between the late nineteenth century and the surrender in 1945, a militaristic national ideology known as State Shinto prevailed, with the Emperor of Japan as a kind of hereditary high priest. This culminated in a period of ultra-nationalism during the 1930s. After 1945, the American victors insisted on freedom of religion and the dissociation of religion from the State – the emperor being demoted to a mere 'symbol of the State' without political influence, reserve powers, or even the right to express opinions. Since then, Japan has become a great capitalist power. The majority of the population are probably happy with the strict secularism of the State, and only a tiny minority still believe that the present emperor – like his father, a Darwinian biologist – is descended from the gods. However, the imperial throne is still valued as a guarantee of continuity with the past after the traumas of the mid-twentieth century. Whereas before the death of Emperor Hirohito (Shōwa Tennō) in 1989 the public knew little about the imperial family behind its palace walls, so that there was a kind of void at the centre of the realm, their lives are now slightly more exposed to the media. When the present emperor, Akihito, was enthroned, ancient ceremonies were publicly performed but they were officially explained as a private matter for the Court. Deprived as the Japanese monarchy may have been of its explicitly religious authority, the very aloofness of the Court from normal human relationships gives it an unmistakable aura of the divine.

Thailand also has a monarchy, but here the king is popularly revered as a living Buddha. Buddhism, the nation and the Thai monarchy are deeply intertwined institutions. The connections go back for many centuries historically, but have been greatly strengthened by the political sophistication of the hugely popular King Bhumibol Adulyadej (Rama IX), who has reigned since 1946. Thailand's critics, internal and external, argue that the regime's pious ideology has screened massive economic corruption, and will come under even fiercer pressure when the king dies than has been evident from recent political upheavals. In the meantime, censorship of internal criticism and self-censorship are thoroughgoing, and insulting the king is a crime punishable by imprisonment. Buddhism is not the State religion, and the king is protector of religions in general, including the large and fractious Muslim minority. But Buddhist institutions, especially the monasteries, play a prominent part of life in Thailand, awarded privileges by the State in return for an understanding that they will stay out of politics. Nonetheless, Thailand is also one of the birthplaces of the Engaged Buddhist movement, which has spread all over the world. For our present purposes, it is enough to note that the religious field extends over much of public life, and is evidently a matter of great concern to those with an interest in national cohesion.

Our fourth example is Indonesia – a newer nation than Japan and Thailand, populous and extremely diverse in cultures and languages. Five religions only are officially accepted as such: Islam, Protestantism, Roman Catholicism, Buddhism and Hinduism. Citizens have to belong to one of these in order to have certain privileges such as voting. During the 1950s Sukarno introduced the doctrine of *pancasila*, the 'five pillars' of Indonesia: belief in a divine Lord, nationalism, democracy, social justice and humanism. This has been praised as a magnanimous expression of religious toleration, but has also been interpreted by analysts as a device to head off the possibility of an Islamic State in a country where at least 80 per cent of the population are officially Muslim. A bloody civil war was fought in 1965, resulting in a massacre of communists. The main political division today is between those who defend the national tradition of multi-culturalism and Islamists who are accused of importing a conservative 'arabized' form of the religion.

So in all these four Asian countries traditional religiosity is, in varying forms, a vital part of the social and political fabric. What of China?

Historically China drew from Confucianism over two millennia a system of official beliefs, and ceremonies carried out by the Emperor and his delegates. This official religion – as it has been called, though by others more neutrally the 'teaching of the scholars' – held that good government by the sovereign guaranteed the cosmic order. This pragmatic philosophy gradually came to predominate over, but also to be mixed with, the more mystical and occult practices associated with Taoism, and later with the influence of Buddhism. According to the official religion, there were three powers: Heaven, the supreme regulator and determiner; Earth, whose fertility was protected by the ancestors; and Man, collectively represented by the Emperor as Son of Heaven, who appointed a small elite to help him administer the State. His correct carrying out of the prescribed rites, such as the seasonal ceremonies and the cult of imperial ancestors, enacted the fundamental virtues of altruism and justice on which harmony depended, and radiated out to bring peace, prosperity and happiness to the people. Drought, floods and rebellion would ensue less from his showing a bad personal example, than from his performing the rites badly.

However, the Mandate of Heaven under which the Emperor ruled was not permanent, but was apt to wear out. Adverse omens, such as abnormal natural phenomena, were signs that it was time to hand over to a new, better-starred dynasty. Mencius (Meng Tseu), the early Confucian philosopher, had held that a king that violated the virtue of altruism was no more than an ordinary person, so that – perhaps uniquely in history – until the end of the dynasties in 1911 Chinese law permitted revolution in certain circumstances.

Other components in the official religion were the idea of *tao* as the ineffable transcendent reality, absolute and pre-existing Heaven and Earth, with which the order of the State must conform. The *tao* is the summation of two modalities, the subordinate *yin* (the feminine, shadowed and negative principle, that of Earth) and the dominant *yang* (representing the masculine, sunny, positive, Heaven).

The official religion was developed by literati and offered only a limited role to the people at large, though they were able to participate in the cult of ancestors and in the worship of the Gods of the Walls and Ditches, a kind of divine bureaucracy with administrators responsible for the well-being of the inhabitants within their demarcated territories. Side by side with the official religion was a popular religion, syncretic in character, tolerated or manipulated by the literati and ever threatening the Confucian insistence on moderation by its outbursts of exaltation. The practices of this popular religion and its conceptions invite comparison with similar phenomena all over the world: reincarnation according to personal merit, sacrifices, prayers and processions, pilgrimages, divination, spirit mediumship, geomancy, talismans, seasonal festivals.

Secret initiation societies were an important part of Chinese popular religion. Over the span of many centuries they provided the template for dissent, and were repressively controlled by the official religion. Whereas the official doctrine was based on the father–son relationship, these societies were typically based on the idea of blood brotherhood. A long history of uprisings under divine sanction goes back to the Red Eyebrows peasants' revolt in 18 CE, through the Taiping (Heavenly Peace) rebellion in the mid-nineteenth century, and up to the Boxer (Righteous and Harmonious Fists) Rebellion of 1900. The success of Maoism, starting as a secret society, in building a revolution from a parareligious ideology may be seen as a recent episode in this historical current.

Early in the twentieth century, Confucianism was abandoned as the State ideology, and was attacked by intellectuals as paternalistic and inegalitarian. A communist revolution was then imposed, depending on the foreign creed of Marxism-Leninism though nominally granting freedom of religion. One of the aims of Mao's disastrous Great Leap Forward in 1958 was to replace the Soviet economic system by a supposedly more Chinese system based on people's communes. The Cultural Revolution followed between 1966 and 1976. This set out to eliminate the 'Four Olds' – 'old ideas, culture, customs, and habits of the exploiting classes', which included Confucianism (but not exploitation by the Communist Party). Attacks on Confucius as an 'upholder of the slave system' were used as allegorical devices to attack supposedly more conservative figures such as Zhou Enlai. All religion was persecuted as backward superstition. Many hundreds of books, paintings, stone steles and graves were destroyed in one site alone, the Confucius Temple in Qufu, Shandong province. On one occasion, a State film crew stood by to record the destruction of Buddhist statues and incense burners in a monastery near Beijing. In 1975, the Muslim village of Shadian, close to the southern border with Vietnam, was razed and more than 1,600 villagers killed.

After the turbulence and killings of the Cultural Revolution, Deng Xiaoping led China into a new era of economic dynamism. Near the end of the first decade of the twenty-first century, it appears that capitalism is being allowed to dominate in a relatively unbridled form that is described officially as 'socialism with Chinese characteristics'. Huge wealth differentials have arisen, and the discrimination against rural populations, with a household pass system controlling migration to the cities, has been called a form of apartheid – based not on race but on the urban–rural divide. These processes must probably be seen as historical constants for the whole Mao period. But it is now clear that the Chinese Communist Party has turned Marxism upside down. For whereas Marx saw ideologies as veils obfuscating the brutality of economic power relations, a tattered Marxism is now the veil itself. All political systems survive through a measure of hypocrisy, but the idea that the Chinese regime is still communist becomes more and more unbelievable. For this reason, it is likely that the last vestiges of communist ideology, as opposed to the one-party system of 'democratic centralism', will soon be gradually sloughed off.

Commentators on the present-day Chinese regime are divided as to whether there is indeed a serious crisis of legitimacy. On the face of it, the State appears to be nearing ideological bankruptcy, if one compares China with the four Asian neighbours whose entanglements with the religious field we have briefly considered in this chapter. Whereas many now regard the entire history of Maoism as an ideological fraud, it was one that millions believed in at the time – including some prominent Western intellectuals.

The official doctrine of the Party has become 'harmony', indicating a return to Confucian values. Chinese nationalism is also very strong, now supported by large numbers of the overseas Chinese in southeast Asia and elsewhere. The orthodox business view is that if the government can sustain the phenomenal growth rate of the last decade, it can keep dissent at bay. China is not ready for democracy: unencumbered State power is necessary to control the social costs of the transition to capitalism. But is this enough of a glue to bind the nation together? Frontier capitalism in nineteenth century America and elsewhere could also be cruel, but it was restrained by Christian ethics. Nations need heroes, but the reputation of twentieth century China's greatest popular hero, Mao, has been tarnished by the admission that he was responsible for the Great Leap Forward famine and the disaster of the

Cultural Revolution, and thus 'only 70 per cent correct' – as the official cliché has it.. An influential body of opinion outside China, led by his biographers Jung Chang and Jon Halliday, contends that there is nothing good to be said about Mao at all (though a less black-and-white portrait is given by scholars such as Roderick MacFarquhar). And is not the present regime clearly terrified, as was Mao's, of uncontrolled religious revivals? Witness the fierce official criticism of the Dalai Lama as a 'splittist' and efforts to impose government control over his next reincarnation; the attempted suppression of the Falun Gong in 1999; and the refusal to allow the Vatican to appoint Catholic bishops, so that there are two Catholic churches in China, the Patriotic Catholic Church which is government approved, and a hierarchy in communion with the Vatican that is technically illegal (though a rapprochement now seems likely).

A closer look at the situation of religion in China reveals a rather more complicated picture. The government recognizes five religions: Buddhism, Protestantism, Catholicism, Islam and Taoism. The criteria for recognition are set out in two alternative lists enshrined in an official document published in 1982. One list mentions as its criteria: a belief in supernatural beings, a set of beliefs and practices relating to that other world, and being organized. The other document states that religion is complex, a mass phenomenon, long lasting, and with important implications for relations with ethnic groups and foreign countries. Confucianism is not covered: Peter Beyer suggests that this is because Christianity was taken as the implicit model for what counted as a religion. By contrast with the accepted religions, the State has introduced a concept of heretical or unapproved teaching – including superstitious practices, sorcerers and witches, confidence artists, phrenologists, fortunetellers and geomancers.

According to one scholar, Vivienne Shue, the traditional components in the logic of legitimation of the Chinese State were: first, transcendent truth; second, benevolent care for the common people; and third, the conscious glorification of the Chinese nation. Despite the political turbulence of the twentieth century, these legitimating norms have been revived in different guises in China:

> ...I believe it makes sense to see the Maoist Party-State's claims to legitimacy based on its possession of a transcendent universal ethical Truth to have been manifested very clearly in the heavy-duty moral instruction of the masses that accompanied the propagation of Marxist theory and Mao Thought during that era. The Party-State's claim to Benevolence in those days took such forms as 'iron rice bowl' guarantees of livelihood, cradle-to-grave subsistence needs met within the capsulized life of the danwei [work unit], and repeated

fervent expressions and demonstrations of state solidarity with the proletariat and the 'poor peasantry'.

(It is political ideology rather than the actual degree of success in creating a Welfare State that she is alluding to here.)

The state's claim to be promoting national Glory then took many interesting forms as well, from the cleansing and militarization of Chinese culture itself, to the obsessions with industrialization, anti-imperialism, and China's pretensions to international leadership within the context of the Third World.

Shue considers that the doctrine of Truth proclaimed by Chinese leaders today is based on scientific empiricism as the necessary path to modernity. Benevolence is manifested in nationwide relief and emergency funds, orphanages and old-age homes, scholarships and the like. About the pursuit of the Glory of China there can be no doubt, but Shue rejects the view that patriotic sentiment is the only popular value on which the present-day State bases its appeal for legitimacy.

Despite the Chinese State's continued formal opposition to popular religion, space has been opened up since Mao's death for a vigorous revival all over China of Christianity, Buddhism, Taoism and numerous syncretic sects. The State is not monolithic, and at a local level there is a 'zone of indifference' towards the highly syncretic local religious observances. The police are supposed to crack down on these, yet (according to Adam Yuet Chau's field study in Shaanxi Province in north-west China) seldom actually do so, but are invited by temple associations to keep order and direct the traffic. Fervent opposition to superstition is associated with the Cultural Revolution and so has a bad reputation.

By contrast, the Falun Gong (or Falun Dafa, the great Dharma of the Wheel of the Law) is suppressed, because it is not merely local but international and combative towards the Chinese high officials. This began as one of the many *qigong* (energy cultivation) groups that sprang up in China in the late 1980s, each with its master. The Falun Gong was originally encouraged by the Chinese government as a homegrown alternative to Western ideas. Li Hongzi (born in 1925) was a former government official who has now retreated to the United States, and is presented as having reached an advanced state of being, like the Buddha. He teaches his followers to free themselves from earthly attachments and ambitions, he demonizes the market and consumerism, and he rejects technological rationality, claiming access to a higher reality. According to Shue, the Falun Gong's challenge cuts to the heart of the post-Maoist government project. Its slogan '*Zhen, Shan, Ren*' ('Truth, Goodness and Forbearance') exposes the

State's narrow empiricist view of truth, its shallow benevolence, and its assumption that glory resides in wealth and power. Therefore it must be eradicated.

Commentators on China focus their debates on whether the current regime is stable on account of the intense cautiousness of the ruling elite, or fragile because of the intuition, dear to Maoists, that 'one spark can start a prairie fire'. Stephan Feuchtwang, one of the most experienced social anthropologists specializing in China, considers that the unifying factor is indeed pride in being Chinese, though this does not necessitate always agreeing with the government. The obverse of the Mandate of Heaven granted to emperors has always been, for the Chinese, the fear of chaos and breakup that the Chinese Communist Party has adeptly manipulated. He disagrees with those who contend that if China does not have a ruling ideology with religious content, its absence must be a weakness. The Party's greatest fear is of different forms of protest, including the pro-Tibet movement, becoming linked to each other laterally in a way that might compete with its power. According to Feuchtwang's research on the posthumous reputation of Mao within China, it is possible for people to accept that, despite his mistakes, which caused serious hardship and victimization, he made a prosperous future possible. Diminished from his former pedestal, he will nonetheless remain a hero within China, with Zhou Enlai and Deng Xiaoping as balancing heroes. Added to the pantheon will probably be leaders of the 1911 republican revolution such as Sun Yat-sen, also Chiang Kai-shek as a defender of China against the Japanese, as well as more recent political leaders.

It seems that protests in China are widespread but, at present, disconnected. A Christian analogue to the Falun Gong is the Huhan Pai, called the Shouters because their congregations are reputedly urged to shout the words 'O Lord, Amen, Hallelujah', and founded by a mainland Chinese who moved to Taiwan before 1949 and later to California. The movement is highly localized and though banned by the Chinese government it has spread to rural areas. The syncretic and inclusive Yiguandao (Tian Dao) movement is centred on worship of the Ancient Mother, the creator of a now imperilled universe, separated from her children, who sends Bodhisattva figures to the earth to help humans to recover their lost birthright. The movement is strong in Taiwan and may be returning to some parts of northern China, where it originated in the 1930s. Its moral but this-worldly philosophy is compatible with the business culture, and might be a template for the kind of eclectic movement that could link protesters in future.

In any case, it is simplistic to view the return of religion in China as due simply to a need for spiritual solace. It should be considered in the same context as the rise in China of movements such as environmentalism and human rights advocacy, which – like strictly religious movements – have no geographical limits and, as has been argued in this book, belong to the field of parareligion.

The Former East German Republic – an Anomalous Case?

If our model is correct, then in the former communist nations of Europe the removal of the political ideology would have resulted in a revival of old religions and in opportunities for religious entrepreneurship. This appears indeed to have happened. According to the World Values Survey, the proportion of people who considered themselves religious rose between 1990 and 1996 in most of the former communist States of Europe (by 25 per cent in Belarus, 19 per cent in Bulgaria, 16 per cent in Russia). There were two exceptions: Poland and Eastern Germany. The case of Poland is easy to interpret: the Catholic Church had acquired great political importance as a spearhead in the destruction of communism, with over 95 per cent adhesion to Catholicism, and under a post-communist regime popular religiosity is declining to more general European norms, with the beginnings of infiltration by groups such as the Jehovah's Witnesses.

Eastern Germany is more difficult to explain. The percentage of self-declared atheists disclosed by the World Values Survey in 1995–97 was as high as 25.4 – the next most atheistic country being Japan at 12.2 per cent, with the Philippines and Bangladesh bringing up the rear at 0.2 and 0.1 per cent respectively. If the 'hydraulic' model is correct – with the religious imagination impelled under pressure to find new outlets – it may be asked what has happened to religion in the former Deutsche Demokratische Republik (DDR).

Two American sociologists of religion, Paul Froese and Steven Pfaff, provide a persuasive and well documented answer – from a perspective derived from rational choice theory. According to them, eastern Germany presents special features: it is a 'desolate' market for religion, while Poland is a 'replete' market.

First of these features in the historical background was the strength of anti-clericalism among German socialists and social democrats in the early twentieth century. They developed a voluntary secular alternative to the Christian ritual of confirmation for adolescents, the *Jugendweihe*, which had been invented in the mid-nineteenth century. Then the nazi regime crushed the independence of the churches and it also oppressed religious minorities – not merely the Jews, but also the Jehovah's Witnesses and the Quakers. Nonetheless, in 1950, shortly after the foundation of the DDR, 92 per cent of East Germans declared themselves in a census as belonging to a religious movement, though the proportion of churchgoers was less in the East than in the West. The peculiarly aggressive atheist policies of the communist regime reduced the proportion of religious adherents sharply, to as little as

40 per cent in 1986. The *Jugendweihe* was made *de facto* mandatory and included a pledge to promote scientific socialism. The Lutheran and Catholic churches were forced into political accommodations with the State, and were infiltrated by the Stasi or secret police. Following the fall of communism, there ensued neither a conspicuous revival of the old East German churches, nor a new religious pluralism.

After reunification in 1990, it became less attractive for eastern Germans to belong to a church because, whereas contributions to churches had been voluntary under the DDR, church membership in West Germany entailed a special church tax that could be avoided by non-adherence. Meanwhile new religious movements such as Scientology were discriminated against and were even subjected to police surveillance. Atheist and Marxist-inspired organizations have flourished in the East, partly out of nostalgia for the DDR, and the *Jugendweihe* has been revived. Froese and Pfaff describe this as atheist competition with religion: 'atheist affiliation is analogous to a conversion and not simply to re-affiliation within a religious market'. They predict that atheist hegemony in East Germany is unlikely to last, and that the field is open for new opportunistic movements. Their own analysis may actually help open the gates to religious entrepreneurship, in that they have set out the issues so clearly.

If comparison with other societies is a guide, it would be surprising if the dominance of out-and-out atheism in the former East Germany were to continue uncontested by new movements – given that its international links are continuing to develop, and that new generations are likely to react against their elders' entrenched positions.

Conclusion

The definition of what counts as religion is, as already argued, partly political. In classical Islam, religious toleration followed a concentric pattern, with true monotheism in the centre and an inner ring of People of the Book – mainly Christians and Jews, with some borderline cases including Hindus, who were to some extent admitted when a small Muslim court found itself governing a huge Hindu population in India. Outside this inner ring was the hated and feared space of *kufr* – barbaric atheism – and *shirk* or polytheism. Christians and Jews were like confessional cousins, allowed subordinate civic rights in the Islamic State.

The recent initiative of King Abdullah of Saudi-Arabia, guardian of Islam's most holy sites and of Wahhabi rigorism, in entering a dialogue with the other two Abrahamic monotheisms came as a surprise: in July 2008 he opened a world conference in Madrid on inter-faith dialogue. But this is consistent with the 'concentric' tradition of toleration in Islam.

Christianity, by contrast, traditionally taught that there was no salvation outside the church and condemned all non-Christian belief systems. Gradually over centuries a more tolerant approach to other religions was developed in some sections of Christendom. Today, even conservative theologians such as Benedict XVI and Bishop Hilarion Alfeyev do not deny the title of religion to Hinduism. Secular regimes frequently grant privileges to a few accepted religions and deny the title of religion to others. Meanwhile individuo-globalism threatens all religious demarcations with the eclectic syncretism that has already been the norm in China and Japan for centuries, but that has frequently been misunderstood or disvalued in the West because of our monotheistic bias.

An inclusive, polythetic definition of religion with its 'grey areas' of parareligion allows us to set all these phenomena in a wide and instructive context.

The active rejection of gods in full-blown atheism can take on some parareligious features – as in the Bulgarian communist marriage ceremony, discussion groups on Mao Thought, or the East German *Jugendweihe* – but it is generally limited by a one-dimensional understanding of the complexity of the religious imperative.

ENVOI

Few subjects are as sensitive as religion. I hope this book will fall into the hands of people who have a wide diversity of backgrounds and beliefs. If anyone who has persevered is offended by its contents, I can only say that it is not the intention to give offence. I have merely tried to follow where the evidence leads. I have started from the proposition that, as John Gray has put it, '[h]uman beings will no more cease to be religious than they will stop being sexual, playful or violent'. Some may be offended by the notion that, in the analysis of nazism as a parareligious movement, full account should be taken of its power at that moment in history to win over large populations – not to speak of a very few indisputably major figures in the European cultural heritage, notably Heidegger and Leni Riefenstahl. But if one believes, as it is perfectly reasonable to do, in the existence of an evil principle in the world, why should we not think of its creating for its own purposes a Mephistophelean simulacrum of religion? It is more sensible to try to understand how Antichrist movements have arisen, and may arise again, than to utter ritual contempt for a movement that ended, except in a few small pockets of revival, six decades ago. This could be specially urgent if, as is forecast by many scientists, environmental problems, aggravated by economic crises, should come to thwart the hopes of the developing world and turn wealthy nations into large-scale 'gated communities'.

Others may be offended by the emphasis given to the fact that many different conservative religious traditions lay claim to absolute truth. It is difficult to study comparative anthropology without being struck by this fact. However, I do not argue that any of these claims is necessarily false. There are deep mysteries at the heart of our existence in the cosmos. The advances of science appear to solve some of these mysteries, but to unpeel others. The analysis presented in this book belongs to the discipline of social research, not polemics for or against any particular religion.

Yet another objection could be that it is trivializing to argue that, say, the animal rights movement or popular archaeology has religioid features. For instance, their adherents are not provided with any supernatural entity that they can pray to for the relief of suffering and misfortune. This may indeed restrict their magnetism as parareligions, since solace in the face of suffering is such an important aspect of religion. However, the receptivity of supernatural beings to prayer is not a necessary feature of religions (witness Unitarianism and the more philosophical forms of Buddhism), and it is balanced in all major religious doctrines by an insistence on the moral responsibility of individuals and on the inadequacy of relying solely on mediation by prayer. If we adopt polythetic criteria for recognizing religion on the lines recommended here, it may help understand how movements such as animal rights and popular archaeology gain their following as partial substitutes for religion in the strict sense.

Though it would be presumptuous to propose any personal inferences that might be drawn from the arguments presented in this book, some suggestions of a general nature may be acceptable.

First, any religious doctrine that opposes the methods of empirical science – rather than trying to complement it, enrich its perspectives, or influence its progress – is unlikely to prosper on a large scale, because these methods are so obviously powerful. It does not follow that those of the world's peoples who are technologically superior are necessarily superior in morality or spirituality. And as argued earlier, a true commitment to science must include an acceptance that the 'religious imperative' is itself part of the necessary subject matter of science.

The Catholic philosopher Charles Taylor, in his erudite *A Secular Age*, argues against 'subtraction stories', by which he means the view that religion has declined simply because science has enabled confining illusions to be sloughed off – the view memorably dramatized by Browning:

> ...cosmogony,
> Geology, ethnology, what not,
> (Greek endings, each the little passing-bell
> That signifies some faith's about to die)...

The historical truth is indeed much more complex. Galileo held that if science conflicted with Scripture, Scripture must be interpreted better. Kepler's aim was to reveal through astronomy God's geometrical plan for the cosmos. Newton was a keen student of the Bible and of the occult; Darwin an agnostic supporter of his local Anglican church; Einstein torn between theism and atheism. Nietzsche's and Freud's vehement opposition to Christianity was motivated by something in addition to their rational response to scientific findings. But it would be hard to deny that organized religion today has to meet its most serious challenge in the advances of biology. My argument is that the antinomy between religion and science can be defused if we accept as a scientific truth the proposition that we are religious animals.

Second, it is otiose to try to escape the religious imperative, and rational to find some way of obeying it. This is what Gell calls the willing submission to selected technologies of enchantment, which he recommends as an alternative to being enslaved by them. The proposition that religious belief can be a preparedness to behave *as if* a given doctrine is true has a philosophical pedigree dating back to C.S. Peirce, and many today find this an acceptable position to adopt. In the same way, we are all susceptible to becoming victims of addiction, and the secret of a relatively ordered life is not to avoid all addictions, but to choose beneficial addictions. If we particularly admire some individuals or their work as exemplary, it is rational to want to follow their lead, and this is an important way in which religious loyalties are attracted. Thus the Orthodox Christian bishop occupies the place of Christ in the Eucharistic gathering; a Muslim philanthropist may become recognized as a 'walking Qur'an', a Buddhist teacher as a Bodhisattva. All these religious doctrines may be embraced as an antidote to mental enslavement, since they all insist on responsibility and self-knowledge.

But religion can also indoctrinate through offering pat nostrums. Those who remain tepid as regards commitment to a religious doctrine are often led to this position by the experience that exceptionally admirable individuals seem to be distributed fairly evenly across religious and cultural boundaries, and to include people who have rejected religious authority for themselves – not only people who are devout or who occupy a religious office. It is a natural consequence to look for meaning and objects of devotion not only in the global repertoire of strictly religious options, but in intellectual or aesthetic pursuits, and/or in a commitment to those causes that have been inelegantly classed in this book as 'religioid'.

We cannot choose to repudiate the religious inclination; but we can choose how to channel it.

NOTES AND REFERENCES

References are to pages.

1: RELIGION AND PARARELIGION

5. Alcoholics Anonymous: second of the Twelve Traditions endorsed by the membership in 1950.
5. Personal growth: Steve Pavlina.com
6. On 'European exceptionalism': Davie, Grace, *Europe: the Exceptional Case: Parameters of Faith in the Modern World* (London: Darton, Longman and Todd, 2001).
6. Wuthnow, Robert, *The Restructuring of American Religion: Society and Faith since World War II* (Princeton: Princeton University Press, 1988), p.67.
   Some other major works by sociologists of religion:
   Berger, Peter, A Rumour of Angels: Modern Society and the Rediscovery of the Supernatural (London: Allen Lane, 1970).
   Wilson, Bryan, The Social Dimensions of Sectarianism: Sects and New Religious Movements in Contemporary Society (Oxford: Oxford University Press, 1990).
   Martin, David, Christian Language and its Mutations: Essays in Sociological Understanding (Aldershot: Ashgate, 2002).
   Beckford, James L., Social Theory and Religion (Cambridge: Cambridge University Press, 2003).
6. On funerals: reliable statistics on the prevalence on non-religious funerals are unavailable. Percentages of 3.5 to 10 per cent for the United Kingdom were suggested in 2007, together with a forecast that this proportion was due to rise sharply (Ward, Lucy, 'C of E or Elvis? Bell tolls for formal funerals', *Guardian*, 14 September). A survey in Belgium conducted by the Free University of Brussels in 2005 concluded that 76.6 per cent of funerals were religious (US Department of State, International Religious Freedom Report, 2007).
7. For an account of the impact of Darwinism and other nineteenth century science on Christianity: Wilson, A.N., *God's Funeral* (London: John Murray, 1999). He aptly observes that nineteenth century Britain was religiously obsessed, as our own age is erotically obsessed (p.57).
   John Paul II had declared in a letter to the Pontifical Academy of Sciences, 1996, that Darwinism was compatible with Catholic doctrine. Cardinal Schönborn,

considered to be a close adviser to Pope Benedict, published an article in the *New York Times*, 7 July 2005, 'Finding design in nature'. In May 2006, Pope Benedict appointed an outspoken advocate for 'intelligent design', Donald Wuerl, as Archbishop of Washington, DC.

7. On some Islamic intellectuals' opposition to Darwinism: Lauzière, Henri, 'Post-Islamism and religious discourse of al-Salam Yasin' [a veteran Moroccan Islamist], *International Journal of Middle East Studies*, 37:2 (May 2005), pp.241–61.

7. On the words 'religion' and 'secular': Bailey, Edward I., 'The implicit religiosity of the secular: a Martian perspective on the definition of religion', in Greil, Arthur L. and David G. Bromley (Eds), *Defining Religion: Investigating the Boundaries between the Sacred and the Secular* (Kidlington: JAI Press, 2003), pp.55–66.

8. On coercion: Asad, Talal, *Genealogies of Religion: Discipline and Reasons of Power in Christianity and Islam* (Baltimore: Johns Hopkins University Press, 1993).

8. On globalization of the Western concept of religion: Beyer, Peter, 'Defining religion in cross-national perspective: identity and difference in official conceptions', in Greil and Bromley (Eds), *Defining Religion...*, pp.163–88.

9. On Judaism: Ruel, Malcolm, 'Christians as believers', in Davis, John (Ed.), *Religious Organization and Religious Experience* (London: Academic Press, 1982).

9. On Confucianism: Spickard, James V., 'Cultural context and the definition of religion: seeing with Confucian eyes', in Greil and Bromley (Eds), *Defining Religion...*, pp.189–99.

9. On the proposition 'religion has no existence apart from the academy': Introduction to Greil and Bromley (Eds), *Defining Religion...*, pp.3–17.

9. *Rigveda* X hymn 129, translated by Macdonell. Quoted in Goody, Jack, 1996, 'A kernel of doubt', *Journal of the Royal Anthropological Institute*, 2:4 (1996), pp.667–81.

10. Minois, Georges, *Histoire de l'athéisme* (Paris: Fayard, 1998), p.587. My translation.

10. Fromm, Erich, *Psychoanalysis and Religion* (New Haven: Yale University Press, 1950). Fromm, Erich, *The Anatomy of Human Destructiveness* (New York: Holt Rinehart & Winston, 1973).

10. Geertz, Clifford, *The Interpretation of Cultures* (New York: Basic Books, 1973) p.100.

11. On repression of the religious: John Gray has a similar thought in *Black Mass: Apocalyptic Religion and the Death of Utopia* (London: Allen Lane, 2007), p.190: 'Like repressed sexual desire, faith returns, often in grotesque forms, to govern the lives of those who deny it'.

11. 'Implicit religion': Edward Bailey is director of the Centre for the Study of Implicit Religion and Contemporary Spirituality and edits the journal *Implicit Religion*.

11. Martin, David, 'Berger: an appreciation', in Woodhead, Linda et al. (Ed.), *Peter Berger and the Study of Religion* (London: Routledge, 2001), p.14.

12. On habitus: Asad, Talal, *Formations of the Secular: Christianity, Islam, Modernity* (Stanford: Stanford University Press, 2003), pp.251–2. The concept is borrowed from Marcel Mauss and Pierre Bourdieu.

13. On Bulgaria: Roth, Klaus, 'Socialist life-cycle rituals in Bulgaria', *Anthropology Today*, 6:5 (October 1990), pp.8–10.

13–15. Binns, Christopher A.F., 'The changing face of power: revolution and accommodation in the development of the Soviet ceremonial system, Part I',

Man (n.s.), 14:4 (1979), pp.585–606. 'A fresh, spontaneous quality…', p.588. 'In the early years…', p.590. On the factory ceremony: *Massovye prazdnestva*, 1926, Leningrad: Akademia, p.82–3, quoted by Binns p.593. Quotations from Trotsky: Binns, p.595.

Binns, Christopher A.F., 'The changing face of power: revolution and accommodation in the development of the Soviet ceremonial system, Part II'. *Man* (n.s.), 15:1 (1980), pp.170–87. 'It is sweet indeed…', p.179. 'Whatever the regime's…', p.183.

15. On football: Chidester, David, 'The church of baseball, the fetish of Coca-Cola, and the potlatch of rock 'n' roll: theoretical models for the study of religion in American popular culture', *Journal of the American Academy of Religion*, 64:4 (1996), pp.743–65.
As if to confirm that Goal has replaced God in contemporary Britain, on 29 June 2008 the television channel BBC1 showed extracts from the European football championship (Euro 2008) accompanied by *Ave Verum Corpus*, the medieval Eucharistic hymn (on transubstantiation) set to music by Mozart.
Bron Taylor points out in his forthcoming *Dark Green Religion* that some surfers, unlike footballers, do consider their sport to be a religion.

16. IBM company song: from IBM Archives website.

16. Amway: in 2007, its British subsidiary faced an attack on its business methods by the British government in the Companies Court, but the case was withdrawn when it agreed to review its practices. The British government had sought to wind up the subsidiary of Amway, on the grounds that it was selling a dream of unachievable wealth. *The Times*, 27 November 2007.

17. Frazer, Sir James, 'The scope of social anthropology', inaugural lecture, University of Liverpool, in *Psyche's Task* (London: Macmillan, 1913), p.171.

17–18. On mistletoe: Frazer, Sir James, *The Golden Bough* (London: Macmillan, 1890). 'Balder and the Mistletoe', LXV. Mabey, Richard, *Flora Britannica* (London: Sinclair-Stevenson, 1996), pp.239–44.

18. Gell, Alfred, 'Technology and magic', *Anthropology Today*, 4:2 (April 1988), pp.6–9. Gell, Alfred, 1992, 'The technology of enchantment and the enchantment of technology', in Coote, Jeremy and Anthony Shelton (Eds), *Anthropology, Art and Aesthetics* (Oxford: Clarendon Press, 1992).

18. On Israel: Weingrod, Alex, 'Dry bones: nationalism and symbolism in contemporary Israel', *Anthropology Today*, 11:6 (December 1995), pp.7–12.

20. On monarchy: Quigley, Declan, 'The paradoxes of monarchy', *Anthropology Today*, 11:5 (October 1995), pp.1–3.

20. Rabinow, Paul, *Essays on the Anthropology of Reason* (Princeton: Princeton University Press).

2: THE FAMILY RESEMBLANCE OF RELIGIONS

21. Classic sociologists of religion: for instance, William James: '…[T]he word "religion" cannot stand for any single principle or essence, but is rather a collective name' (*The Varieties of Religious Experience* (London, Longmans Green, 1928 [1902]), p.27).

Two anthropologists, to which this discussion is much indebted, have sketched out criteria for the polythetic definition of religion:
Southwold, Martin, 'Buddhism and the definition of religion' *Man* (n.s.) 13:3 (September 1978), pp.362–79.
Saler, Benson, *Conceptualizing Religion* (Oxford: Berghahn, 2000, second edition with new preface).
A recent list of suggested polythetic criteria, with commentary, may be found in Taylor, Bron R., 'Exploring religion, nature and culture: introducing the *Journal for the Study of Religion, Nature and Culture*', *Journal for the Study of Religion, Nature and Culture*, 1:1 (2007), pp.5–24. This is refined further in Chapter One of *Dark Green Religion*, a book he expects to be published in 2009.

21. On prototype semantics: Coleman, Linda and Paul Kay, 'Prototype semantics: the English word Lie', *Language*, 57 (1981), pp.26–44. Quoted in Saler, Benson, *Conceptualizing Religion*, page x.

22. On the Aymara: Bastien, J.W., *Mountain of the Condor: Metaphor and Ritual in an Andean Ayllu* [community] (Long Grove, IL: Waveland, 1978).

22. On the Uduk: James, Wendy, *The Listening Ebony: Moral Knowledge, Religion and Power among the Uduk of Sudan* (Oxford: Clarendon Press, 1999).

22. Boyer, Pascal, 'Functional origins of religious concepts: ontological and strategic election in evolved minds', *Journal of the Royal Anthropological Institute*, 6:2 (June 2000), pp.195–214. On spirits and zombies, p.212.

22. Littlewood, Roland, 'Living gods: in (partial) defence of Euhemerus', *Anthropology Today*, 14:2 (April 1998), pp.6–14.

23. On Sri Lankan popular Buddhism: Leach, Edmund, in Stephen Hugh-Jones and James Laidlaw (Eds), *The Essential Edmund Leach* (New Haven: Yale University Press, 2000 [1962]), vol.2, p.96; Southwold, 'Buddhism…', pp.364–5.

23. On Mao: Buruma, Ian, 'Cult of the chairman', *The Guardian*, 7 March 2001.

24. Buccellati, Giorgio, 'Ethics and piety in the Ancient Near East', in Sasson, Jack M., (Ed.), *Civilizations of the Ancient Near East* (New York: Macmillan Reference Library, 1995), III:1, pp.685–1, 696.

25. Hardy, Thomas, 'On a Fine Morning', 1899.

25. Taylor, Charles, *A Secular Age* (Cambridge, MA.: Belknap Press, 2007), p.5.

25. Gray, John, *Black Mass…*

26. On St Thomas Aquinas and St Augustine: Martin, Raymond and John Barresi, *The Rise and Fall of Soul and Self: An Intellectual History of Personal Identity* (New York: Columbia University Press, 2006), pp.101, 74.

26. 'Limbo consigned to history books': Owen, Richard, *The Times*, 30 November 2005.

26. On Islamic rules on eating animals: Benkheira, Hocine, 'Le rite à la lettre: régime carné et normes religieuses', in Bonte, Pierre et al. (Eds), *Sacrifices en islam: Espaces et temps d'un rituel* (Paris: Éditions du CNRS, 1999), pp.63–91.

27. On the absence of doctrine in philosophical or Western Buddhism: Thomson, Garry, *The Sceptical Buddhist* (Bangkok, River Books, 2000). Thomson argues that Buddhism is totally compatible with scientific openmindedness, quoting from the early Sutta Nipāta text: 'Nothing is assumed, nothing rejected. He [the Buddha] has washed all beliefs away' (p.26).

27. On the Dogon: Maybury-Lewis, David, *Millennium* (New York: Viking, 1992), pp.163–72 – drawing on research by Walter van Beek.

27. On the Kalasha: Lièvre, Viviane and Jean-Yves Loude, *Le Chamanisme des Kalash du Pakistan* (Lyons: Éditions du CNRS, 1990). The ethnographer was Peter Snoy.

28. Firth, Raymond, *Rank and Religion in Tikopia* (London: Allen & Unwin, 1970), p.351.

29. Headley, Stephen C., 'Sembah/Salat: the javanisation of Islamic prayer; the islamisation of Javanese prayer', in Parkin, David and Stephen C. Headley (Eds), *Islamic Prayer across the Indian Ocean: Inside and Outside the Mosque* (Richmond: Curzon, 2000).

29. Bohm, David, *Wholeness and the Implicate Order* (London: Routledge, 1980).

30. On Emerson: Fromm, Harold, 'Overcoming the Oversoul: Emerson's evolutionary existentialism', *Hudson Review*, LVII:1 (Spring 2004).

30. Proust, Marcel, *À la Recherche du Temps Perdu*, Pléiade 1954 edition, 1:820, Scott Moncrieff translation. All references to the *Recherche* are to this three-volume edition.

30. Browning, Robert, 'Bishop Blougram's Apology', 1855.

31. Agus, Aharon, *The Binding of Isaac and Messiah* (Albany: State University of New York Press, 1988), pp.1, 58, 67. This does not appear to be a mainstream position in the Orthodox tradition to which Agus belonged. For a near-existentialist world-view in authoritative Jewish Orthodox teaching, see Soloveitchik, Joseph, *The Lonely Man of Faith* (New York, Doubleday, 1992). For the crisis in Jewish theology since the Shoah, see Breitman, Zachary, *(God) After Auschwitz: Tradition and Change in Post-Holocaust Thought* (Princeton: Princeton University Press, 1998).

31. Bellow, Saul, *Herzog* (London: Alison Press, 1964), p.289.

31. Tolstoy, Leo, 'Religion and morality', in *'A Confession' and other religious writings* (London: Penguin, 1987 [1893]).

31. Steiner, George, *Real Presences* (London: Faber, 1989), pp.228–9. In his more recent published reflections on religion, Steiner has disavowed his earlier interest in a 'negative theism', of God as in some mode of recession or coming into being. 'Now such tropes seem to me more or less fatuous. ... What I have come to feel with compelling intensity is the absence of God.' *My Unwritten Books* (New York, New Directions, 2008), pp.205–8.
The historical roots of modern atheism may be traced back to the deism of the Enlightenment and arguably to St Thomas Aquinas's and Luther's concept of the *deus absconditus* (hidden God). See Depoortere, Frederiek, *The Death of God: An Investigation into the Western Concept of God* (London: T. and T. Clark, 2007).

32. Merleau-Ponty, Maurice, *La Phénoménologie de la Perception* (Paris: Gallimard, 1945), p.221. My translation.

32. On gods of the Ancient Near East: van der Toorn, Karel, 'Theology, priests, and worship in Canaan and Ancient Israel', in Sasson (Ed.), *Civilizations...*, III:1, pp.2043–58.

32. Pocock, David, *Understanding Social Anthropology* (London: Athlone, 1998, revised Edition), pp.160–1.

34. World Union for the Propagation of Judaism: founded by Dr Israel Ben-Zeev of Bar-Ilan University in 1955. For its recent activities: 'Japanese Jew', *Time*, 18 February 2008.

34. Calvin: Dillenberger, John (Ed.), *John Calvin: Selections from his Writings* (Missoula: Scholars Press, 1975), p.110.

34. Barker, Eileen, *The Making of a Moonie: Choice or Brainwashing?* (Oxford: Basil Blackwell, 1984).

34. Firth, Raymond, 'Conversion from paganism to Christianity: the Tikopia case', *Royal Anthropological Institute News*, 14 (May–June, 1976), pp.3–7.

35. Lambek, Michael, *Knowledge and Practice in Mayotte* (Toronto: University of Toronto Press, 1993), p.21.

35. Wilson, A.N., *God's Funeral*, p.4.

35. Firth, Raymond, *Religion: a Humanist Perspective* (London: Routledge, 1966), Chapter 8, 'Paradox in religious systems'.

36. On the Trinity: St Augustine is said to have met, while wandering along the seashore, a young angel filling a shell with sea water and pouring it into a hole in the sand. When the Saint asked him why, the boy replied that he was showing it is easier to empty the sea into a hole than explain a single iota of the mystery of the Trinity. (Freeman, Charles, *AD 381: Heretics, Pagans and the Christian State* (London: Pimlico, 2008), p.165.)

36. Liogier, Raphaël, *Le Bouddhisme mondialisé …*, p.56.

37. Georg Cantor (1845–1918): he believed his transfinite mathematics, which gave a rigorous mathematical foundation to the concept of infinity, to have been directly communicated to him by God.

37. Kurt Gödel (1906–78) found that in a mathematical system based on a finite number of axioms there will always be statements that can be neither proved nor disproved.

37. The computer simulation argument: www.simulation-argument.com

37. Mithen, Steven, 'The origins of anthropomorphic thinking', *Journal of the Royal Anthropological Institute* (n.s.), 4:1 (March, 1998), pp.131–2.

38. On Russian seminaries: Alfeyev, Bishop Hilarion, *Orthodox Witness Today* (Geneva: WCC Publications, 2006), pp.71–5.

38. Lilla, Mark, *The Stillborn God: Religion, Politics, and the Modern West* (New York: Knopf, 2007), p.53.

38. On Durkheim: Liogier, Raphaël, 'Devenir de la légitimité chrétienne: le christianisme face au schizo-humanisme', in Chélini-Pont, Blandine and Raphaël Liogier (Eds), *Géopolitique du christianisme* (Paris: Ellipses, 2003), p.173.

38. van Gennep, Arnold, *The Rites of Passage* (Chicago: University of Chicago Press, 1960 [1908–9]).

39. Ritual as conservative: Bloch, Maurice, *From Blessing to Violence* (Cambridge: Cambridge University Press, 1986).

39. Leach, Edmund, 'Once a knight is quite enough' in *The Essential Edmund Leach…*, vol.1, pp.194–209.

39. On St Ignatius: Barthes, Roland, 'Loyola', in *Sade, Fourier, Loyola* (Paris: Le Seuil, 1971).

40. On whirling dervishes: de Vitray-Meyerovitch, Eva, 'Derviches tourneurs', *Dictionnaire de l'Islam* (Paris: Albin Michel, 1997), pp.231–2.

40. Liogier, Raphaël, *Le Bouddhisme mondialisé...*, p.57

41. Oldstone-Moore, Jennifer, *Taoïsme* (Paris: Grund, 2004), p.90.

41. Cardinal Lustiger, quoted by Weber, Eugen, *Apocalypses et Millénarismes* (Paris: Fayard, 1999), p.278.

42. On spiritual procreation ('pseudo-procreation'): Shapiro, Warren, 'Ritual kinship, ritual incorporation and the denial of death', *Man* (n.s.), 23:2 (1998), pp.275–97, and Shapiro, Warren and Uli Linke (Eds), *Denying Biology: Essays on Gender and Pseudo-Procreation* (Lanham, MD: University Press of America, 1996).

42. On Christian martyrdom: Norris. R.A., Jr., 'Patristic Ethics', in *A New Dictionary of Christian Ethics*, ed. Childress, James and John Macquarrie (London: SCM Press, 1986), p.454.

43. On Tibet: Liogier, Raphaël, *À la rencontre du dalaï-lama: mythe, vie et pensée d'un contemporain insolite* (Paris: Flammarion, 2008).

44. On the Bishop of Carlisle: *Sunday Telegraph*, 1 July 2007.

44. On Satan: Rousseau, Henri, 'Satan', in *Dictionnaire de la théologie chrétienne* (Paris: Albin Michel, 1999), pp.730–4.

44. Firth, Raymond, *Religion: a Humanist Perspective*, p.190.

45. On Confucianism: Spickard, James V., 'Cultural context...', pp.189–99.

45. Martin, Raymond and John Barresi, *The Rise and Fall of Soul and Self: An Intellectual History of Personal Identity* (New York: Columbia University Press, 2006), pp.302–3.

46. On the superego: Freud, Sigmund, *The Ego and the Id* (London: Hogarth Press, 1927 [1923]).

47. On the Monde du Graal: www.mondedugraal.com

48. Definitions of 'sect' and 'church': Stackhouse, Max L., '*Church* and *sect*', in Childress, James and John Macquarrie (Eds), *A New Dictionary of Christian Ethics..*, pp.90–1, 566–7. See also: Champion, Françoise and Martine Cohen (Eds), *Sectes et Démocratie* (Paris: Le Seuil, 1999). Mary Douglas does not seem to have used Troeltsch as an explicit source but she probably absorbed his ideas as part of her Christian background.

49. On Lefebvre: Tincq, Henri, 'Le pape rallie ses intégristes', *Le Monde*, 29 September 2006.

49. On freedom of religion : Saudi-Arabia is not the only Muslim State to disregard it. In Algeria, though a small Christian community of 30,000 out of a population of 35 million is tolerated, proselytism on behalf of a non-Muslim religion is punishable by prison sentences and fines ('Condamnation de deux Algériens convertis au christianisme', *Le Monde*, 3 July 2008). In Iraq, Christians were treated relatively well under Saddam Hussain but have been persecuted since his downfall ('Iraqi Christians' long history', BBC News, 13 March 2008).

51. On religion as a weapon: Liogier, Raphaël, 'Le facteur religieux dans la géopolitique transnationale', in Chélini-Pont, Blandine and Raphaël Liogier, *Géopolitique...*, p.9.

51. On the sacred: Leach, Edmund, in *The Essential Edmund Leach...*, vol.1, pp.348–50.

51. The Roman concept of *Homo sacer*, a person excluded from all civil rights and entitled only, if at all, to 'bare' life, has been revived by the Italian philosopher

Giorgio Agamben in his criticism of present-day authoritarianism: *Homo Sacer: Sovereign Power and Bare Life* (Stanford: Stanford University Press, 1998).

52. Liogier, Raphaël, *Le Bouddhisme mondialisé...*, p.57. See also Étienne, Bruno and Raphaël Liogier, *Être bouddhiste en France aujourd'hui* (Paris: Hachette, 1997).

52. On 'the poet's way of life': Proust, Marcel, *Les Plaisirs et les Jours*, in *Jean Santeuil* (Paris: Gallimard, 1971 [1896]) p.104. On the mother's goodnight kiss: *Recherche* 1:13. On Bergotte's death: 3:188. On cider and cherries: 3:479. On coffee and the newspaper: 3:568.

52. Joyce, James, *A Portrait of the Artist as a Young Man* (London: Cape, 1956 [1916]), p.225. Quoted in Ziolkowksi, Theodore, *Modes of Faith: Secular Surrogates for Lost Religious Belief* (Chicago University of Chicago Press, 2007), p.82.

53. Lewis, I.M., *Ecstatic Religion* (London: Routledge, 1989, second edition), pp.34, 118.

53. On glossolalia, see Firth, Raymond, *Religion...*, pp.175–6.

54. Herbrechtsmeier, William, 'The burden of the Axial Age: transcendentalism in religion as a function of empire' in Greil and Bromley (Eds), *Defining Religion...*, pp.109–26. The concept of the Axial Age was formulated by Karl Jaspers.

3: THE RELIGIOUS FIELD AND ITS SHIFTING NEIGHBOURHOOD

57. Taylor, Bron R., 'Exploring religion...'

58. Douglas, Mary, 'Self-evidence', *Proceedings of the Royal Anthropological Institute*, 1972, pp.27–43.

59. On fundamentalism: Marty, Martin E. and R. Scott Appleby, 'Introduction' to *Fundamentalisms and Society*, Marty, Martin E. and R. Scott Appleby (Eds), (Chicago: University of Chicago Press, 1993), p.3.

60. McNeill, William H., 'Epilogue: Fundamentalism and the World of the 1990s', in Marty and Appleby (Eds), *Fundamentalisms...*, pp.558–73.

60. Non-violence: leaders of some of the greatest non-violent movements have died as a result of violent acts: Jesus, Gandhi and Martin Luther King.

60. On Christianity and Islam: Partner, Peter, *Two Thousand Years: The First Millennium: The Birth of Christianity to the Crusades* (London: Granada Media, 1999), pp.117–18.

61. McCutcheon, Russell T., 'The category "religion" and the politics of tolerance', in Greil and Bromley (Eds), *Defining Religion...*, pp.139–62.

63. Quinn, Malcolm, *The Swastika: Constructing the Symbol* (London Routledge, 1994), p.135.

64. Bourdieu, Pierre, *Méditations pascaliennes* (Paris: Le Seuil, 2003, revised edition), pp.16, 149, 190.

66. On Mao: Macfarquhar, Roderick and Michael Schoenhals, *Mao's Last Revolution* (Cambridge, MA.: Harvard University Press), pp.262–8.

66. Hinton, William, *Fanshen: A Documentary of Revolution in a Chinese Village* (New York: Monthly Review Press, 1966), pp.vii, 610. This book gave valuable information about daily life at the grass roots, but Hinton's account of the relationship between theory and practice is, according to Jon Halliday, unreliable at all levels (personal communication).

67. Marcuse, Herbert, *Soviet Marxism: A Critical Analysis* (Harmondsworth: Penguin, 1971 [1958]).

68. Paxson, Margaret, *Solovyovo: the story of memory in a Russian village* (Bloomington: Indiana University Press, 2006).

68. On nazism and Christianity: Burleigh, Michael, *The Third Reich: A New History* (London: Macmillan, 2000), pp.13–14, 191–7, 254–61, 719–20.

69. On the two swastikas: Quinn, *The Swastika…*, pp.128–30.

69. On nazism as political religion: Burleigh, *The Third Reich…*, pp.9–10, 265, 812. See also Kershaw, Ian, *The Hitler Myth: Image and Reality in the Third Reich* (Oxford: Oxford University Press, 1987). On the 'illegitimate brothers' of religion: Burleigh, Michael, *Sacred Causes: Religion and Politics from the European Dictators to Al Qaeda* (London: HarperPress, 2006), p.37.

71. On Hitler as a posthumous comedian: *Hitler: the Comedy Years*, Channel Four Television programme, 2007. On Hitler's language: Steiner, George, *Language and Silence* (London, Faber and Faber, 1967), p.121.

71. On slavery: no biblical text explicitly condemns it, though some passages refer to the freeing of captives (*Luke* 4:18) or to slave and master becoming brothers in Christ (*Galatians* 3:28).

73. 'The cords of all…': Joyce, James, *Ulysses* (London, The Bodley Head, 1960 [1922]), p.46.

74. On Islamic calligraphy: Khatibi, Abdelkabir and Mohammed Sijelmassi, *The Splendour of Islamic Calligraphy* (London: Thames and Hudson, 1994), pp.100–1, 142–3. The underlying principles of Ibn Muqla's innovations were unlocked by an Egyptian artist and scholar, Ahmed Moustafa, in his 1989 doctoral thesis on the scientific foundation of the Arabic letter-shapes.

74. On the evolution of Western painting: Borchert, Till-Holger, 'Introduction: Jan van Eyck's workshop', in Borchert, T.-H. (Ed.), *The Age of Van Eyck: The Mediterranean World and Early Netherlandish Painting, 1430–1530* (London: Thames and Hudson, 2002), pp.8–31, and North, Michael, 'Art markets', *ib.*, pp.52–63.

74–5. On Cézanne: Verdi, Richard, *Cézanne* (London: Thames and Hudson, 1992), p.202. 'I work obstinately': Cézanne, Paul, *Letters*, ed. John Rewald (Oxford: Cassirer, 1976, fourth edition), p.292. Reff and Schapiro: cited in Cachin, Françoise et al. (Eds), *Cézanne* (London: Tate Publishing, 1996), p.474.

75. Steiner, George, *Real Presences*, p.218.

75. On music and the mysteries of existence, evoked by a leading contemporary French novelist: Millet, Richard, *La voix d'alto* (Paris: Gallimard, 2001), p.66.

75. Proust, Marcel, *Recherche*, 1:349–50. Scott-Moncrieff translation, slightly modified.

77. Watkin, David, *Morality and Architecture* (Chicago: University of Chicago Press, 1977), pp.13, 56. Watkin, David, *Morality and Architecture Revisited* (London: John Murray, 2001).

77. Jencks, Charles, *The Language of Post-Modern Architecture* (London: Academy Editions, 1977).

78. Jencks, Charles, *The Iconic Building: the Power of Enigma* (London: Frances Lincoln, 2005).

78. Rosenberg, Harold, *The Tradition of the New* (London: Thames and Hudson, 1962), pp.30–1.

78. On Pollock: Marquis, Alice Goldfarb, *The Idler*, 3:54, 12 March 2001.

79. Sontag, Susan, *Against Interpretation* (New York: Noonday Press, 1966), p.42.

79. Reise, Barbara, 'The stance of Barnett Newman', *Studio International,* February 1970, pp.49–55.

79. Catalogue introduction by Greenberg: Marquis, Alice Goldfarb, *Art Czar: The Rise and Fall of Clement Greenberg* (Aldershot: Lund Humphries, 2006), p.169. See also Greenberg, Clement, *Art and Culture* (London: Thames and Hudson, 1973).

80. Newman on the political implications of his work: Temkin, Ann (Ed.), 2002, *Barnett Newman,* chronology of Barnett Newman's life by Melissa Ho (Philadelphia: Philadelphia Museum of Art, 2002), pp.318–35.

81. On the Rothko chapel: Ashton, Dore, 'The Rothko chapel at Houston', *Studio International,* June 1971, pp.272–5; Novak, Barbara and Brian O'Doherty, 'Rothko's dark paintings: tragedy and void', in *Mark Rothko* (Washington, DC: National Gallery of Art, and Yale University Press, 2000), pp.265–81. Reportedly, the paintings have now seriously deteriorated, owing to the poor quality of the paint and glue, and their power to evoke emotion is almost lost. Some have drawn inferences from the fact that Rothko, Newman, Rosenberg and Greenberg were all (secular) Jews, e.g. (of Greenberg and Rosenberg): 'As secular Jews, they had moved from the faith of their fathers to a belief in the significance and centrality of culture and its critique' (McCaughey, Patrick, 'Events on canvas', *TLS,* 20 June 2008.

82. On art and reality: Nabokov, Vladimir, *Pale Fire* (London: Penguin, 2000 [1962]), p.106.

82. On the Romantic image of the artist: Williams, Raymond, *Culture and Society 1780–1950* (Harmondsworth: Penguin, 1958), Chapter 2.

83. Proust on altruism: *Recherche,* 1:1036.

83. Lévi-Strauss, Claude, *Regarder Écouter Lire* (Paris: Plon, 1993), pp.168–76.

84. Proust on music: *Recherche,* 3:253, 256.

84. On literature in general: Theodore Ziolkowski's *Modes of Faith…* is an impressive work focussed mainly on notable individual writers.

84. Leavis, F.R., *The Great Tradition* (London: Chatto and Windus, 1948), and several other works. It has been pointed out that George Eliot's *Daniel Deronda* was one of the most politically influential novels ever written, in that it dramatized and to a great extent endorsed political Zionism.

85. Grass, Günter, *Peeling the Onion* (London: Harvill Secker, 2007), p.97.

85. Steiner, George, 'A new literacy', Eighth Athenæum Lecture (London: The Athenæum, 2005). See also his commentary on Adorno's view, 'No poetry after Auschwitz', in *Language and Silence.*

85. Bellow, Saul, *Herzog,* p.238.

86. On the British Museum: Hunt, Tristram, 'How one cultural vision has lessons for the whole world', *The Observer,* 6 July 2008.

4: THE HUMANITARIAN MOVEMENT

88. On *waqf:* Barnes, J.R., *An Introduction to Religious Foundations in the Ottoman Empire.* (Leiden: Brill, 1987), p.83; Benthall, Jonathan and Jérôme Bellion-Jourdan, *The Charitable Crescent: Politics of Aid in the Muslim World* (London: I.B.Tauris, 2003), pp.29–37.

89. On alms in India: from a panegyric text addressed to a local notable, written by a Brahmin in Poona district on behalf of those affected by famine: Deshpande, Gopal Narsingh Frao, *Dushkal ke Bakhat Bhagirath Prayatna* [Herculean efforts during a famine], Poona 1877. Quoted in: Sharma, Sanjay, *Famine, Philanthropy and the Colonial State: North India in the Early Nineteenth Century* (New Delhi: Oxford University Press), pp.171–81.

90. On humanitarianism: Rufin, Jean-Christophe, *L'aventure humanitaire* (Paris: Gallimard, 1994); Ryfman, Philippe, *La question humanitaire: histoire, problématiques, acteurs et enjeux de l'aide humanitaire internationale* (Paris: Ellipses, 1999).

91. On the churches and humanitarianism: the role of Christian and Jewish lobbies in making possible the founding of the United Nations was arguably effaced because of the need for support from Muslim, atheist and other governments See Linden, Ian, 2008, 'The language of development: what are international development agencies talking about?', in Clarke, Gerard et al. (Eds), *Development, Civil Society and Faith-Based Organizations* (Basingstoke: Palgrave Macmillan, 2008), pp.72–93.

91. On the YMCA: Muukkonen, Martti, 'Framing International Aid: A Case of the YMCA'. Presentation to the conference on *Religious NGOs, Civil Society and the Aid System*, Oslo, 8–10 November 2006. Muukkonen, Martti, *Ecumenism of the Laity: Continuity and Change in the Mission View of the World's Alliance of YMCAs, 1855–1955* (Joensuu: University of Joensuu Publications in Theology, 2002).

91. On Special Purpose Groups: Wuthnow, Robert. 1988. *The Restructuring...*, pp.100–31.

93. On the overreaction against Islamic charities: Benthall, Jonathan, 'Islamic charities, Faith-Based Organizations, and the international aid system', in Alterman, Jon B. and Karin von Hippel, *Understanding Islamic Charities* (Washington, DC, CSIS Press).

94. Liogier, Raphaël, 'L'ONG comme agent institutionnel optimal du champ religieux individuo-globalisé', in Duriez, Bruno et al. (Eds), *Les ONG confessionnelles: religions et action internationale* (Paris: L'Harmattan, 2007). The idea of individuo-globalism (not the word) was partly foreshadowed in 2001 by Heelas, Paul, 'Homeless minds today' in Woodhead (Ed.), *Peter Berger...*, p.43.

95. Tvedt, Terje, Paul Opuku-Mensah and T. Ronnow, 'Religious NGOs and the international aid system: an analysis of roles and relationships with special focus on the European arena', draft research proposal, Bergen/Oslo, December 2006.

95. A typology of FBOs is attempted by Gerald Clarke 2007, 'Faith-Based Organizations and international development: an overview', in Clarke et al. (Eds), *Development, Civil Society...*, pp.17–45.

95. Secular NGOs as Faith Based Organizations: Stephen Hopgood's *Keepers of the Flame: Understanding Amnesty International* (Ithaca: Cornell University Press, 2006) is a sophisticated ethnographic interpretation of this leading human rights organization as a religoid movement. More generally, Hopgood argues that the awe and reverence arrogated by quasi-sacred bodies such as the United Nations need to be constantly questioned and undermined by means of a determined rationalism ('Sacredness and social reproduction in global civil society', Re-public re-imagining democracy, no date, www.re-public.gr).

96. Since drafting this section on MSF, I find that it has started to become a favoured object of research by cultural anthropologists. See: Redfield, Peter, 'A less modest witness: collective advocacy and motivated truth in a medical humanitarian movement', *American Ethnologist*, 33:1 (February 2006), pp.3–26; and Fassin, Didier, 'Humanitarianism as a way of life', *Public Culture*, 19:3 (2007), pp. 499–520.

96. On the name: the question as to whether Médecins Sans Frontières or Jeux Sans Frontières, the long-running European television stunt game, came first is not one that is easy to ask in Paris, but my research indicates that Jeux Sans Frontières was founded six years earlier, in 1965. According to legend, it resulted from the wish of General de Gaulle, then President of the French Republic, to unite the youth of Europe, especially France and West Germany, in a competition that would be joyful and amusing. Already a programme called Intervilles had been shown since 1962, when two French towns competed in a game involving a swimming pool and a herd of calves.

97. Vallaeys, Anne, *Médecins Sans Frontières: la biographie* (Paris: Fayard, 2004). English translations are mine. On the Biafran war: Vallaeys, *Médecins...*, p.53.

98. Brauman on MSF France: Vallaeys, p.497.

98. Emmanuelli, Xavier, *Les Prédateurs de l'Action Humanitaire* (Paris: Albin Michel, 1991).

99. On security risks: Stoddard, Abby and Adele Harmer and Katherine Haver, *Providing aid in insecure environments: trends in policy and operations*, HPG Report 23 (London: Overseas Development Institute), September 2006. The authors found that since 1997, the absolute number of major acts of violence committed against aid workers each year had nearly doubled. However, when the number of victims was compared to the population of aid workers in the field, which increased by an estimated 77 per cent from 1997 to 2005, the global incidence trend of violence against aid workers was found to have risen only slightly.

100. On Geneviève: Vallaeys, *Médecins...*, p.197; on Gilles: Vallaeys, *Médecins...*, pp.380–4.

101. On Barry Gutwein: Campbell, Tom, *Purdue Agriculture Connections*, 15:1 (West Lafayette, Indiana: Purdue University, Winter 2006).

102. 'Florid expressions...': Benthall, Jonathan, *Disasters, Relief and the Media* (London: I.B.Tauris, 1993), p.132.

102. Emmanuelli on medical ethics: quoted in Vallaeys, *Médecins...*, pp.196, 253.

102. 'Only in MSF...': Rowan Gillies, International Council President, 'Where is MSF today' (internal discussion paper, summer 2005).

104. On MSF's current policies on publicity: Brauman, personal interview, Paris, 21 October 2005.

104. On French fantasies over MSF: Vallaeys, *Médecins...*, p.461. On its early history: Vallaeys, *Médecins...*, pp.183–93).

104. On MSF's visual imagery: Hugo Slim, in MSF internal discussion paper, summer 2005, quoted by permission.

105. On 'what is man?': Brauman, Rony, *Humanitaire: le dilemme* (Paris: Textuel, 2002), p.60.

105. Camus, Albert, *La Peste* (Paris : Gallimard, 1971 [1947]), p.151. This novel was criticized by Sartre and others, when it was first published, for its use of

emotive metaphor. In its quest for classical purity, eliminating female and Arab characters, it is now ripe for dissection in the terms of Mary Douglas's *Purity and Danger*. However, it is also an extraordinarily potent allegory for our times.

106. On fund-raising, ritual and rhetoric, I am indebted to an article by Simon Harrison, who wrote in an article 'Ritual as intellectual property', *Man* (n.s.), 27:2, June 1992, that 'Ritual is to everyday action, as rhetoric is to discourse, as luxuries are to goods'.

106. MSF and public controversies: for instance, it has led a campaign against big pharmaceutical companies in defence of the interests of HIV/AIDS patients in poor countries, and has been in conflict with the Hudson Institute, Washington, DC, which claims that MSF has been using unproven anti-HIV drugs in Africa. Again, a Swiss court has been hearing evidence in a lawsuit wherein the government of the Netherlands is suing MSF–Switzerland over ransom money of € 1 million that the former paid to release one of MSF–Switzerland's staff, a Dutch citizen, who was held as a hostage for almost two years since August 2002 in Russia's Dagestan province (the longest period an aid worker has ever been held in captivity).

5: ANIMAL RIGHTS AND ENVIRONMENTALISM

110. On the number of anglers: *Public Attitudes to Angling* (Bristol: Environment Agency, 2005).

110. On circuses and the film industry: see website of PAWSI (Performing Animals Welfare Standards International), www.pawsi.org

110. Brophy, Brigid, 'The Rights of Animals', *Sunday Times*, 10 October 1965.

111. Singer, Peter, *Animal Liberation: A New Ethics for our Treatment of Animals* (New York, Random House, 1975).

111. Regan, Tom, *The Case for Animal Rights* (Berkeley: University of California Press, 1983).

111. Garner, Robert, *Animal Ethics* (Cambridge: Polity, 2005).

111. Ingold, Tim, 'An anthropologist looks at biology', *Man* (n.s.), 25:2 (June 1990), pp.208–29.

111. Darwin, Charles, *The Descent of Man*, 1871, Chapter 3.

113. Bentham, Jeremy, *An Introduction to the Principles of Morals and Legislation*, 1789.

113. Kete, Kathleen, 'Beastly agendas: an interview with Kathleen Kete' (by S. Najafi), *Cabinet Magazine Online*, 4 (Fall 2001).

114. Collectif anti-spéciste de Paris: http://antispesite.free.fr [my translation into English]

115. 'Arguments from Marginal Cases': comparable issues arise in the complex debate about abortion law.

116. Groce, Nora Ellen and Jonathan Marks, 'The Great Ape Project and disability rights: ominous undercurrents of eugenics in action', *American Anthropologist*, 102:4 (2001), pp.818–22.

116. On the Samo: Héritier, Françoise, 'L'identité samo', in Lévi-Strauss, Claude (Ed.), *L'Identité* (Paris: Grasset, 1977).

116. On the Algonquian: Hornborg, Alf, 2001, *The Power of the Machine: Global Inequalities of Economy, Technology, and Environment* (Walnut Creek, CA.: Altamira Press, 2001).

116. On 'interlocked forms of abuse': Ascione, Frank R. and Phil Arkow, (Eds), *Child Abuse, Domestic Violence, and Animal Abuse: Linking the Circles of Compassion for Prevention and Intervention* (West Lafayette: Purdue University Press, 1999).

117. Jamison, Wesley V., Caspar Wenk and James V. Parker, 'Every sparrow falls: understanding animal rights activism as functional religion', *Society and Animals*, 8:3 (2000), pp.305–30.

118. On feminism and the animal rights movement: Monro, Lyle, 'Caring about blood, flesh, and pain: women's standing in the animal protection movement', *Society and Animals*, 9:1 (2001), pp.43–61.

118. On fur: Emberley, Julia V., *Venus and Furs: the Cultural Politics of Fur* (London: I.B.Tauris, 1998).

119. The Auden poem is quoted by Robert Grant in a review article, 'Red in tooth and claw', *TLS*, 13 January 1995.

119. On von Uexküll: see Hornborg, *The Power of the Machine...*, pp.175–90.

119. Kalland, Arne, 'Whale politics and Green legitimacy: a critique of the anti-whaling campaign', *Anthropology Today*, 9:6 (December 1993), pp.3–7.

120. International Dolphin Watch website: www.idw.org

120. Servais, Véronique, 'Enchanting dolphins: an analysis of human–dolphin encounters', in Knight, John (Ed.), *Animals in person: cultural perspectives on human–animal intimacies* (Oxford: Berg, 2005).

121. Douglas, Mary: see note to p.131.

123. On Thoreau: Gould, Rebecca Kneale, 'Thoreau, Henry David', in Taylor, Bron R. *Encyclopedia of Religion and Nature* (London: Thoemmes Continuum, 2005), pp.1634–6. For further information on early American conservation, see the Introduction to this *Encyclopedia* and the entries on Muir (pp.1126–7) by Steven J. Holmes and on Pinchot (pp.1280–1) by D. Keith Naylor.
Two other excellent works in this well covered field are Worster, Donald, *Nature's Economy: A History of Ecological Ideas* (Cambridge: Cambridge University Press, 1985); and Pepper, David, *Modern Environmentalism: An Introduction* (London: Routledge, 1999). Taylor devotes a chapter to this history in Chapter 3 of *Dark Green Religion*, and provides an analysis of radical environmentalism in Chapter 4.

124. On love of green: Lee, David, *Nature's palette: the science of plant color* (Chicago: University of Chicago Press, 2008).

124. On Leopold: Meine, Curt, *Aldo Leopold: His Life and Work* (Madison: University of Wisconsin Press, 1988).

124. On Carson: McCay, Mary, *Rachel Carson* (New York: Macmillan, 1993).

124. de Beauvoir, Simone, *Privilèges* (Paris: Gallimard, 1955), p.192.

125. White, Lynn, Jr., 'The historical roots of our ecologic crisis', *Science*, 155 (1967), pp.1203–7.

126. Tuan, Yi Fu, 'Our treatment of the environment in ideal and actuality', *American Scientist*, 58:3 (1970), pp.244–9.
For discussions of the evidence for and against the Lynn White thesis, see Pepper, *Modern Enviromentalism...*, pp.148–55, and articles by Bron R. Taylor

('Environmental ethics', pp.604–6), James D. Proctor & Evan Berry ('Social science on religion and nature', pp.1571–7) and Elspeth Whitney ('White, Lynn – thesis of, pp.1735–7), in Taylor (Ed.), *Encyclopedia of Religion and Nature*.

126. Foltz, Richard C., *Islam and Ecology: A Bestowed Trust* (Cambridge, MA: Harvard University Press, 2003). Foltz, Richard C., *Animals in Islamic Tradition and Muslim Culture* (Oxford: Oneworld, 2006).

127. Palmer, Martin et al., *Faith and Nature* (London: Rider, 1987). See also the ARC web-site: www.arcworld.org

128. Sweetman, William, 'Romanticism – Western toward Asian religions', in Taylor, (Ed.), *Encyclopedia of Religion and Nature*, pp.426–7. See also Kalland, Arne, 'The religious environmentalist paradigm', in the same *Encyclopedia*, pp.1367–71.

129. Ellen, Roy, 'What Black Elk left unsaid', *Anthropology Today*, 2:6 (December 1986), pp.8–12.

129. On Soka Gakkai: Liogier, *Le Bouddhisme mondialisé…*, pp.13–14, 260–7, 351, 531.

130. On the Dalai Lama: Liogier, *À la rencontre du dalaï-lama…* On western Buddhism: Liogier, Raphaël, 'Buddhism', in Iriye, Akira and Pierre-Yves Saunier, *Dictionary of Transnational History* (Basingstoke: Palgrave Macmillan, 2008).

130. On Buddhist environmentalism: see also the entries on Soka Gakkai and the Earth Charter (by David W. Chappell, pp.1580–1), Thich Nhat Hanh ['Thich' is a term of respect for Vietnamese monks] (by Sallie B. King, pp.1202–3); Dalai Lama (by John Powers, p.443); Sierra Club (by Gavin Van Horn and Bron Taylor, pp.1544–7); David Brower (by Gavin Van Horn and Brent Blackwelder, pp.225–6), and Greenpeace (by Paul Wapner, pp.727–8), in Taylor (Ed.), *Encyclopedia of Religion and Nature*.
For a generally sympathetic analysis of New Age ecology, neo-paganism and similar movements, see: Greenwood, Susan, *The Nature of Magic: an Anthropology of Consciousness* (Oxford: Berg, 2005), and Pike, Sarah, *New Age and Neopagan Religions in America* (New York: Columbia University Press, 2004).

131–3. The discussion here of grid–group or 'cultural theory' looks back to many years of absorbing the ideas of the late Mary Douglas, beginning with her Institute of Contemporary Arts lecture in 1970, 'Environments at Risk', *TLS*, 30 October; reprinted in Benthall, Jonathan (Ed.), *Ecology, the Shaping Enquiry* (London: Longman, 1972), published in the USA as *Ecology in Theory and Practice* (New York: Viking). See also Chapter 7, 'Verbal weapons and environments at risk', in Fardon, Richard, *Mary Douglas: An Intellectual Biography* (London: Routledge, 1999). More recent texts relied on here are:
Douglas, Mary, 'Grid and group: new developments', paper prepared after workshop in honour of Michael Thompson on Complexity and Cultural Theory, London School of Economics, 27 June 2005.
Verweij, Marco and M. Douglas, R. Ellis, C. Engel, F. Hendriks, S. Lohmann, S. Ney, S. Rayner and M. Thompson, 'The case for clumsiness', Introduction to Verweij, Marco and Michael Thompson, *Clumsy Solutions for a Complex World: Governance, Politics and Plural Perceptions* (Basingstoke: Palgrave Macmillan, 2006).

135. Lovelock, James, *Gaia: A New Look at Life on Earth* (Oxford: Oxford University Press, 1979). Lovelock, James, *The Revenge of Gaia* (London: Allen Lane, 2006).

136. On neo-paganism: see Partridge, Christopher, *Encyclopedia of New Religions* (London: Lion Publishing, 2004).

136. On the Charity Commission and Paganism, see York, Michael, 'Defining Paganism in England and Wales', in Greil and Bromley (Eds), *Defining Religion...*, 265–74.

136. See entries on Anarchism (by John Clark, pp.49–55), and on Earth First! & the Earth Liberation Movement, and Radical Environmentalism (by Bron Taylor, pp.518–24, 1326–35), in Taylor (Ed.), *Encyclopedia of Religion and Nature*; as well as Chapter 4 in *Dark Green Religion*; and for radical environmentalism globally see Bron Taylor (Ed.), *Ecological Resistance Movements: The Global Emergence of Radical and Popular Environmentalism* (Albany, New York: State University of New York Press, 1995.)

138. Voluntary Human Extinction Movement: www.vhemt.org

138. Lomborg, Bjørn, *The Skeptical Environmentalist: Measuring the Real State of the World* (Cambridge: Cambridge University Press, 2001), pp.3, 321, 351.

138. On scientists' beliefs about religion: Larson, Edward J. and Larry Witham, 'Scientists' belief in religion', *Scientific American*, September 1999; 'Leading scientists still reject God', *Nature* (6691) 23 July 1998, p.313; Britt, Robert, 'Scientists' Belief in God Varies Starkly by Discipline', Livescience.com, 8 November 2005.
For recent research, see Ecklund, Elaine Howard, 2007, 'Religion and spirituality among university students', SSRC essay forum, www.religion/ssrc.org/reforum

138. Max Perutz, quoted in Patel, Kim, 'Perutz rubbishes Popper and Kuhn', *Times Higher Education Supplement*, 25 November 1994.

139. A sense of the sacred in the cosmos: this is a key argument in Bron Taylor's *Dark Green Religion*.

140. Bron Taylor points out that in environmental ethics, the idea of 'clumsy solutions' is represented by the work of Bryan Norton, inspired by the pragmatic philosophy of John Dewey, e.g. his *Sustainability: A Philosophy of Adaptive Ecosystem Management* (Chicago: University of Chicago Press, 2005).

6: SOME HUMANE DISCIPLINES AS RELIGIOID MOVEMENTS

141. The terms psychoanalysis, psychotherapy etc. have been used here in a generic sense, though to professionals each term is related to a specific therapeutic tradition.

141. Gould, Stephen Jay, *Rocks of Ages: Science and Religion in the Fullness of Life* (New York, Ballentine Books, 1999).

142. On science as a cultural system: Franklin, Sarah, 'The anthropology of science', in MacClancy, Jeremy (Ed.), *Exotic No More: Anthropology on the Front Lines* (Chicago: University of Chicago Press, 2002).

142. Gellner, Ernest, *The Psychoanalytic Movement* (London: Paladin, 1985).

143. Jones, Ernest, *Sigmund Freud: His Life and Work* (London: Hogarth Press, 1955), pp.172–5. See also Littlewood, Roland, 'Science, shamanism and hermeneutics: recent writing on psychoanalysis', *Anthropology Today*, 5:1 (February 1989), pp.5–11.

145. On the counter-transference: Gay, Peter, *Freud: A Life for Our Time* (London: Dent, 1988), pp.253–4; Carnochan, Peter, *Looking for Ground: Countertransference and the Problem of Value* (Hillsdale, NJ: Analytic Press, 2001).

145. Turner, Philip, 'An unworkable theology', *First Things: The Journal of Religion, Culture, and Public Life*, June/July 2005, pp.10–12.

146. On New Age movements, see articles by Michael York ('New Age traditions', pp.308–12) and Elizabeth Puttick ('The Human Potential Movement', pp.399–402), in Partridge (Ed.), *Encyclopedia of New Religions*.

147. 'The discipline of archaeology…': Roderick Beaton reviewing Yannis Hamilakis's *The Nation and its Ruins: Antiquity, archaeology, and national imagination in Greece* (Oxford University Press), *TLS*, 1 February 2008.

147. On contemporary archaeology: Fox, Robin, 'One World Archaeology: an appraisal', *Anthropology Today*, 9:5 (October 1995), pp.6–10.

148. Tomášková, Silvia, 'A site in history: archaeology at Dolní Věstonice/Unterwisternitz', *Antiquity*, 69:263 (1995), pp.301–16.

148. On Gimbutas: review of *The Civilization of the Goddess* by Ruth Tringham, *American Anthropologist,* March 1993, 95:1, 196–7. Gimbutas as mother goddess: Maskell, Lynn, 'Goddesses, Gimbutas and "New Age" archaeology', *Antiquity*, 69:262 (1995), pp.74–86.

149. On Goddess figurines: Ucko, Peter J., *Anthropomorphic Figurines: Of Predynastic Egypt and Neolithic Crete with Comparative Material from the Prehistoric Near East and Mainland Greece* (London: Royal Anthropological Institute, 1968).

149. Piggott, Stuart, *The Druids* (London: Thames & Hudson, 1968).

149. Daniel, Glyn, 'The forgotten milestones and blind alleys of the past', *Royal Anthropological Institute News*, 33 (August 1979), pp.3–6.

149. Williams, Stephen, *Fantastic Archaeology: the Wild Side of American Prehistory* (Philadelphia: University of Pennsylvania Press, 1991).

150. On Stonehenge: Chippindale, Christopher, *Stonehenge Complete* (London: Thames and Hudson, 1983), pp.248–9; Worthington, Andy, *The Battle of the Beanfield* (Lyme Regis: Enabler Productions, 2005).

150. *Incidents of Travel in Chichén Itzá* is distributed by Documentary Educational Resources, Cambridge, MA. (www.der.org)

151. On James Mellaart: Mallett, Marla, 'A weaver's view of the Çatal Hüyük controversy', *Oriental Rug Review*, 10:6, August/September 1990, pp.32–43; 'The Goddess From Anatolia: an updated view of the Çatal Hüyük controversy', *Oriental Rug Review*, 13:2 (December 1992/January 1993), pp.24–31 (accessible on www.marlamallett.com). He published a lavishly illustrated four-volume work with co-authors but the data were never defended in academic journals, and the publication is omitted from his 2007 *Who's Who* entry. (Mellaart, James and B. Balpinar and U. Hirsch, *The Goddess from Anatolia* (Milan: Eskenazi, 1989).

151. See the Çatalhöyük website www.catalhoyuk.com. Quoted by kind permission.

152. Holtorf, Cornelius, *From Stonehenge to Las Vegas: Archaeology as Popular Culture* (Lanham: Altamira Press, 2005).

152. Lucas, Gavin, *The Archaeology of Time* (London: Routledge, 2005), p.134; Lucas, Gavin, 'Forgetting the past', *Anthropology Today*, 13:1 (February 1997), pp.8–14.

152. On the changing family tree of *Homo sapiens*: Marks, Jonathan, 'Anthropological taxonomy as subject and object: the consequences of descent from Darwin and Durkheim', *Anthropology Today*, 23:4 (August 2007), pp.7–12.

152. On Louis Leakey: Knight, Chris, Review of Virginia Morell, *Ancestral Passions: the Leakey Family and the Quest for Humankind's Beginnings*, in *Journal of the Royal Anthropological Institute*, 13:2 (June 1997), p.388.

153. On Easter Island: Rainbird, Paul, 'A message for our time? The Rapa Nui (Easter Island) ecodisaster and Pacific Island environments', *World Archaeology*, 33:3 (2002), pp.436–51.

154. On early State societies and their environments: Scarre, Chris, n.d., 'A disaster waiting to happen? Sustainability, degradation, and environment in early state societies', Stanford University website, 'The archaeology of contemporary issues'.

155. Hiscock, Peter, 'The New Age of alternative archaeology of Australia', *Archaeology in Oceania*, 31:3 (1996), pp.152–64.

155. Teilhard de Chardin, Pierre, *The Human Phenomenon* (Brighton: Sussex Academic Press, 1999), originally published as *The Phenomenon of Man* in 1960.
American Teilhard Association: www.teilharddechardin.org
British Teilhard Association: www.teilhard.org.uk
Association des Amis de Pierre Teilhard de Chardin: www.teilhard.org

156. Medawar, Peter, Review of *The Phenomenon of Man*, republished in *The Art of the Soluble* (London: Methuen, 1967 [1961]).

158. Eiseley, Loren, *Darwin's Century: Evolution and the Men Who Discovered It* (London: Gollancz, 1959). Eiseley, Loren, *Francis Bacon and the Modern Dilemma* (Freeport, NY: Books for Libraries Press, 1970). Eiseley, Loren, 'The Angry Winter', in *The Unexpected Universe* (London: Gollancz, 1970), pp.93–119.
Loren Eiseley Society: www.eiseley.org
'The inward skies of man...': Eiseley, Loren, 'The Inner Galaxy', in *The Star Thrower* (London: Wildwood House, 1978), p.299.
I am grateful to Professor Benson Saler, who was a friend and colleague of Eiseley's, for his stimulating thoughts on Eiseley's work, and specially for his insight, as a long-term resident of Concord, Massachusetts, that Thoreau and Emerson, like Eiseley, were more 'enchanters' than systematic thinkers.

159. Social and cultural anthropology: these were often treated as separate sub-disciplines in the mid to late twentieth century, but the distinction is now less observed.
Knight, Chris, *Blood Relations: Menstruation and the Origins of Culture* (New Haven: Yale University Press, 1991). He has written many articles since, including 'The wives of the Sun and Moon', *Journal of the Royal Anthropological Institute*, 3:1 (1997), pp.133–53.
See also: Radical Anthropology Group: www.radicalanthropologygroup.org

161. On Kipling: Mason, Timothy, 'Evolution or revolution? A review of Chris Knight's *Blood Relations*', 2000. www.timothyjpmason.com

161. 'The conditions for a sex-strike in late 20th-century America...': Bell, Diane, Review of *Blood Relations* in *American Ethnologist*, 21:4 (November 1994), p.903.

163. The 'tribal mirror': see Knight, John, '*The Mountain People* as tribal mirror', *Anthropology Today*, 10:6 (December 1994), pp.1–3.

164. On Margaret Mead: MacClancy, Jeremy, Introduction to MacClancy, Jeremy (Ed.), *Popularizing Anthropology* (London: Routledge, 1996), p.25. Other articles in this collection are relevant.

165. Gustaaf Houtman comments (personal communication) that the Buddhist tradition of *vipassana* claims to go beyond philosophy, which working through language is already shaped by conventional assumptions. Moreover, language cannot match the rapidity with which human beings perceive and act. In *vipassana*, practitioners learn to sub-divide and identify very short changes in perception, and to understand them in the context of awareness of the universals of impermanence, non-self and suffering. The aim is to end up with a depersonified experience of all particulars as universally constituted irrespective of their cultural context.

166. On anthropology in general: MacClancy, Jeremy (Ed.), *Exotic No More...*; and Benthall, Jonathan (Ed.), *The Best of 'Anthropology Today'* (London: Routledge, 2002).

166. On earlier Indian anthropology: Ratnam, Bala (Ed.), *Anthropology on the March* (Madras, The Book Centre, 1963).

167. On Australian Aboriginals: Glowczewski, Barbara, 'Dynamic cosmologies and Aboriginal heritage', *Anthropology Today*, 15:1 (February 1999), p.6. A select list of modern anthropologists who have worked on the relationship between religion and nature may be found in Sponsel, Leslie, 'Spiritual ecology: one anthropologist's reflections', *Journal for the Study of Religion, Nature and Culture*, 1:3 (2007), pp.340–50. These include Roy G. Rappaport, Gerardo Reichel-Dolmatoff, Philippe Descola, Brian Morris, Kay Milton and Piers Vitebsky.

7: THROW RELIGION OUT OF THE DOOR: IT FLIES BACK BY THE WINDOW

169. Dawkins, Richard, *The God Delusion* (Boston: Houghton Mifflin, 2006).

170. Lilla, Mark, *The Stillborn God...*

170. Smith, James A.K., 'The last prophet of Leviathan', www.ssrc.org/blogs/immanent_frame, 27 December 2007.

171. On the 'Next Age': Liogier, Raphaël, Article 'New Age', in *Dictionary of Transnational History*. On 'euphemization', see Liogier, Raphaël, 'L'ONG comme agent institutionnel...' Liogier borrows the term from Fath, Sébastien, 'Les ONG évangéliques américaines, ou les ruses de la Providence', in the same collection.

172. For an attempt to apply statistical research methods, based on an on-line international questionnaire, to exploring possible correlations between New Age beliefs and adherence/non-adherence to established religions, see Bainbridge, William S., 'After the New Age', *Journal for the Scientific Study of Religion*, 43 (2004), pp.381–94.

172. Alfeyev, Bishop Hilarion, *Orthodox Witness Today* (Geneva: WCC Publications, 2006), pp.1–11, 216–49. Alfeyev is also an internationally acclaimed liturgical composer.

173. On Islamic feminism: Roald, Anne Sofie, 'Feminist reinterpretation of Islamic sources: Muslim feminist theology in the light of the Christian tradition of

feminist thought', in Ask, Karin and Marit Tjomsland (Eds), *Women and Islamization* (Oxford: Berg, 1998), pp.17–44. Some Islamic feminists go much further in re-examining Islamic sources with the aim of achieving equal rights for women. For references and a balanced assessment of the opportunities and problems inherent in this exercise, see Mirsa, Qudsia, 'Islamic feminism and gender equality', *ISIM News*, 21 (Summer 2008), pp.30–1.

173. On Muslim gays and neo-Sufi brotherhoods: Roy, Olivier, *Globalised Islam: The Search for a New Ummah* (London: Hurst, 2002), pp.195, pp.220–31. On the gay Muslim counter-culture, see Habib, Samar, 'Queer-friendly Islamic hermeneutics' *ISIM News*, 21 (Summer 2008), pp.32–3.

175. On the persecution of the Russian Church under communism: Alfeyev, *Orthodox Witness Today*, p.112.

175. On Leo Strauss: Gray, *Black Mass...*, p.133.

176. On the relative rigidity of the Orthodox churches: François Thual, *Le Monde*, 20 January 1998.

176. Liederman, Lina Molokotos, 'Le rôle des ONG humanitaires orthodoxes dans l'action sociale et le développement international: le cas des organisations orthodoxes', in Duriez et al. (Eds), *Les ONG confessionnelles...*
The Ecumenical Patriarch: the Orthodox Church is currently divided, not like the Anglican Church by quarrels over sex and gender issues, but principally by the large Russian Church's refusal to accept the Ecumenical Patriarch as having more than a 'primacy of honour' over the other Patriarchs.

177. On Russian émigré Orthodoxy in Paris: Williams, Rowan, 'Sharp questions for the Orthodox', *TLS*, 11 April 2008.

176. On the world in its entirety as the liturgy: Chryssargis, John, 'Orthodox spirituality', in Taylor (Ed.), *Encyclopedia of Religion and Nature*, p.336; Clément, Olivier, 'L'Église Orthodoxe', in Peuch, Henri-Charles (Ed.), *Histoire des Religions* (Paris: Gallimard, 1972), vol. 2, p.1035.

178. On Hinduism and Indianness: Varenne, Paul, 1976, 'L'hindouisme contemporain', in Peuch (Ed.), *Histoire des Religions*, vol. 3, pp.180–84.

178. On Hinduism as a default religion in India: Beyer, Peter, 'Defining religion ...', pp.179–80.

178. Macfarlane, Alan, *Japan through the Looking-Glass* (London: Profile, 2005).

179. On new Japanese religions: Reader, Ian, 'Japanese new religions', in Partridge (Ed.), *Encyclopedia of New Religions*, pp.224–30.

179. On Darwinism and Japan: personal conversation with H.M. Emperor Akihito of Japan, Wimbledon, 1998.

179. On State Shinto: Renondeau, Gaston, 'Le Shintō d'État', in Peuch (Ed.), *Histoire des Religions*, vol. 3, pp.511–19.

179. On the death of Hirohito and succession of Akihito: Crump, Thomas, 'The end of the Showa era', *Anthropology Today*, 5:5 (October 1989), pp.21–2; and 'The making of an Emperor', *Anthropology Today*, 7:2 (April 1991), pp.14–15.

180. On China: Dunstheimer, Guillaume, 'La Chine depuis les Han' in *Histoire des Religions...*, vol. 3, pp.371–443. I am much indebted to this excellent article.

181. On the Cultural Revolution: Macfarquhar, Roderick and Michael Schoenhals, *Mao's Last Revolution*, pp. 366–70 (on Confucianism), pp.118–22 (on destruction of national treasures), pp.387–8 (on the Shadian incident).

182. On the urban–rural divide: Alexander, Peter and Anita Chan, 'Does China have an apartheid pass system?', *Journal of Ethnic and Migration Studies*, 30:4 (July 2004), pp.609–29. According to more recent reports, the household pass system has been gradually eroding in response to the realities of the labour market ('A dynamic new China sheds old restraints', *International Herald Tribune*, 2–3 August, 2008).

182. Chang, Jung and Jon Halliday, *Mao: the Unknown Story* (London: Cape, 2005).

183. On the criteria for recognition of religion in China: Beyer, Peter, 'Defining religion…', pp.174–7.

183. Shue, Vivienne, 'Legitimacy crisis in China?', in Gries, Peter Hays and Stanley Rosen (Eds), *State and Society in 21st-century China: Crisis, contention, and legitimation* (New York and London: RoutledgeCurzon, 2004), pp.39–41, 46–7.

184. Chau, Adam Yuet, *Miraculous Response: Doing Popular Religion in Contemporary China* (Stanford: Stanford University Press, 2006).

184. On the Falun Gong: Hilton, Isabel, 'Great thinkers of our time: Master Li Hongzhi', *New Statesman*, 14 July 2003.

184. Feuchtwang, Stephan, personal communication, 2007.

185. On the Shouters and Yiguandao: Irons, Edward, in Partridge (Ed.) 2004, *Encyclopedia of New Religions*, pp.241, 245–6.

186. Froese, Paul and Steven Pfaff, 'Explaining a religious anomaly: A historical analysis of secularization in Eastern Germany', *Journal for the Scientific Study of Religion*, 44:4, 2005, pp.397–422; 'Replete and Desolate Markets: Poland, East Germany, and the new religious paradigm', *Social Forces*, 80:2, December 2001, pp.481–507. The statistics given here are borrowed from their two articles. Paul Froese's *The Plot to Kill God: Findings from the Soviet Experiment in Secularization* (Berkeley: University of California Press, 2008) was due to be published soon after the present book went to press.
It is argued above in this chapter that the high apparent incidence of atheism in Japan has special features.

187. On the contrast between Christian and Islamic toleration: Benthall, Jonathan, 'Confessional cousins and the rest: the structure of Islamic toleration', *Anthropology Today*, 21:1 (February 2005), pp.16–20.

187. Inter-faith conference in Madrid: *Le Monde*, 16 July 2008.

ENVOI

189. Gray, John, *Black Mass…*, p. 208.
190. Browning, 'Bishop Blougram's Apology'.
191. On belief 'as if': Wilson, A.N., *God's Funeral*, p.328.

INDEX

Frequently occurring words such as 'religion', 'spirituality', 'faith', 'Christian(ity)', 'anthropology', 'science' and. 'art' have not been indexed; nor have geographical references to Britain.